A CAVALCADE OF QUEENSLAND'S CRIMES AND CRIMINALS

SCOUNDRELS, SCALLYWAGS & PSYCHOPATHS

The Colonial Years
and Beyond
1859 - 1920

By the same author

The St Helena Story
True Tales of Old St Helena
More True Tales of Old St Helena
The Wild Men of St Helena
The Escapes from St Helena
The St Helena Island Prison
Managing Your School: Vol. 1
Managing Your School: Vol. 2
Managing Your School: Vol. 3
The Educator's Book of Enlightening Lists
True Tales from the Classroom
More True Tales from the Classroom
Did I Really Say That?

With Neil Flanagan
Management in a Minute
Just about Everything a Manager Needs to Know
The Management Bible
The Manager's 100

With Barry Bamford
The Classroom Teacher's Book of Management Essentials

A CAVALCADE OF QUEENSLAND'S CRIMES AND CRIMINALS

SCOUNDRELS, SCALLYWAGS & PSYCHOPATHS

THE COLONIAL YEARS
AND BEYOND
1859 - 1920

JARVIS FINGER

Boolarong Press

Conversion tables

Money
One pound (£1) = 20 shillings (20/-)
= two dollars ($2)
One guinea = £1/1/0 = 21 shillings

Length
1 inch = 2.54 cm
1 foot = 12 inches = 30.38 cm
1 yard = 3 feet = 0.914 m
1 mile = 1760 yards = 1.6 km

Area
1 acre = .405 hectares

Weight
1 ounce (1 oz) = 28.35 gm
1 pound (1 lb) = 16 ozs = 0.453 kg
1 ton = 2240 lbs = 1.02 tonnes

Capacity
1 pint = 0.568 litres
1 quart = 2 pints = 1.136 litres
1 gallon = 4 quarts = 4.544 litres

Acknowledgements

The author wishes to acknowledge the assistance provided by the following in the preparation of this book:

Queensland State Archives; State Library of Queensland; John Oxley Library; Queensland Parliament House Library; Queensland Police Museum; Queensland Newspapers; National Library of Australia's Trove Service

Published by
Boolarong Press in association with Fernfawn Publications

National Library of Australia
Cataloguing-in-Publication entry

Author: Finger, Jarvis.

Title: A cavalcade of Queensland's crimes and criminals: Scoundrels, scallwags & psychopaths – The colonial years and beyond 1859-1920 / Jarvis Finger.

ISBN: 9781922109057 (pbk.)

Subjects: Crime--Queensland--History.
Criminals--Queensland--History.
Criminals--Queensland--Biography.
Law enforcement--Queensland--History.
Justice, Administration of--Queensland--History.

Dewey Number: 364.9943

A CAVALCADE OF QUEENSLAND'S CRIMES AND CRIMINALS

The Colonial Years and Beyond 1859 - 1920

Introduction ix

1859 ***The slaughter of three St Helena fishermen*** 2
Unsolved, *Murder*

1860 ***They didn't need the hangman*** 5
Troopers Gulliver, Toby and Alma, *Murder*

1860 ***The ex-convict killer*** 8
Thomas Woods, *Murder*

1861 ***That tell-tale bump*** 10
Georgie, *Rape*

1862 ***Three for the gallows*** 12
Tommy, *Murder*
Kipper Billy and Billy Horton, *Murder*

1863 ***Death on a sheep station*** 15
Michael Turley, *Murder*

1864 ***Murder most cowardly on the Darling Downs*** 18
Alexander Ritchie, *Murder*

1864 ***When Fagan's gang ran wild*** 21
Peter Fagan, Daniel Webster, Thomas Howson, *Robbery under arms*

1865 ***The Wild Scotchman*** 24
James Macpherson, *Mail robbery under arms*

1866 ***Man overboard!*** 27
William Domane, *Manslaughter*

1866 ***The Frenchman, bushranger*** 29
Henry Hunter, *Mail robbery under arms*

1866 ***Assault on the high seas*** 31
William Griffiths, *Assault*

1866 ***The Crocodile Creek Chinese riots*** 33
John Stone, Daniel Galvin, Abraham

Soloman, John O'Sullivan, *Riot, unlawful assembly and affray*

1867 *The Ipswich Mail hold-up* 35
William Jenkins,
Mail robbery under arms

1867 *The Clermont gold escort killings* 38
Thomas Griffin, *Murder*

1868 *The Imbil incident* 41
William Troden, Joseph Blake,
Robbery under arms

1868 *The avenging public servant* 44
Frank Bowerman, *Assault with intent to murder*

1869 *The lure of Halligan's gold* 47
George Palmer, Alexander Archibald,
John Williams, *Murder*

1870 *The hunt for Herrlich, the Hun* 50
James Herrlich, *Murder*

1871 *The murder of Simon Zieman* 53
Patrick Collins, Murder

1872 *The pure white bull* 56
Henry Redford, *Cattle duffing*

1873 *The downfall of a young nipper* 59
John Ruddy, *Larceny*

1874 *The Ipswich riot* 61
Ryan, Keogh, Shaw & others,
Riotous assembly and assault

1875 *The stranger who never was* 63
Charles Pritchard, *Murder*

1876 *The brute from the Belyando* 66
Frederick Wheeler, *Murder*

1877 *The missing bank notes* 69
Victor Townsend, *Larceny/ Bank robbery*

1878 *Gory goings-on at Gilbert River* 71
Gilbert River aborigines, *Murder*

1879 *Caught... down a mineshaft* 74
Joseph Mutter, *Murder*

1880 *The tree-climbing bank robber* 76
Joseph Wells, *Robbery and wounding under arms*

1881 *The tell-tale letter* 79
Michael Minnis, *Manslaughter*

1882 *Murder in the fowl house* 82
Margaret Spillane, *Murder*

1883 *The Mackay Racecourse riot* 84
George Goyner,
Assault and battery

1884 *The South Sea slavers* 86
Neil McNeil, Bernard Williams and others
Murder and Kidnapping

1885 *The Muttaburra murder* 89
Walter Gordon, *Murder*

1886 A brotherly bullet? 91
Wong Tong, *Murder*

1886 *A woman on the gallows* 92
Ellen Thompson and John Harrison, *Murder*

1887 *The American killer* 95
Christopher Pickford, *Murder*

1888 ***A right royal ruckus over stolen boots*** 98
Benjamin Kitt, *Theft*

1888 ***Murder – and the Normanton riot*** 101
Sedin, *Murder*

1889 ***The strychnine scones*** 104
Elizabeth Hyde, *Murder*

1890 ***It's only a pumpkin I found*** 107
Maurice Lonergan & Percy Matthews, *Theft*

1890 ***The law would show no mercy*** 108
Michael Barry, *Murder*

1891 ***The Union conspirators*** 109
William Hamilton and others, *Conspiracy*

1892 ***Bones in his bed*** 112
Leonardo Moncardo, *Murder*

1892 ***Death among the pearl divers*** 114
George Gleeson, *Murder*

1893 ***The burning body*** 116
George Blantern, *Murder*

1894 ***Death of a swagman*** 119
Mi Orie and Narasemai, *Murder*

1895 ***The hallucinating husband*** 121
Charles Gibson, *Attempted murder*

1896 ***The Snob*** 123
Edward Hartigan, *Forgery*

1896 ***Marie, the mission matron*** 126
Marie Christensen, *Manslaughter*

1897 ***Double death at the asylum*** 127
Tommy Ango, *Murder*

1898 ***The murder of Warder Dodd*** 128
William Archer, *Murder*

1898 ***The Gatton mystery*** 131
Unsolved, *Murder*

1899 ***The Wooloongabba murder*** 134
Unsolved, *Murder*

1900 ***The fake suicide*** 138
Charles Beckman, *Murder*

1900 ***The jockey who sought revenge*** 140
Jack Smith, *Attempted murder*

1901 ***Bullets in the boardroom*** 142
David Brown, *Murder*

1902 ***The railway rascals*** 145
John Campbell & James Henderson, *Fraud and perjury*

1902 ***"The very man I wanted to meet"*** 146
Edgar H.W. Whitehouse, *False pretences*

1902 ***The last of the bushrangers*** 148
Patrick Kenniff & James Kenniff, *Murder*

1903 ***One killing was not enough*** 151
Sow Too Low, *Murder*

1903 ***The Longreach Cinderella*** 154
Florence and Angus Macdonald, *Murder*

1904 ***The Boonah publican*** 156
Robert Denner, *Manslaughter*

1905 ***One crime too many*** 158
James Warton, *Murder*

1905 ***Death of a policeman*** 161
Johannes, *Murder*

1906 ***Dobbed in by his wife and son*** 164
August Millewski, *Murder*

1906 ***The threepenny murder*** 167
Look Kow, *Murder*

1906 ***A killing in the kitchen*** 168
Twadiga, *Murder*

1907 ***The Townsville railway station robbery*** 169
Unsolved, *Robbery*

1908 ***The bungling bank robber*** 171
Arthur Ross, *Murder*

1909 ***The Carron River killings*** 174
Alexander Bradshaw, *Murder*

1909 ***Bismark, the murdering blacktracker*** 177
Bismark, *Murder*

1910 ***Tragedy in a tent*** 179
William Denton, *Murder*

1911 ***Butchery on a Sarina cane farm*** 181
George Silva, *Murder*

1912 ***The Turkey Station mystery*** 184
Unsolved, *Murder/Abduction*

1913 ***The last man to hang in Queensland*** 185
Ernest Austin, *Murder*

1914 ***The Mayne timber yard tragedy*** 188
Henry Hopgood, *Murder*

1915 ***The Oxley Creek infant murder*** 190
Ambrose Butwell, *Murder*

1916 ***Acid attack on the Victoria Bridge*** 193
Denis Buckmaster, *Grievous bodily harm*

1917 ***The missionary murderer*** 195
Burketown Peter, *Murder*

1918 ***Murder on the breakwater*** 198
John La Hay, *Murder*

1919 ***The Red Flag riot*** 200
15 protesters, *Exhibiting a red flag*

1920 ***The empty chamber*** 203
James Comerford, *Murder*

Commit the crime, do the time 206
Queensland's major prisons: The colonial years and beyond

From prison records... 208

References 210

Index 214

Introduction

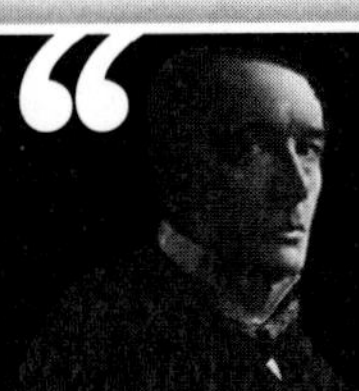

"Crime is an interest for many people of intellect and imagination. Indeed, how could it be otherwise? Rob history and fiction of crime, and how tame and colourless would be the residue![1]

Harry Brodribb Irving (1870-1919), lawyer and author

There's something about a crime that grabs our attention.

Perhaps we relate in some way to the victim (or the felon) – it's called the 'that-could-so-easily-have-been-me' factor. Or maybe it is our irrepressible urge to snoop, unobserved, into the offender's life – to wonder how the lawbreaker, motivated by greed, passion, anger, jealousy or hatred, could commit such an unlawful, even appalling act. Or maybe sometimes it's just the mystery or the 'who-done-it' component of it all!

Herbert Bloch and Gilbert Geis offer their explanation:

> 'Much of what appears to be morbid curiosity about crime and criminals may stem from our need to repress our own impulses toward lawlessness and violence. Concern with

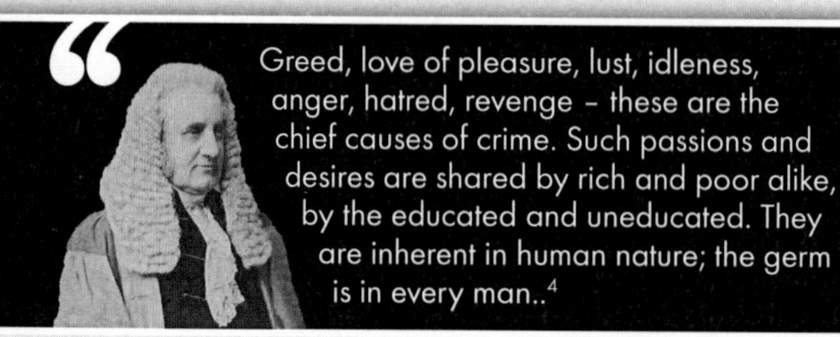

A French judge, cited in H.B.Irving's *A Book of Remarkable Criminals*

crime is said to represent a vicarious interest in wide-ranging motivations which actuate us all, and a tacit recognition that the impulses which turn some men towards lawless behaviour are really not so much different from the urges which law-abiding persons frequently experience, but manage to extinguish.

As well, crime appeals to the popular interest because it varies the humdrum of the normal and routine that is so much a part of daily life.'[2]

And, for some reason, the further back in time, the more fascinated with the crime we become – especially in an age when the authorities knew nothing of blood types, fingerprints, DNA or other modern-day crime-busting technologies. We can but marvel at the number of crimes they *did* solve back then!

This book focuses on six decades of criminal episodes – the four decades of Queensland as a colony, following its separation from New South Wales in 1859, and the first couple of decades of the twentieth century, from 1901 as one of the federated States. What becomes apparent is that early Queensland crimes not only provide a rich source of knowledge about the frailty and vulnerability of some human beings in those times, but also about the evolving societies of which they were a part – a proposition echoed by Carole McCartney and others:

> 'The prevalence and type of crime in any society can reveal (and is revealed by) wider social, political, economic and environmental conditions.'[3]

The history of Queensland in colonial times, among other things, is one of dispossession of and resentment, indeed retaliation, by indigenous peoples, of gold rushes, bushranging, blackbirding and racial tension, and of the spread of settlement, pastoralism, the sugar industry, and railways. Indeed, it is stimulating to reflect for a few moments upon how criminal behaviour in those days so colorfully footnotes, illuminates and annotates those evolutionary components of the state's genesis…

The *violent dispossession of indigenous peoples*, and their bitter struggle with colonizers, continued well into the 19th century. Thousands of Aborigines were brutally killed during that period, as were, in retaliation, many Europeans and other races. Colonial records are peppered with criminal files illustrative of those unfortunate times – for example, the pursuit and slaughter by native troopers of a party of Aborigines suspected of murdering pioneer gold fossicker Manuel Yous at Gilbert River (1878); the arraignment of the sadistic Lieutenant Frederick Wheeler of the Queensland Native Mounted Police for whipping and beating to death a young aboriginal lad (1876); the killing of three Europeans by Aborigines when fishing for dugong in Moreton Bay (1859), the murder of newly-wed Fanny Briggs near Rockhampton (1860) and rape of Bridget Ryan near Ipswich (1861), and the decapitation of a Presbyterian missionary and the besieging of his associates by Aborigines on Mornington Island (1917).

In the 1860s, Queensland was facing bankruptcy due to drought and the fall in wool prices. *The discovery of gold* saved the new colony. And with the gold came crime, usually motivated by greed, as many files reveal – including the cold-blooded murder of police troopers Power and Cahill by Gold Commissioner Thomas Griffin near Clermont (1867); the ambush and killing of gold-buyer Patrick Halligan (1869); the Mount Morgan Gold Mining Company gold-theft case (1893); and the Charters Towers Pyrites Company boardroom shooting (1901).

With the discovery of gold, *the bushranging epidemic* also reached Queensland and, while the colony avoided the notorious bushranging episodes that occurred in the southern colonies, many of Queensland's own brand of highwaymen also attained 'hero' status – The Fagan Gang (1864), The Wild Scotchman (1865), The Frenchman (1866), William Jenkins who held-up the Ipswich- Brisbane mail coach (1867), and others. But the authorities were determined to stamp out the problem – by introducing sentences of up to 25 years in gaol, the first two or three in irons!

The spread of *the pastoral industry* throughout the colony brought with it the cattle duffer. Cattle duffing was a major problem in the 1870s, with thousands of head 'going missing' in western frontier

districts. The most notorious of the cattle duffers was Harry Redford, widely believed to be the Captain Starlight character in Rolf Boldrewood's novel *Robbery Under Arms*. Redford and two accomplices drove 1000 stolen cattle over 1000 miles across uncharted country from Aramac into South Australia – only to be found 'not guilty' by a sympathetic Roma jury (1872), a finding that caused Australia-wide bewilderment.

Indeed, crime would lower its sinister hand on many of *the colony's infant industries* – the sugar industry was rocked when a mother and her five children were butchered by a cane worker on a Sarina cane farm (1911); wool-washer Walter Gordon shot dead the manager at a sheep station outside Muttaburra (1885); in the Torres Strait, pearl diver George Gleeson opened fire on a fellow worker, because he was bored (1892); and a rowdy 18-year-old wheat farm worker was slain by an irate publican at Emu Vale (1920)… to list but a few examples.

> Convicted criminals are just like other people; in fact, I often think that, but for different opportunities and other accidents, the prisoner and I might very well be in one another's places.[6]

A British judge, cited in H.B.Irving's *A Book of Remarkable Criminals*

In the 1880s, seeking cheap labour for the colony's cotton and sugar plantations, *blackbirders* raided South Sea Islands, kidnapping tens of thousands of islanders. Those who resisted they murdered in cold blood. At a show trial (1884), and beyond, a political battle raged over the innocence or otherwise of the convicted crew of the *Hopeful*, who were imprisoned for long terms on St Helena Island for murder and kidnapping. A dark and controversial episode in colonial Queensland's history.

The shadow of *racism* also loomed large in colonial Queensland. Initially directed against indigenous peoples, it later focused on South Sea Islanders (kanakas), Chinese and other Asians. Such groups were seen as posing an economic threat: they were willing (or required, in the case of conscripted kanakas) to work long hours for low pay. This, coupled with problems of language, assimilation and, most of all, social acceptance, was the source of much disruption, violence and lawbreaking.

Many were derided for 'being involved in opium and gambling dens, brothels and reputedly having "hot tempers and wild ways", committing murders and ending their days on the colonial gallows'[5] – Chinese Tommy was executed for stabbing to death the man who had killed his dog (1862); as were Wong Tong for killing his brother who owed him money (1886), Mi Ori and Narasemai for hacking to death an old swagman selling matches (1894), So Too Low who murdered

CADBURY'S COCOA ESSENCE

QUEENSLAND FIGARO PUNCH

TITBITS OF EVERYDAY ABOUT EVERYBODY, AND EVERYTHING WITH A PEEP AT SOCIETY, SCIENCE, SPORT, AND THE DRAMA.

BRISBANE: SATURDAY, DECEMBER 4, 1886.

THE CHINESE PLAGUE.

C. REESE,

In colonial times, press acrimony did much to heighten racial tension and foster associated law-breaking.

12-year-old Alice Gunning near Mackay and a few months later a warder in Mackay Gaol (1903), Johannes who stabbed a policeman to death (1905), and Look Tow, who tomahawked-to-death a fellow gambler over a threepenny wager (1906).

The situation was not helped by an overtly racist press. *Figaro* visualised the Chinese as a plague of grasshoppers, 'pests' that needed to be 'exterminated'; and the *Charters Towers Eagle* depicted them as 'a yellow agony' and likened them to 'the spread of a lasting pestilence'. According to the *Brisbane Courier*, South Sea Islanders were 'savages, dark-minded and cruel-hearted'.

Not surprisingly, such press acrimony frequently provoked isolated eruptions of racial tension that inevitably saw the conviction of many for 'riot, unlawful assembly and affray'. Crocodile Creek near Rockhampton was the first goldfield in Queensland where white diggers would eject the Chinese, after burning down and destroying Chinese Street and their market gardens (1867). Kanakas were the target of white anger at the Boxing Day riot at Mackay Racecourse (1883). There was more mob violence in Normanton when white miners, fishermen and merchants torched a large Malay camp and drove 'the terrified aliens' out of town (1888).

Not that racism in those early days was the motivation for all rioting and the subsequent gaoling of ringleaders and exuberant followers. It seems that striking workers and demonstrators have a history of clashing with police in Queensland – protesting Roman Catholics used chair legs, cudgels and shillelaghs on a Protestant crowd in Ipswich (1874); some twenty unionists spent up to three years on St Helena Island following the

The ultimate colonial punishment – death by hanging

Great Shearers' Strike (1891); and the Red Flag Riot saw returned soldiers clashing with police and Bolsheviks on the streets of South Brisbane (1919).

This period also embraces the age of *capital punishment* in Queensland, when nearly ninety men (and one woman) were hanged for their crimes. The stories on the pages that follow reference many of these harrowing executions, including the triple hanging that never was (1862); the botched execution of the only woman to be hanged in the colony, for assisting in the murder of her husband (1886), and of the scaffold's youngest victim, 17-year-old Frank Horrocks (1892); the hanging of two kanaka murderers, witnessed by fourteen of their countrymen who were forced to watch, lined up in front of the scaffold in 'extreme anxiety and horror', lest in the future they too 'be tempted to take the life of a fellow man' (1894); and the State's last hanging, that of Ernest Austin, for the killing of 12-year-old schoolgirl Ivy Mitchell at Samford (1913).

Many of colonial Queensland's crimes attracted Australia-wide attention – the unsolved Gatton paddock mystery where three Murphy siblings were brutally murdered (1898); the capture of the death-dealing Kenniff brothers, the 'last of Queensland's bushrangers', and their trial and its aftermath (1902); and Moncardo (1892), the murderer who chopped up his victim and took the bones to bed!...

But if such atrocities hold our attention because of their notoriety, other lesser known offences retold in *A Cavalcade of*

Queensland's Crimes and Criminals are no less absorbing – such as that of the Cunnamulla bank robber who was caught after being chased up a tree by a yapping sheep-dog (1880); or of John Kitt's imprisonment for stealing two pairs of boots, an act that would bring down the Government a few months later (1888); or of the courageous police magistrate Willie Hill who crawled in darkness along an abandoned mineshaft in pursuit of murderer Joseph Mutter (1879); or of the 'paralysed' rascal who, having 'fallen out of a train', presented the Queensland government with a £10,000 writ (1902); or of the suave Edgar Whitehouse who, among other things, impersonated a Congregational parson and was 'admired, feted and trusted by the cream of Gympie society' – until he was exposed and gaoled for false pretences (1902)…

All are real-life episodes that span the sizeable patchwork of Queensland's criminal past. They are but a few of the dozens of stories that feature in *A Cavalcade of Queensland's Crimes and Criminals: Scoundrels, Scallywags and Psychopaths – The colonial years and beyond.* ■

On the pages that follow, for every year after the colony's separation from New South Wales – from 1859 to 1920, Queensland's most notable crimes are recounted.

Six decades of murder, robbery, theft, bushranging, assault, stabbing, rape, riot, kidnapping, fraud, arson, conspiracy, forgery, cattle duffing…

Some of the perpetrators would never be brought to justice. Many of the offenders would serve long periods in prison. Others would receive the ultimate penalty – death by hanging.

Turn the page, and begin your stroll through the colony's early years, through its dark side, through a cavalcade of Queensland's crimes and criminals.

And, in doing so, here's something to reflect upon: it is but *one* very brief selection of our State's many thousands of scoundrels, scallywags and psychopaths – a few of whom are also depicted here…

Conspiracy 3 yrs

False pretences 18 mth

Illegally using horse 6 mths

Burglary 5 yr

Breaking/entering 18 mths

Wife desertion 1 y

Murder Death

Perjury 5 yrs

Assault 14 days

Obscene language 6 mths

llegal pawning 6 mths
Bigamy 2 yrs
Vagrancy 6 mths
Murder Life
Shooting w. intent 10 yrs
Vagrancy 6 mths
Larceny 6 mths
Arson 7 yrs
Loitering w. intent 6mths
Forgery 18 mths
Manslaughter 2 yrs
Murder Death
Embezzlement 3 yrs
Larceny 12 mths
Forgery 3 yrs
Destruction of property 1 yr

The slaughter of three St Helena fishermen

At noon on Thursday, 27 January 1859, as the steamer *Hawk* made its way from Moreton Bay into the Brisbane River, the bloated body of a man was seen on the bank near Luggage Point, just on the high water mark.

Captain Twine sent two men ashore in the ship's boat, and the badly decomposed corpse was retrieved and taken aboard the *Hawk* to Brisbane.

The corpse 'presented a ghastly appearance'. The right arm, neck and chest had been hacked 'by not a very sharp cutting instrument – perhaps a tomahawk'. The bones of the face and jaws were smashed.

There was no doubt that the deceased had been 'foully and brutally murdered', and it was feared that, whoever this was, the state of the body would prevent recognition.

But the distinctive shirt and boots, and a gold digger's belt with many pockets in it, led to early identification by friends and family. It was Bob Hunter *alias* Robert Collins.

TWO weeks earlier, Hunter, accompanied by a man named Morgan, and a recently arrived unknown Dutchman, a net-maker, had set out for Moreton Bay to hunt dugong. They were provisioned for about nine days.

Hunter was experienced in 'the Bay trade'. He was well known to the local Aborigines and often used them in his dugong hunts.

Suspicion initially fell upon Aborigines. According to Hunter's wife: "They had no blacks on board when they started, but they would have blacks with them afterwards, as they could not well manage without them. They said they were going to take some in."

And did not the evidence point to a native tomahawk as the possible murder weapon?

OF immediate concern was the whereabouts of Hunter's two white companions. Had they shared the same fate?

A search of the Bay and river over the days that followed found no clues. In the ensuing weeks, several scenarios were canvassed in the press…

> 'Suspicion points to Ballow, a blackfellow, who could give some clue to the mysterious tragedy; and the rumours in circulation, as to the threats used by this notorious black against the deceased, make out a sufficient *prima facie* case to justify his arrest…'

> Collins and Morgan and the foreigner were not good friends, 'because they had spent the foreigner's money' and misstated the rate of wages – sufficient grounds for suspecting a quarrel between them. Was the foreigner the killer?…

> A Mr Izzam of Amity Point claimed

that 'a Ningi Ningi gin, who was in the boat with Collins and his party, told him: "The party first went to Bribie Island, where they stayed for a few days without catching anything. While there, they had a disturbance with a party of seven or eight Ningi Ningi blacks, but on their return to Brisbane…, they carried these blacks over to the mainland at their own request and left them there.

When they reached the Pine River, Collins put in there, and stretched his nets across the stream for the night. At a very early hour the next morning, the party were surprised in their sleep by the seven or eight blacks, and all three of the whites were murdered, and their bodies thrown into the river…"'

The newspaper dubiously concluded: 'Our readers can place their own construction on this version of the catastrophe.'

The press, like everyone else, was at a loss, concluding: 'Granted that mystery surrounds the whole tragedy, it appears to us to be too early to suspect the whites or the blacks…'

IN March, Tom Petrie, the respected brother of John Petrie, Brisbane's first mayor (1859-1862), brought some finality to the episode. His Aboriginal friends had told him the three fishermen were murdered by Aborigines on St Helena Island *(see box below)*, who then dragged the bodies to the low water mark, and left them there:

> 'They then took the boat over to Bribie, and from thence to Maroochy Doore river. The boat

STORY OF THE MURDERED MEN.—The story of the way in which Collins, Morgan, and the Dutchman met their death is revived. Mr. T. Petrie, from his knowledge of the aboriginal language, is enabled to corroborate the published account in which the poor fellows met their death, differing only in slight details. The public are satisfied of their end; and they know, also, that the blacks have escaped punishment.

TOM PETRIE was the fourth son of the Moreton Bay settlement's well known builder, Andrew Petrie. Tom had arrived in the new colony with his family as a boy in 1837, at a time when the settlement on the Brisbane River was little more than a village 'of about ten buildings'. He was brought up amongst the Aborigines of the area, learned their language and habits, and was accepted in their circle as a trusted friend. Petrie claimed he knew the full story of the 1859 killings, told to him by the offender, whom he named as Billy Dingy. His account was later recorded in his published reminiscences[1]...

Three men were murdered at St Helena Island by aboriginals and this is the account given to me by 'Billy Dingy', one of the blacks concerned.

Billy said that he and two other young men, each with a young wife, were taken in a boat by three white men, who had promised to land them at Bribie Island, as it was then the great 'bunya season', and the Aborigines always met there before travelling to the Bunya Mountains (to feast ▶

on wild bunya nuts)... Well, these men, instead of doing as they had promised, landed on St Helena, and there set their nets for catching dugong, acting as though they had not the slightest intention of going near Bribie. They also took possession of the young girls, paying no heed to Billy, who pleaded for their wives and to be taken to Bribie as promised.

So Billy, poor soul, didn't know what to do and at last he determined to kill them.

He did it in this way:

Some distance from where they were camped, a cask was sunk in the sand for fresh water and Billy, in broken English, called to one of the men, Bob Hunter by name:

'Bob, Bob, come quick, bring gun, plenty duck sit down longa here.'

Bob went to Billy all unthinking and, passing the cask in the sand, knelt to drink. There was Billy's chance and he took it, striking the man from behind with a tomahawk on the back of the head. Bob threw up his arm to save himself, only to be cut on the arm, and then again on the head and was killed. Billy then dragged him down to the water. And that was the end of that man.

On returning to the camp after this 'deed of darkness', Billy told the gins in his own language what had happened, that he meant to finish by killing the other two, and that they could all get away together. The gins begged him not to kill the others, but his mind was fixed and remained unmoved.

Fortune favoured him surely, for he found one man sitting alone by a camp fire, smoking, and, creeping up stealthily behind him, cut open his head with the tomahawk. This man's body was in turn dragged to the water.

There now remained but one other and he at that time was away in the scrub shooting pigeons. Billy followed and, watching his opportunity, struck the white man as he stooped to go under a vine. This last was also dragged to the water, and that was the end of the three.

After the white men were thus disposed of, the natives all got into the boat and came to the mouth of the Pine River, where they left the boat and, walking round on the mainland opposite Bribie, swam across to the island.

Bob Hunter's body was afterwards recovered, and it had a cut arm even as Billy described. The other bodies were never found and it was thought they were eaten by sharks.

I had these three men – Billy and the others – working for me afterwards till their death and I was alone for days with Billy in the forest looking for cedar timber. I found them all right.

Who can say the blacks were wholly to blame on St Helena Island that day?"

has been brought back to Kaloundra by the three blacks, who were afraid to bring it any further, fearing the whites might imagine *they* were the guilty parties. They say there is a gun, two pistols, harpoons, sails, and a tent, oil tins and blankets, all the same as left by the deceased...' [*sic*]

Although there were some who called for retribution, the murderers of the three fishermen were never brought to justice: Prior to the mid-1870s, statements made by Aborigines were not admissible in Court, nor were they allowed to appear in the courtroom as witnesses. ■

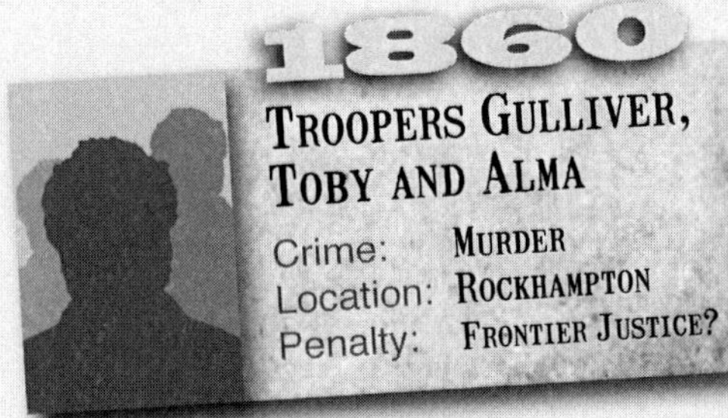

They didn't need the hangman

Newly-weds Johnny Watts and Fanny Briggs lived in a comfortable homestead on the Rockhampton-Gracemere Road in the late 1850s. The couple ran some horses and cattle, and Johnny conducted a butchering business in town.

The crime

ON the morning of 6 November 1860, after Johnny had ridden off to attend his business in Rockhampton, 22-year-old Fanny, as usual, rode off in search of stray horses…

When Johnny returned home that night, and finding no trace of his wife, he immediately organised a search party. They could not locate her.

The next day others joined the search, including the detachment of local Native Police troopers.

Five days later, Fanny's mutilated body was found near Scrubby Creek. It was clear to the examining medico that Fanny had been 'murdered, abused and mutilated in the fashion of Aborigines', a finding that 'caused much alarm in the neighbourhood' and served to intensify racial hatred in the area.

The murder exposed

SOME time after the discovery of Fanny's body, the Native Troopers were sent to quell a disturbance at a Rockhampton pub. Drunk themselves, the troopers bashed an Aboriginal woman who, in retaliation, loudly threatened that she would tell the police who had murdered Fanny, 'the white Mary'!

Word reached the police and the woman was interviewed. Native troopers Gulliver, Toby, and Johnny Reid (who was later released through lack of evidence) were arrested; trooper Alma was away on patrol at the time but was soon escorted back to Rockhampton.

A newspaper report later revealed the terrible tale:

> Fanny Briggs was on horseback that morning near the scrub, about one and a half miles from her residence, where five troopers and three gins were catching opossoms. She asked one of them who had come outside the scrub if he had seen any horses. He answered, 'Yes,' and whistled to his mates. She was then pulled

Left: *Gulliver's Waterhole today, outside Dululu in central Queensland, where Trooper Gulliver was shot while trying to escape capture. He was one of three Native Police Troopers arrested for the murder of Fanny Briggs at Scrubby Creek near Rockhampton.*

> from her horse, taken into the scrub, ravished by these scoundrels, and then brutally murdered – or as they themselves express it, when they found they had gone too far – 'Blackfellow too much frightened, white Mary directly yabber; then blackfellow kill him white Mary'. To confirm their guilt, of which there can be no doubt, her handkerchief was found with Toby's gin, in the police camp. This handkerchief had a peculiarly broad hem, and has been sworn to as the property of Fanny Briggs…

Retribution

THE three suspects were never brought to trial.

Following his arrest, trooper Gulliver agreed to show police where Fanny was murdered and to reveal where some of the girl's clothes were hidden.

Accompanied by two armed constables, at Scrubby Creek he dragged some of Fanny's items from a hollow log. Her veil, he said, was hidden in a hole high in a tree, but he would need to climb it and use a tomahawk to enlarge the hole.

Handcuffs removed and, up the tree, Gulliver soon had wood chips flying into the faces of the constables below, 'forcing them to move back'. The prisoner sprang from the tree, knocked the men down, and fled into the scrub. The police fired but failed to fell the fugitive.

Over the next few days, police and trackers followed Gulliver's trail for some fifty miles, to Westwood and further south. Along the way, Gulliver had been stealing food, blankets, tomahawks and pistols from shepherds' huts. They finally caught up with him at the Dee River where Dululu now stands, but he heard them approaching and he fled once more.

Good news for the police next morning – they were told that teamsters, overnight, had captured Gulliver near the Dee River crossing. One report stated:

> As some drays had crossed the river going to Rockhampton, Gulliver apparently thought his best chance of getting away was to double back. With these drays was a tame blackfellow named Remus whom Gulliver cautiously approached and asked to be sheltered under the tarpaulin of the dray, as the police were after him for "killing a white

Mary" at Rockhampton. Remus promised to do so saying, "All right, you bin come up longa night."

Gulliver agreed to do so and when it grew dark he came up to the drays, where he was given some gin to drink. They supplied him with drink until he was intoxicated, and then the teamsters fell on him and securely bound him.

When the police prepared to start back to Rockhampton with their prisoner, Gulliver refused to walk a step, and shouted, "Shoot me here, you bastards."

A man passing in a buggy was called on in the Queen's name for assistance and Gulliver was transported as far as a waterhole at the junction of the road to Mount Morgan.

There, 'in trying to escape', Gulliver was shot dead.

TROOPER Toby's fate is somewhat obscure; it is said that the troopers 'escorted him out into the bush and came back without him, presumably shot'.

Trooper Alma's death is also puzzling. The lockup keeper at the Rockhampton stockade took him down to the river to get water, handcuffed and wearing leg irons. The constable reported that, when Alma stooped to dip his bucket in the water, he plunged into the river and tried to escape, even though weighed down with leg irons and handcuffs. The constable shot him dead. There were those who found this explanation hard to accept; many believed that Alma was shot on the bank and thrown into the river.

Retribution, 1860s style, for the violation and death of dainty little Fanny Briggs! ■

Handcuffs with history?

Ten years later:
Sydney Morning Herald, 4 March 1870:

'THOSE were wild times, and the shooting down of the three blacks who were supposed to have committed the deed of atrocity against Fanny Briggs was looked upon as retribution and, in fact, as necessary, in order to prove to the aborigines that the white man was not to be wronged with impunity...

Trooper Alma was handcuffed and told to go down to the river, which was running not many yards below the barracks where he was confined, and fetch a pail of water. When the poor fool reached the bank he made a dash for his freedom and plunged into the river; hardly had he risen to the surface, when a bullet from the trooper's rifle killed him dead. He sunk like a stone, and nobody looked for him, or cared what became of his body. This was near ten years ago.

On Saturday a person was fishing in the Fitzroy over the spot where the black sunk. He felt something heavy at the end of his line, pulled up, and found that the hook had caught, what appeared at first to be a lump of stone and mud, but upon looking more closely it was found to be a pair of handcuffs, the connecting chain of which was perfectly hidden by rust, mud and pebbles, but in the centre of the chain, imbedded in one of the links, was a small round black substance which when scraped with a knife was found to be lead. There is a firm belief that the handcuffs were those on the wrists of the unfortunate trooper Alma who was shot ten years ago.

The theory is that the bullet passed through the man's body and lodged in the third link of the chain. We, of course, give no opinion upon this subject; there is a probability that the prevailing idea is correct, as the spot where the handcuffs were fished up was precisely the same as that where the black was shot, and the bullet goes to show that whoever wore these must have met a violent death.'

The ex-convict killer

Thomas Woods was a former convict who, in 1827, barely a teenager, had been transported to Van Diemen's Land for stealing a coat in Bristol. After serving out his sentence, he moved as a free man to the mainland where he spent his time, in the vernacular of the day, 'knocking about'.

In the late 1850s Woods found himself west of Gayndah in Queensland, as a bullock driver working for Archibald Campbell at Coonambula station.

On 30 March 1860, Woods spent the night in the hut of a fellow worker, shepherd Gabriel Morell, where he by chance found out that his host had a moderately large sum on money in his possession – sufficient, the contemporary press later reported, for Woods to plot 'a cold-blooded deed, a murder most foul, strange and unnatural'.

£50 REWARD
or
CONDITIONAL PARDON
For the arrest of the suspected murderer of Gabriel Morell, at Coonambula, in the district of Gayndah.

The description of the fugitive is as follows:— Name—Thomas Woods (or Wood); age—about 42 years; calling—bullock driver; height—about 5 feet 8 inches; complexion—sallow; hair—sandy, intermixed with grey, bald over forehead; remarks—sandy whiskers under the chin; an Englishman; speaks in a drawling manner; dress when last seen, Scotch twill shirt, moleskin trousers, blucher boots, Panama hat.

NEXT morning, Morell started out for one of Campbell's sheep runs, about seven miles from his hut. Woods offered to accompany him most of the way, saying he was going to a neighbouring station.

The pair had to pass through some thick scrub. Here Woods fired at Morell from behind with a pistol, the ball entering his back and lodging in his stomach. The horse bolted and Morell soon fell from the saddle.

Badly injured, but still with sufficient strength, Morell made for open ground. He was overtaken by Woods who threatened to drag him 'back into the scrub and finish him'.

"Oh, for God's sake," said Morell, "don't kill me! I suppose it is my money you want – here it is," handing him a pocketbook, containing cheques and loose change – amounting to £97.

Woods took the money, and said, "You had better come back anyway."

Back in the scrub, and knowing Woods' intention, Morell made another desperate break through the scrub and fortuitously came across his horse, which he mounted and rode in agony to the station.

Doctor and police were sent for. Morell was rapidly sinking from the effects of his wound but was able to give the details of his harrowing ordeal. Despite assiduous care, he died a couple of days later.

Meanwhile Campbell, two Aborigines and a constable were already on the track of the murderer. He eluded them.

Woods, well known in the district, was apprehended some weeks later, and was brought to trial in Brisbane on 16 November 1860 for the murder of Gabriel Morell. He was found guilty and sentenced to death.

ON THE EVE of his execution, the first for the new colony of Queensland, Woods continued to protest his innocence – even complaining that someone, eight months earlier, had taken *his* £97, the exact amount he had stolen from his victim, Morell.

Present at Woods' hanging at Brisbane Gaol, Petrie Terrace, on 7 December 1860 were some thirty citizens, who were admitted by ticket. Outside the walls, in the boughs of trees at the back of the building, there were other spectators and, according to the *Moreton Bay Courier*, 'as is usual on such occasions, the females exhibited no less anxiety to gratify their morbid curiosity than the men'.

The *Courier* continued: 'The drop fell and Thomas Woods was instantly launched into eternity with no spasmodic convulsion of the body, which ordinarily indicates the struggle that takes place between life and death'. ■

Sidelight

GALLERY OF THE SUPREME COURT. Yesterday whilst the trial of Woods was being proceeded with, the bannister of the gallery immediately over the Judge's head gave unmistakeable indications of a precipitate descent and, as his Honor did not desire to see Mr. Abraham and perhaps the Attorney-General converted into martyrs on behalf of their country, he judiciously directed the police to remove the large body of people from that portion of the gallery from whence the danger was anticipated. There are some persons of such morbid curiosity that they would gaze on the face of a blood-thirsty criminal forever, and it was in the gratification of this desire that the rush took place which occasioned the alarm, and which caused the hairs of Attorney-General Pring's wig to stand on end.

— *Moreton Bay Courier*, 17 November 1860

1860. IN June the mutilated body of a shepherd Garrick Burns was found face down in grass on Clifton Station near Toowoomba. Suspicion immediately fell upon Kimboo, a Chinese swagman with a violent temper and a razor-sharp butcher's knife. Arresting police found blood stains on his trousers, swag and knife – and Kimboo's face bore fresh scratch marks. The evidence against him was circumstantial, but police argued the murder was the result of an argument over a blanket. Kimboo's death sentence was later commuted to life imprisonment.

In 1871, while in Brisbane Gaol, the bad-empered Kimboo killed a fellow prisoner, 70-year-old Michael Turley [see page 15], bashing in his skull with a broom handle.

That tell-tale bump

Bridget Ryan lived at Little Ipswich*. On the evening of 11 October 1861 she left home to look for stray calves. She crossed over the One Mile bridge and, turning off the road to the left, she saw the calves in a hollow.

A contemporary newspaper continues the tale:

> Bridget went towards the calves, and on her way found that a blackfellow was running after her, with his hands open, as if to catch her. She was frightened, and screamed, and when the blackfellow attempted to seize her, she gave him a push, which caused him to fall down. He got up again, and after a violent struggle, succeeded in committing a ravishing of the most disgusting barbarity. He beat her about the head and face with a boot and a spur. The blackfellow had a distinguishing bump upon his body.
>
> The man was with her about two hours. When he left, she crawled on her hands and knees until she came to the One Mile bridge; it was then moonlight.
>
> She was almost blinded by the blood which streamed from the wounds on her head and face. When she reached the bridge she called to two men who were passing, and subsequently her husband and some neighbours came and bore her home.

It was said that Bridget threw up nearly two quarts of blood when she reached the house. Initially, her condition was grave. She was regularly visited by Dr Challinor and was unable to stir without assistance for three weeks.

ON THE DAY after the incident, police and local men returned to the scene, where they found boots, a bag and a spur. There was plenty of blood on the ground.

Suspicion immediately fell upon an aboriginal man named Georgie, an employee of Colin Peacock of nearby Warrell Creek. Peacock had that day sent Georgie on a message in that direction. He identified the boots, bag and spur as being with the Aborigine when he left for Ipswich that day. And, yes, Georgie had an identifiable protuberance [unspecified] on his body.

In the meantime, the suspect had made himself scarce, and he eluded police over the days that followed.

Colin Peacock also employed two aboriginal bullock drivers, Brandy

* In the 1860s Little Ipswich was an area near One Mile bridge, now West Ipswich, which was divided into small farmlets and allotments for vegetable gardens. The nearby inn accommodated bullock drivers who camped their teams there overnight enroute to Toowoomba.

and Billy Ross. He told them about Georgie and offered them a reward if they could capture him.

Supplied with leg irons, the pair set out in a dray for Little Ipswich, where they left the dray outside Balbi's inn. Nearby, in an aboriginal encampment, they knew Georgie was hiding. They managed to lure the suspect to the inn with the promise of liquor. A press report related what followed:

> Brandy seized him, drew him to the door, called out to Mr. Balbi, and then threw him into the bar by main force. He then held him down and tied him, Mr. Balbi fastening his legs, and Mr. George Macdonald and Brandy his arms.

As reward for the capture of the fugitive, the government provided inn-keeper Balbi with £25 (which he donated to Ipswich Hospital) and Brandy with '£5, two suits of clothes, five pounds of tobacco, and blankets &c'.

IN EARLY November, Georgie, heavily chained and accompanied by two constables, was taken down to Brisbane by Ipswich steamer to Petrie Terrace Gaol.

At the Supreme Court on 11 November 1861, he was tried for having raped Bridget Ryan, found guilty, and sentenced to be hanged.

Bridget's identification of that tell-tale 'protuberance on his body', was a key factor in his conviction. ■

A desperate act

FOLLOWING his trial, the condemned man, 'showing great symptoms of dread', had been returned to his cell, with his arms handcuffed behind him.

Immediately, in great despair, Georgie succeeded in getting his arms in front of his body, and began rubbing the handcuffs to and fro over the small lump somewhere on his body, by which he had been identified as the rapist, apparently with the aim of obliterating that tell-tale mark. A doctor was needed to attend to his bleeding wound.

He was hanged on 5 December.

Fragments from The FILES of FELONS

1861. IT was a Saturday night in June when James Carnill stealthily entered the Brisbane residence of Jeremiah Scanlan through a bedroom window. Inside, just as he found a cash box, he was discovered.

He leapt back through the window, cash box under his arm, and fled. Chased by Scanlan and his son, he jumped a couple of garden fences, and discarded the box, before being felled by his pursuers, who held him down until police arrived. When taken into custody, police found a pick-lock and skeleton keys in his pocket.

For the actual robbery, Carnill was later sentenced to six months imprisonment – and for having skeleton keys in his possession, he received an additional eighteen months hard labour!

1862. IN December, an ill German Frederick Strauss claimed he had been bailed up and robbed of everything on the Gowrie-Jondaryan Road. Inquiries later revealed he had lied – in an attempt to get admitted into hospital as a pauper patient. He was sentenced to a week in the cells.

Three for the gallows

It would be Queensland's first triple hanging, so the year 1862 provided a noteworthy event for the new colony, particularly for those who planned to climb trees outside the walls of Brisbane Gaol on Petrie Terrace to witness the occasion. Three men – a Chinaman and two Aborigines – were scheduled to face the gallows on 2 April of that year.

Tommy

TOMMY was a Chinese immigrant who worked as a shepherd on a property at Apis Creek near Duaringa. He had been arrested on a charge of wilful murder for stabbing to death another employee, George Lang, whom he accused of killing his dog.

Tommy was a confused individual who failed to understand his predicament. Before and during the trial, he wavered between confessing his guilt and denying his involvement. Through an interpreter, he invariably mixed up issues of wages with the affair and said that he hoped the trial would soon be over because he 'only wants to be allowed to take another situation and get money'.

In mid-March, Tommy was tried at the half-yearly sittings of the Supreme Court in Maryborough, found guilty of murder, and sentenced to death. According to the press, the sentencing 'created some excitement' when the judge 'did not don the black cap as usual on such occasions, which circumstance gave rise to a considerable amount of gossip among the spectators'.

In the end, Tommy knew he was going to die, but insisted that he would not be hanged, and that he would oppose it to the end. As the contemporary press wrote: 'We fear that the resistance of the poor wretch will avail him little when the fatal hour comes'.

Time would tell.

Billy Horton and Kipper Billy

IN the 1860s, the land on the Brisbane River, around Fernvale today, was cut into small blocks and opened to settlers, who were subsidised by the Government to grow cotton. The area was known as Fernie Lawn. In 1861, the Raes were one of those families pioneering the district.

Just before Christmas of 1861, Mrs Jane Rae had been washing down at the river and about noon went back to the family hut to put the kettle on.

When fetching some wood chips at the saw-pit nearby, she was approached from behind by an Aborigine, who grabbed her by the hair. He was joined by another who also appeared out of the surrounding scrub.

"These two pulled me down," she later said, "when another came out of the scrub, wearing a clean blue

Scotch twill shirt and holding up his trousers; he beat me and committed an offence upon me, while the first two held me down, one by my head, the other by my arms. Then another big blackfellow, the fourth and naked, pulled the first off me."

Later she was dragged to the river, 'insensible', but could recollect screaming as loud as she could.

When her son, hearing the screams, came riding to the scene, the Aborigines dived into the river, swam across, and disappeared into the scrub opposite.

Son Edward later gave his version of the ordeal:

> Being attracted by the screams at the river, I saw my mother near the scrub; her hair was hanging down her back, her arms were bleeding and her dress was nearly torn off her back... She made the complaint to me. I fetched my sisters from up the river. I returned to my mother twenty minutes after I first saw her, and found her raving and screaming, and trying to get the mare down to the river. I went across the river to see my father, while another man got my mother back to the hut.

In a disoriented state, Mrs Rae provided descriptions of her attackers to the police, sufficient for constables and native troopers to begin a search of the district.

Two hours after the assault, the aboriginal group was seen on the Pritchards' property, four miles away. In time, Billy Horton was found hiding under a dray; later, Kipper Billy was located near the river at Wivenhoe.

Both were committed to trial for the capital offence of rape.

Initially, Mrs Rae stated that Billy Horton was present while two others committed violence on her, but that he took no part in it. Later she affirmed on oath that he was the very one who committed the crime.

One point made in the trial was clear, as defence counsel Bramston was to argue: 'There is great difficulty in identifying blacks'.

At the trial Billy Horton himself pleaded: "Your Honour and jury gentlemen – This woman came before magistrates one time, she say me not the blackfellow at all; another time she come before magistrates and said me be blackfellow who did it. She not know what to think."

Billy Horton was known in the district and his involvement seemed dubious to some. John Petrie, then mayor of Brisbane, said that he knew Billy Horton 'when quite a lad, and he was then one of the most well-disposed and well-behaved of the Aborigines frequenting the streets of the town'.

On the other hand, Kipper Billy was a stranger – although a letter was received from F. E. Bigge, offering to give evidence as to Kipper Billy's character, describing him as 'a black of the worst character possible, a great villain, and so cunning that he was hardly ever found out, &c.'

On 4 February 1862, a jury found both men guilty of the rape of Mrs Jane Rae. The judge pronounced sentence separately:

> You shall be taken from where you are now to the place from whence you came, and thence to the common gaol in Brisbane, and there, on such day as it shall please his Excellency the Governor, with the advice of his Executive Council, to appoint, you shall be led to the place of execution, and to be there hanged by the neck until you are dead. And may God have mercy on your soul.

And in April 1862, the citizens of the new colony would be witnessing their first triple hanging... ▶

Three appointments with the hangman

Three executions were scheduled for 2 April 1862 at Brisbane Gaol on Petrie Terrace.

Tommy

First to face the hangman was Tommy. The prisoner was led out shortly before nine o'clock on that Wednesday morning. Courageous before the event, he vowed that he 'was a very good fellow' and that he would 'go to the sky', for a white man had told him so.

But the small amount of fortitude he had mustered deserted him at the foot of the gallows. He rolled and writhed on the ground, sobbing heavily and shouting that he would not die.

Two Aborigines were made to carry him up the steps of the scaffold. With Tommy refusing to stand up, the hangman adjusted the rope while he lay on the drop; the bolt was drawn, and in a minute the murderer of George Lang was a lifeless corpse.

Billy Horton

Observing proceedings that morning, through the grating over the doorway of his cell, was Billy Horton, one of the two Aborigines sentenced to death for the capital offence of rape. But at the eleventh hour, the Under-Sheriff and the chaplain approached his cell and advised him that the Governor had granted him an absolute pardon: evidence had come to light that Billy had been wrongly identified by the confused victim as one of the perpetrators of the crime.

The press reported that, 'as the heavy irons on his legs were stricken off, and as the last rivet fell, the poor fellow heaved a long sigh of relief, his countenance was overspread with an expression of joyfulness which very rarely is witnessed in every day life'.

Kipper Billy

Convicted rapist Kipper Billy also missed his appointment with the hangman that day. On 5 March, the condemned man had made a dash across the exercise yard at Petrie Terrace gaol, scaled the surrounding fence – and was shot dead by one of the guards.

The missing head

Kipper Billy was buried in unconsecrated ground, in land promised to the Church of England. In April, a rumour circulated: someone had removed the skull from the corpse! Controversy erupted when, after the body was exhumed and the rumour confirmed, church wardens, on information they had received, accused parliamentarian and well known local chemist, T. S. Warry, of the deed, a claim he vehemently denied. The press had a field day.

Death on a sheep station

In the early 1860s, a young Gordon Davidson was station manager at Mitchell Downs in the Maranoa District.

On 21 April 1863, Davidson, accompanied by two shepherds, Walter Stack and James Connolly, rode to an out-station where another shepherd, Michael Turley, had been left in charge of a large flock of sheep.

On arrival, they found no trace of Turley at his hut where he should have been, but located him and the sheep a few miles further on.

That day, Davidson was a little ill-tempered.

"Why have you driven the sheep all through this scrub?" he snapped at Turley.

The exchange continued for a time, Davidson speaking to the man as a manager of a large sheep station might do when he found that his worker had blatantly neglected the mustering entrusted to him.

Davidson then ordered the men to take the flock to a yard about half a mile away to be counted.

When Turley offered advice on how to make the count, Davidson again raised his voice: "Hold your clatter, Turley!" More heated words.

Once the sheep were counted, the manager told Connolly and Stack to take the sheep to the head station some four miles away. He told Turley to return to the head station as well: "There I will pay you off – and then you can leave!"

NOW Michael Turley was regarded by fellow workers as 'an old man', somewhat eccentric, and had the disturbing habit of carrying several firearms with him at all times. He was, it was said, 'subject to fits of temporary aberration of intellect or, to use other and more homely language, perhaps, was "cranky"'. In hindsight, this was not the kind of person Davidson should push to the edge.

AS Connolly and Stack turned to head the flock back to the main station, they heard a gunshot from behind them.

Turning, they saw Davidson falling

from his horse. In Turley's hand was a large horse pistol – somewhat like a hand shot-gun, still pointing at the man.

Standing beside the body, Turley in a low but audible voice said, "Now he's done for!"

Connolly launched himself at Turley, to be joined by Stack, and the pair wrestled the gun from his grasp.

Leaving Connolly to handle the old man, Stack ran to Davidson's aid. The manager was near death, his head perforated by pellet wounds, each about half-an-inch in diameter, 'from which the man's brain was oozing'.

Despite his age, Turley broke free from Connolly and ran to grab Davidson's horse; the men were reluctant to tackle him, fearing he still had another smaller weapon in his coat.

As he rode off into the scrub, Turley shouted, "I'll go and give myself up." He didn't.

Davidson was on the verge of death. Connolly rode off to the head station for a wagon while Stack remained with the victim to keep crows and dingoes away. Three hours later Davidson's limp body was being lifted onto a cart. Fifteen minutes into the return journey he was dead.

TWO days after the murder, some thirty miles from Mitchell Downs, a detachment of native troopers under Lieutenant Frederick Carr tracked down Michael Turley. Surrounded by troopers with carbines aimed, he had little choice than to lower his weapon

Michael Turley, who was convicted at the last Toowoomba Assizes of murdering Mr G. W Davidson, has had the sentence of death passed upon him commuted to imprisonment for life—it being supposed that he was subject to temporary fits of insanity.

Commutation and commotion

ONE month after Michael Turley was sentenced to death, Executive Council commuted his death sentence to life imprisonment.

'Why?' Brisbane's leading newspaper *The Courier* demanded to know. Why was the Government so inconsistent in granting reprieves?

ONLY two weeks before old Turley shot dead Gordon Davidson at Mitchell Downs, another murderer, of questionable sanity, much like the 'eccentric' Turley, was hanged.

In April 1863, at the 'Bend of the Burnett River' near Gayndah, the body of a German swagman, Fritz Lenhan, had been found. Investigations revealed that he had been bludgeoned and stabbed by his young Irish travelling companion, Matthew McGuinness.

In addition to a pre-trial confession, the evidence focused on the fact that McGuinness had purchased from a local store a shirt, moleskin trousers and a pair of boots, and paid for them with a blood-smeared cheque for £5 15s 4d. The same cheque had been made out to the swagman a week earlier.

While the judge was delivering his sentence, the prisoner fell into a ten-minute epileptic fit – his sixth for the trial. During one fifteen-minute episode, six policemen had to hold him down.

After the trial, the Governor received a petition:

> "We feel called upon to express our opinion as to the state of mind of the said Matthew McGuinness, having had ample opportunities of observing his conduct during the very protracted voyage of the *Erin Go Bragh* to Moreton Bay.
>
> We believe him to be of unsound mind and under excitement most dangerous, apparently having no control over his actions, particularly after fits to which he is very subject."

Their pleadings fell on deaf ears and McGuinness was hanged.

BUT *The Courier* sought answers:

> 'We feel ourselves bound to recognize the peculiar anomaly exhibited between

and surrender.

At his trial in Toowoomba in July 1863, with two witnesses to the shooting, the case against Turley was clear cut.

Notwithstanding the evidence, Turley's defence argued that the shooting may have been the result of an accident. Failing that, 'looking at the great age of the prisoner, and his childish habit of carrying several firearms about him, and his known eccentricity', perhaps his mind was in a state that he could not be held accountable for his actions.

It took the jury 45 minutes to return a guilty verdict. Chief Justice Sir James Cockle, despite constant interruption from the prisoner, sentenced Turley to death. ■

the cases of McGuinness, the last man executed, and of Michael Turley.

In the first, the youth McGuinness, without money and a new arrival in the colony, is unfortunately tempted and executed for murder and robbery; in the other, the old man Turley, convicted of a most cold-blooded and deliberate murder, is reprieved...

Have not the parents of Davidson a right to demand some explanation from the Queensland government for the extraordinary exercise of their prerogative which they have exhibited? Have they not a right to demand why the murderer of their son... should not suffer the same penalty as that inflicted upon the poor unfortunate boy, McGuinness?...

We have a right to enquire why leniency should be shown in any particular case without sufficient cause for it being assigned."

The Executive Council failed to respond.

Sidelight

Not that Michael Turley escaped his death sentence... as a prisoner in 1871, the 70-year-old Turley was bashed to death with a broom handle wielded by a fellow inmate. (see page 9)

1863. AT a timbergetters' camp in the Bunya Bunya Mountains near Dalby, two drunken sawyers, Thomas Hardgraves and John McCormick, had to be separated on the morning of 22 December as the pair fought outside one of the huts.

Fifteen minutes later, a shot rang out – and fellow sawyers found Hardgraves lying near his hut with 'a wound below the stomach and his entrails protruding'. He was 'pulling at his entrails with his hands, and tearing them in pieces'. He soon died.

Next morning, a constable from Dalby arrested John McCormick, whom he found asleep and very drunk in his hut. McCormick claimed Hardgraves had attacked him with the timber handspike which was found several yards from the body.

Found guilty of manslaughter, McCormick was sentenced to '10 years hard labour on the roads and other public works of the colony'.

1863. ON 30 July, Thomas Connors, the homestead cook at Canning Downs station on the Darling Downs, was dismissed. Ten days later he returned under cover of darkness, broke a window pane in the kitchen wing where the butler slept, and stole various items including a watch and locket. Next morning in Warwick he sold his plunder for 10 shillings to Caroline Johnson. Her husband turned the items over to the police. Found guilty of larceny, Connors spent the next 18 months in Brisbane Gaol at Petrie Terrace.

Murder most cowardly on the Darling Downs

The town of Leyburn on the southern Darling Downs grew up as a centre to service the surrounding gold mining camps. By the mid-1860s it boasted a number of hotels and general stores, and a school, post office, police station and courthouse.

Charles Owen was the magistrate at Leyburn courthouse. He was a well-liked local resident and manager of nearby Yandilla Station.

The station flourished under his management, as he sub-divided the land into grazing paddocks and replaced older quarters with new sawn-pine buildings.

In mid-1863, work had begun on building a new kitchen adjacent the house of the property's North Branch overseer, John Pierce. A contract had been signed with an Irish carpenter named Alexander Ritchie to erect the kitchen for £20.

The trigger to tragedy

HALFWAY through the job, Ritchie became increasingly dissatisfied with the terms of the agreement, saying he could make more money elsewhere.

Pierce soon became fed up with the Irishman's complaining and abuse – and he sacked him without pay. This enraged the carpenter and he left, only to return a few days later to try to claim his pay.

In the meantime, Pierce had notified Owen of the situation, asking him to bring a cheque over for Ritchie, to be rid of him.

Owen arrived at the outstation to hear Ritchie's complaints and asked the carpenter why he took on contracts he could not finish. Ritchie became rude and abusive. Annoyed, Owen then showed him the cheque he had brought with him, and tore it up in front of the Irishman.

"You have no claim on it. You did not carry out your agreement," he said testily.

An infuriated Ritchie stormed off.

Revenge

LATE in 1863, through a lawyer, Ritchie summonsed both Pierce and Owen over the $20 payment. He lost the case. From that point, Ritchie focused his seething anger on Owen, the manager of Yandilla Station.

On 29 April 1964, magistrate Charles Owen was at work in Leyburn, hearing a case in the courthouse. He lunched at Mrs Murray's Royal Hotel across the street.

It was there he came across Ritchie and they had a brief and heated conversation on the veranda of the hotel. When Owen went inside, Ritchie reminded Mrs Murray that Owen owed him £20.

"If Mr Owen owes you £20, in honesty he would pay you," she

"Owen was instantly launched into eternity by the hand of a demon in human form…"

responded.

"Never mind, I'll have it out of him in a day or two – one way or another…," he replied.

At 4 o'clock that afternoon, Owen set off for the Yandilla homestead. With him was Rev. William Thackeray who was going to spend some time with his parishoners at the station.

Earlier that afternoon, Ritchie had been parading up and down the main street boasting to all who would listen that he was going to take revenge on the magistrate. He had also purchased a single-barrelled gun and a tin of powder, 'to use on some stray dogs'.

The fatal shot

ON hearing that Owen had left town, Ritchie pursued on horseback. He caught up with Owen's buggy some four miles out of Leyburn. According to the *Darling Downs Gazette* of 19 May:

> About 6.10 p.m. when nearly quite dark… without the slightest warning, Owen was instantly launched into eternity by the hand of a demon in human form who… had cowardly stolen up close behind the carriage and fired the fatal shot, which severed the spinal cord and passed out his mouth.

With horses bolting, the buggy ran into a tree, freeing the horses and hurling the clergyman to the ground. The *Gazette* continued:

> The murdered magistrate was held in the vehicle by his coat, being caught by a bolt outside the carriage. The clergyman jumped up, lifted the wounded man, bleeding profusely, out of the buggy and laid him on the ground. He found life extinct.

The culprit had galloped off into the dense timber, but not before being seen by two riders following a few hundred yards behind the buggy.

They saw 'a man wearing a distinctive old hat'.

Ritchie became the prime suspect, but he proved to be elusive – until five days later he was arrested in his cottage, minus his beard and moustache.

But the police needed the 'distinctive old hat' to prove their case. The only hat they found in the cottage was brand new.

Making inquiries in Leyburn drapery stores, they discovered that Ritchie's wife had only recently purchased a new hat. With persistent questioning, she finally admitted to having burnt her husband's old hat. The police had their man.

The end of a demon

ON 11 July, a Toowoomba jury found Alexander Ritchie guilty of wilful murder. Judge Alfred Lutwyche addressed the prisoner: "A more cold-blooded and heartless murder... has seldom come under my notice. I entreat you to look for no hope of mercy this side of the grave; but address yourself to the consolations of religion for the short period that is allotted to you in this world." That said, he sentenced Ritchie to death.

Three weeks later, the government hangman did the deed, the first hanging at the still-under-construction Toowoomba Gaol. At a few seconds after 8.00 a.m. on 1 August, the drop fell and Ritchie died instantly. After hanging for 20 minutes, the criminal's body was cut down and buried at Drayton Cemetery outside Toowoomba. ■

1862. IN the 1860s, the famous clipper, ***The Flying Cloud (below)***, made several voyages to Brisbane with British immigrants on board.

On 20 February, the ship was met in Moreton Bay by the colony's Health Officer, Dr William Hobbs. From the steamer ***Settler*** alongside, Hobbs began questioning the ship's medical officer George Sandiford:

Q. Have you any infectious or contagious disease on board ?

A. No.

Q. Have you any fever on board?

A. No.

Q. What was the date of the last death, and the cause of it ?

A. Dysentery...

Three months later, Sandiford would be facing trial in Brisbane's Supreme Court for giving false answers to certain questions put to him as to the causes of death of twenty persons who died on board in the course of the voyage.

The court heard that there was indeed 'fever on board, and the cause of the last death was not dysentery; there were at the time more than four persons sick on board, and they were suffering from the contagious and infectious disease – typhoid fever...'

Hobbs' inspection of the vessel two days after his initial questioning had revealed the extent of the disease. Sandiford had been doing his best to cover up the on-board outbreak since the captain was keen not to have the ship held over in Moreton Bay for a lengthy quarantine period.

Justice Lutwyche, 'although believing him to have been made the tool of a more artful man than himself', sentenced Sandiford to six months in gaol. The artful captain escaped penalty.

1864

Peter Fagan and Daniel Webster

Crime: Robbery under arms

Location: Rockhampton district

Penalty: 20 years hard labour

Thomas Howson

Crime: Robbery under arms

Penalty: 12 years hard labour

When Fagan's gang ran wild

Four men broke out of an understaffed Rockhampton gaol on 6 May 1864.

A few days earlier, the leader of the pack, Peter Fagan, had been imprisoned for forgery. Fagan and his cellmates Daniel Webster (forgery), John Wright (horse theft), and Thomas Howson (forgery) scaled the wall after overpowering an ailing principal warder.

The gang of four

THE four escapees, fired up by the exploits of the New South Wales bushranger Frank Gardiner, who had been captured at Apis Creek, 140km north-west of Rockhampton only a month earlier, began eight weeks of law-breaking adventure that turned them into local folk heroes.

With mounted police and native troopers in hot pursuit, the Fagan gang plundered central Queensland during the reckless weeks that followed.

Travellers were bailed-up and relieved of their horses, saddles and guns. Hotels and stores were ransacked for provisions and liquor. Mailmen were forced to hand over cash and valuables. When the gang's horses tired, fresh ones were simply stolen.

The gang's bravado was boundless. For example, after demanding replenishment of supplies at the Bell property near Canoona, Fagan boasted to the owners that their next target would be the hotel in Woodville near Yaamba – and true to his word, the gang held up the Woodville Inn. There, after being reluctantly treated to a grand evening meal by the publican, they departed with more general supplies and grog.

And with every report of a new strike, a small army of police and native trackers, under Sub-Inspector Foran and mockingly known as 'Foran's Army', was soon on the trail – but invariably with no success. It

The Fagan gang forced the proprietor of the Westwood hotel to wait on them, and to slake their endless thirst in a long carouse.

helped little that local and Brisbane newspapers ridiculed the police for their inability to apprehend the desperadoes.

In mid-May, in rollicking style, the gang kicked up the dust at Westwood, some 30 miles west of Rockhampton. Giving vent to their exuberant spirits, they fired their guns at random and sent the few startled inhabitants scrambling for shelter as they galloped with pounding hooves to the door of the hotel.

Flourishing their pistols in playful fashion at the few shearers and teamsters at the bar, they herded them into one of the back rooms and, after having locked them in, made themselves at home in the parlour. The proprietor was forced to wait upon them with food and drink and, after enjoying themselves for several hours, they ransacked the till and robbed everybody at the hotel, before unsteadily mounting their horses and whooping away.

ON 20 May, Foran's party finally caught up with the gang at Walloon. The mounted posse charged into the Fagan camp, where the quartet was sleeping off a hangover. Fagan, Wright and Webster had time to mount their horses and disappear into the bush. Howson wasn't so lucky. He stumbled into the scrub – and still managed to flee the bumbling police. A few days later, foodless, unarmed and exhausted, Howson was found hiding in a bush shanty not far from Gladstone, and was taken into custody.

And then there were three

ON the night of 9 June, Fagan, Wright and Webster were 'shouting the bar' at the Cornish Mount Hotel. Sub-Inspector Foran, warned of their presence, sent in plain clothed constables and also surrounded the pub and outbuildings.

The watchers saw a man move furtively along the front veranda before making a dash to the back yard.

"That's Webster!" was the shout and rifle shots crackled.

The fugitive fell to the ground with a bullet in his leg.

Again, to the embarrassment of the pursuers, Fagan and Wright slipped out of the hotel into the darkness and rode off.

And then there were two

FOR two weeks the remaining duo kept out of sight. On 25 June, the bushrangers robbed a mailman near Princhester and again stuck-up the Woodville Inn.

Four days later, a Clermont businessman, Henry Paton, was held up west of Apis Creek and the contents of his drays were ransacked. Furious, he organised his own posse and a couple of days later located the pair. Fagan was captured but had time to shout a warning to Wright who rode off.

And then there was one

JOHN Wright was the last of the Fagan gang to be accounted for – and again it was at the hands of Henry Paton.

On July 6, Paton and his teamsters were camped by the Mackenzie river when a man approached on foot. It was Wright, intent on surrendering. As Wright was being tied up, Paton's pistol accidentally discharged, Wright was shot in the chest and, crying 'My God! What was that for?', died moments later.

The local heroes

FROM May until July 1864, the central Queensland community was in a state of excitement at the exploits of the Fagan gang, and eagerly sought news of each new move and counter-move by the bushranging quartet.

They were unlike other bushrangers. They killed no one. They robbed no mail coaches. They bailed-up no gold escorts. To the locals, they were harmless and good-natured, intent only on keeping themselves well-provisioned with cheap tucker and liquor. And, importantly, they continually embarrassed the police, who were always one step behind the gang.

Indeed, when Peter Fagan was recaptured, and was on his way under a strong police escort back to Rockhampton Gaol, the posse passed through Apis Creek, Marlborough, Princhester and Yaamba. Along the streets people gathered in groups – some to cheer their hero, others to jeer at the police.

The boys of the Fagan gang were seen by many as the first dyed-in-the-wool central Queensland bushrangers – just the thing, the locals claimed in the 1860s, to put Rockhampton on the map!

ON 14 October 1864, Fagan, Webster and Howson faced the court on a string of bushranging charges. The outcome of the trial was a foregone conclusion and the jury took ten minutes to return guilty verdicts. Judge Cockle sentenced Fagan and Webster to twenty years, and Howson to twelve.

Ringleaders Fagan and Webster were released from prison on St Helena Island after nine years, 'on account of good conduct and industry'. ■

In October 1864, Sir James Cockle, the first Chief Justice of Queensland, pronounced sentence upon the three surviving members of the Fagan bushranging gang.

1864. THE 'horrible murder!' at Jandowae caused a stir in the contemporary press.

One correspondent wrote: "I was not astonished at such violence taking place as it did in the licensed public-house, the only building in Jandowae… Are public-houses of such paramount importance that they may be established in such lonely districts… miles from police protection?"

Another: "The public-house in which the murder was committed has been a source of crime since its first erection… It is such wretched shanties in the interior… that are the cause of nine-tenths of the crime that appears in the criminal calendar…"

And the 'horrible murder'?

On 15 September, five travellers began drinking at sundown and by 11 o'clock that night were arguing loudly, quarrelling, fist-fighting, throwing things, and chasing each other wildly around the establishment and surrounds. One, John Corbett, was struck across the forehead with a thick stick by Michael Behan, and his profusely bleeding head needed treatment by the publican. Next morning Behan's body, with seven stab wounds, was found on the verandah.

In January 1865, Corbett was found guilty of manslaughter and sentenced to 12 months in prison.

1865

MACPHERSON

JAMES MACPHERSON
Crime: MAIL ROBBERY UNDER ARMS
Location: QUEENSLAND
Penalty: 25 YEARS PENAL SERVITUDE

The Wild Scotchman

Throughout the 1860s, James Alpin Macpherson, an impetuous young firebrand, became the colony's most colourful bushranger, a legend in his own time, being popularly referred to as 'The Wild Scotchman'.

As a lad, James Macpherson attended a Brisbane school where his diligence pleased the teachers. He learnt some French and German, and became a fluent and entertaining speaker. He attended the Brisbane Mechanics' School at night and achieved prominence in its debating class. Apprenticed to the builder, John Petrie, he impressed people as an intelligent and industrious worker.

Then, one day in 1863 he shocked everyone: he left town with a couple of other wild spirits from the shearing sheds – 'to take up bushranging', he said.

Bushranging

IN the wake of gold discoveries in the 1860s, a rash of bushranging activity flared throughout the eastern colonies. Wild young colonials, skilled at gun-play, accomplished with horses, and possessing an uncanny ability to melt into the trackless retreats of rugged bushland, became brash and brazen through the public notoriety of their exploits. Mailmen, gold coaches, hotels and travellers on roads around the colonial settlements and goldfields were fair game for this new breed of outlaw. They came in various moulds, being described as both brave and cowardly, mean and generous, brutal and kind, and were viewed with a curious mixture of awe and horror, hatred and hero-worship.

The bushranging epidemic reached Queensland in the mid-1860s and the authorities made it clear that such activity would not be allowed to thrive in the infant colony. Indeed, while a good many miscreants took to the roads of the colony at one time or other, their careers were mostly cut short, ending in very lengthy terms in gaol, for the law provided severe penalties to discourage would-be bushrangers.

A bushranging career

IN his first recorded criminal exploit, Macpherson robbed at gunpoint the Willis pub and store at Houghton River in North Queensland. Shots

were fired. Then he reputedly joined southern bushrangers, staging hold-ups in company with Ben Hall and John Gilbert.

While in New South Wales, he encountered the head of police in the colony, Sir Frederick Pottinger, and some troopers, exchanging shots with them and getting slightly wounded during the affray.

He returned to Queensland and began making a name for himself in his home colony by robbing overland mails, sticking up travellers and hotels, and stealing racehorses.

In February 1865, he was captured and despatched to Sydney to stand trial for the Pottinger shootings – but the charges were dropped when Pottinger was accidentally killed on his way to the trial.

Macpherson was taken back to Queensland to stand trial for the Houghton River hold-up and other charges. En route by ship to Rockhampton, under escort in irons to stand trial, he escaped overboard, leg irons and all, while his guard slept. He swam to shore. His irons and a file were found next morning under a tree to which was pinned this note:

> *Presented to the Queensland Government with the Wild Scotchman's best thanks, that gentleman having no further use for them, the articles being found to be rather cumbersome to transit in this age of enlightenment and progress – the nineteenth century. Many thanks. Adieu.*

Legends were made of such stuff.

At large once more, Macpherson resumed his rampage throughout central and southern Queensland – stealing horses, robbing the mailmen and mail coaches en route to such places as Maryborough, Gayndah, Roma, Banana, and Toroom, and holding up several travellers. As always, he was able to elude his pursuers.

On 30 March 1866, a man answering to the Wild Scotchman's description was seen by two men on the Gin Gin road. They immediately reported their suspicions to the manager of a nearby cattle station, who joined them and another person, and immediately set off in pursuit. After a short chase on horseback, Macpherson surrendered at gunpoint.

A couple of days later, the Maryborough court house was crowded with spectators 'amongst whom,' reported a contemporary newspaper, 'there seemed to be some disappointment at the appearance of this legendary prisoner. Some because he was not so "flash", and others because he was not so ferocious-looking as they expected.'

'The prisoner, however, answers to the ordinary description of a bushranger,' it continued, '– a bushman, hardy, strong, and supple; in Macpherson's case, we should say of more than ordinary intelligence and courage.'

Some months later Macpherson was brought to trial in Maryborough for armed robbery and bushranging. He was found guilty and sentenced by Judge Cockle to two terms of twenty-five years hard labour, to be served concurrently.

He was imprisoned on the prison hulk *Proserpine* at the mouth of the Brisbane River for a few years, and thence to the newly-opened St Helena Island prison in Moreton Bay.

Even there, for a time, his adventurous spirit wasn't quelled... ▶

Macpherson's St Helena episode

ST HELENA Island played host to the Scotchman from 20 February 1870 until he was released five years later at the age of 33 years after a petition, containing the names of prominent clergymen, Justices of the Peace and Members of Parliament, was presented to the Governor. The petitioners had argued that the ex-bushranger's sentence was a severe one in order to deter others and, in this regard, it had been most successful.

In the last years of his life, Macpherson was known for his anecdotes, poetry and ready wit, regaling listeners with stories of his bushranging days and his time on St Helena Island, including a far-fetched account of his attempted escape.

Supposedly, one dark night he broke out of his cell, overpowered the guards and, taking a wooden sugar cooler about eight feet square and one foot deep, he dragged it to the shoreline. Bravely he negotiated the choppy waters of the Bay and the menace of circling sharks, only to be recaptured just before reaching the mainland.

So romantic and so different from what really happened – he and a few prisoner mates simply stormed out through the stockade gate, only to be recaptured shortly afterwards. But then, such exaggerated claims helped to create the daredevil legend of Queensland's Wild Scotchman.

The legend grows

THE Wild Scotchman was a legend in his own lifetime, and even today the Macpherson reputation lingers – although a large part of this was invented by the bushranger himself during his own lifetime.

Repeatedly he claimed that, during his bushranging days, his gun was either never loaded, or filled with blanks. At other times he said that he only carried a loaded gun so that he could suicide if captured.

He told a story of how he once held up a mailman with his pipe! He insisted that he robbed the rich to give to the families of poverty-stricken shepherds, thereby earning for himself the title 'Robin Hood of the Burnett'. In later years he claimed that *he* was the bushranger on whom Rolf Boldrewood based his character 'Starlight' in the novel *Robbery Under Arms*. (Another James MacPherson was involved.) And he even had his own version of the 'escape' from St Helena prison *(see box, above)*.

In 1874, when James Macpherson turned his back on St Helena, he had served only eight years of his 25 year sentence. He was 33 years old.

He became a stockman in western Queensland where he married before settling down in Burketown in 1885 with his family. It was in Burketown ten years later that he was killed at a friend's funeral when his horse bolted and fell on him. Until his death he had been a hard-working and law-abiding citizen of Burketown where he now lies in an unmarked grave.

James Macpherson

Man overboard!

The best 'road' between Ipswich and Brisbane in the early days was the Brisbane River, a smooth and easy trip compared with the bumpy dirt tracks that often became impassable in wet weather.

By the 1860s, paddle steamers plied this profitable passenger and cargo route and included the *Mary Anne, Emu, Hawk, Swallow, Ipswich, Breadalbane, Bremer* and *Settler*. And they continued to do so until the railway opened in 1875.

IT BEGAN as just another day for the *Settler* as she set out from Ipswich on the morning of 27 August 1866, under the command of Master Alexander Rooney. Depending on the wind and tide, it would be a four- or five-hour trip for the forty passengers. This day, however, it would take a little longer.

Among the passengers were William Domane and a few of his friends. Midway through the trip, around 1 o'clock, they found themselves in the dining cabin for a meal and refreshments. Domane ordered two bottles of beer and brandy for himself and his companions. Another passenger, William Sewell, joined them. He ordered a small bottle of ale.

At one stage during the meal, the conversation got a little heated, particularly after Sewell emptied 'some of his slops' from his glass into Domane's glass.

Angry words continued to be exchanged, such that the Master had to intervene and tell the group to calm down, which they did. After dessert some fifteen minutes later, they all went back on deck.

By 2 o'clock, the *Settler* had reached Twelve-mile Reach (Indooroopilly). The Master Rooney was on deck collecting tickets when he heard shouts and the splashing of water. Looking quickly back along the side of the vessel he saw 'a man in the water just going by the stern wheel of the boat'.

"I immediately stopped the steamer and ordered the small boat to be lowered away. For nearly an hour we searched for the body but could not find it," he said later.

What had transpired was the result of a prank gone wrong…

THE diners that day had vacated the dining saloon a few minutes before

The paddle steamer Settler, *one of a number of vessels that used the busy Brisbane-Ipswich route in the 1860s*

2 o'clock. Domane was standing on the starboard side, smoking his pipe, when he was approached by Sewell. For several minutes, more angry words passed between the pair.

In the end, a steward heard Domane say to the 21-year-old, "Go on, you damn puppy, I could pitch you overboard… and why shouldn't I!"

With that, he grabbed the smaller man around the legs and heaved him over the side.

Sewell, weighed down with boots and coat, managed a few strokes, and then sunk beneath the water. A search for him by the crew found nothing.

Domane was taken into custody when the *Settler* reached Brisbane.

Next day police dragged the river for half an hour, and Sewell's body was located.

THE MURDER TRIAL of William Domane took place in November 1866. In his defence, the jury was told that the prisoner had acted "in a moment of excitement or passion. There was no malice prepense. The deceased was annoying the prisoner and he 'chucked' him overboard to get a wet jacket – to get rid of him as he might a fly."

On 19 November, the jury returned a finding of manslaughter. In passing sentence, Judge Lutwyche said that he had taken into account "the considerable provocation the prisoner had received. He had used every means to prevent any altercation, till at last, stung by insults, in a moment he seized and pitched the deceased overboard; he had then not the slightest intention of depriving the deceased of his life. It was an act for which he was very very sorry."

He sentenced Domane to twelve months with hard labour. ■

Fragments from the FILES of FELONS

1866. ON 11 September a rowdy afternoon meeting of over 100 unemployed workers was held at Green Hills (Petrie Terrace). From the back of a cart, a rabble-rousing William Eaves suggested the crowd should reassemble that night, when 'the police would have less chance of spotting us'. The rendezvous would be the Treasury Hotel (known then as the Dunmore Arms, *below*) in George Street – 'because there are plenty of stones there' and they could 'take over the streets'. And he promised 'plenty of bloodshed'.

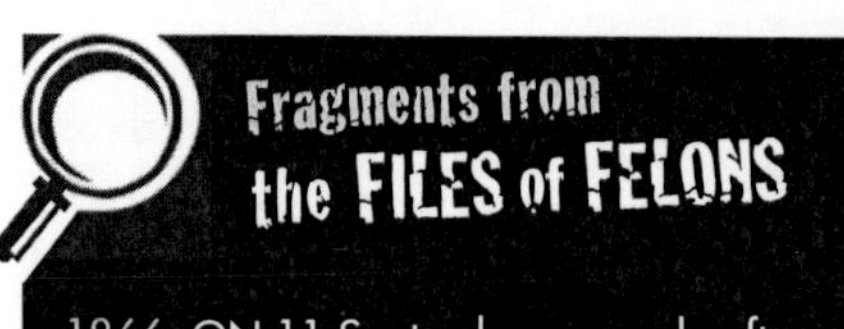

That night over 400 people crowded the intersection, where Eaves, Henry Parker and John Murray stirred up the crowd. Cheered by the mob, "Bread or blood!", they cried.

Soon the uproarous crowd was marching on the Government Stores in William Street. There they began hammering away at the door, and several people were injured by projectiles and stones. Police formed in line and managed to drive the masses back down Elizabeth Street. There Police Magistrate Massie read the Riot Act – and was hit in the eye with a stone while doing so. Peace was restored by midnight.

Eaves, along with co-agitators Parker and Murray, were charged with 'having, with divers other persons, being armed with stones and other offensive weapons, unlawfully assembled riotously and did then disturb the peace of the liege subjects of Her Majesty'. The trio was found guilty and sentenced to twelve, six and three months hard labour respectively.

The Frenchman, bushranger

When 22-year-old Henry Hunter was gaoled in 1866, the mailmen of central and southern Queensland breathed a sigh of relief. Known popularly as 'The Frenchman' because of his cultivated French accent and good manners, for six explosive months in that year, he became a regular hazard on the isolated mailruns near Springsure and Condamine.

Hunter, a tall man of dark complexion, and sporting a small brown beard, was invariably dressed in a tweed coat, moleskin trousers worn inside his Wellington boots, and a cabbage tree hat with black band. He usually brandished a revolver in each hand - and was not afraid to use them.

A man of letters

THIS wild colonial was apparently a man of education and culture as well. More than once he rode off after having removed from mailbags three or four newspapers and postage stamps 'so he could write some letters'.

Indeed, Hunter became quite famous for his 'letters to the editor'. In exchange for the gold and cash they were carrying, his mailmen victims were frequently given letters, sealed with wax, and imprinted with the muzzle of one of his revolvers.

In one such letter to the editor of the Rockhampton *Morning Bulletin*, Hunter called on all bushrangers to surrender, provided the Government of the day promised to pardon them. They could then be employed by the Government 'to keep the northern Aborigines in subjection', he wrote. He had second thoughts, however:

> But supposing we did surrender, what have we really to expect? At least twenty years on Government rations! With such a life as that in store, there is little hope of us giving ourselves up willingly. No! Much sooner have an ounce of lead to digest!

And lead he almost did digest, on more than one occasion.

A man of weapons

ON 3 April 1866, for example, on the Clermont Road at the Dawson crossing, Hunter held up mailman William Duncombe and off duty police constable Michael Mahoney.

Brandishing a pair of guns, he ordered both men to go further down the creek where he told them to sit down and hold their horses. There Hunter ransacked the mailman's five mailbags, putting over a hundred letters into one booty bag.

In conversation, as he was rifling through the bags, Hunter was asked who he was - to which he brazenly replied, "Why, I'm Henry Hunter, the Frenchman bushranger!"

Mahoney asked the bushranger if

the pair could now continue their journey. Not yet, was the reply.

"Then could I smoke my pipe?" asked the constable. Hunter nodded.

The constable drew a revolver from his swag and called on Hunter to surrender.

The bushranger sprang to his feet, gun in hand. The policeman fired and Hunter returned the fire. Three more shots from the constable; and four more from the bushranger before he dropped the mailbag and bolted for the protection of the scrub.

The unnerved mailman meanwhile scrambled off in the other direction. As the constable headed off after Hunter, he shouted back to the mailman for assistance. No response.

Hunter managed to elude the pursuing policeman who later caught up with the unnerved mailman – to discover that neither of them had retrieved the mailbag that Hunter had stuffed with letters.

Returning to the scene, they could find no mailbag. Hunter had earlier returned to collect his plunder.

TWO months later, another gunfight brought about Hunter's downfall.

For nearly two hours on 12 June 1866, The Frenchman shot it out with a police sub-inspector and an aboriginal tracker near Condamine. With two bullets remaining and police reinforcements scrambling through the nearby scrub, Hunter threw down his guns, walked into the open, and surrendered.

A Rockhampton jury took only eight minutes to find him guilty of his bushranging crimes. In passing sentence, the Chief Justice concluded:

> "I very much regret having to pass such heavy sentences on young men but the crime of which the prisoner stands convicted must be repressed at all cost. It is, therefore, my duty to pass upon the prisoner a sentence of 22 years penal servitude."

Henry Hunter, 'The Frenchman', was released from St Helena Island prison in 1881, a little over a year after the notorious Ned Kelly was hanged in Melbourne Gaol. ■

A model for Madden

ONE of Henry Hunter's victims was mailman William Madden, whom the bushranger bailed-up no fewer than four times in 1866 near Springsure. Madden was impressed with Hunter's style – he too took up bushranging. But in 1871, he was caught and found guilty of sticking up the Springsure Mail. Sentenced to 15 years on St Helena Island, he no doubt found the time there to discuss with his mentor where they both went wrong.

Australia's most iconic bushranger Ned Kelly was still a boy when Queensland's Henry Hunter was putting his criminal talents into practice. Clearly, at least in this 1980 comic strip, Ned misconstrued his colonial predecessor's approach.

Assault on the high seas

LIFE aboard the early immigrant ships to Queensland and the sailing ships of the merchant marine in the 1850s and 1860s was far from pleasant. Many have been justly labelled by some writers as 'hell ships', with brutal captains and swaggering mates holding ruthless sway over crews of men, many of whom were still being shanghaied or tricked into service against their will. Such viciousness of course bred fear and enmity, with the result that many of the sailors were as nasty as their officers.

In circumstances such as these, the authorities in Brisbane were called upon to enforce maritime law at home and on the high seas. In 1859, a unit of Water Police was formed. The Water Police had their own magistrate, court, and a floating gaol for the detention of sea-faring prisoners, the old hulk *Proserpine*, which was moored at the mouth of the Brisbane River. It continued to operate as a floating prison until the late 1860s, after which, from 1871, it became a reformatory school for boys.

The sailing ship *Maryborough* departed Glasgow in early May 1866. On board, bound for Brisbane in the distant colony of Queensland, were over 400 people, enthused by a vigorous program to attract immigrants from the British Isles.

The vessel arrived in the new colony on 7 August 1866. A fortnight later the second mate of the *Maryborough* stood before Magistrate McDonnell in the Water Police Court in Brisbane. He had been charged with assaulting the ship's surgeon.

AT AROUND 8 o'clock on the night of 1 July, passenger Alexander Livingstone was on deck, taking the night air. It was quite dark as he approached the poop deck, to the rear of the ship.

At that moment, the ship's second mate, a tough and somewhat unruly character by the name of William Griffiths, exited the petty officers' quarters carrying a belaying pin. He then dressed himself in oil-skins and head cover. Moments later, Dr Hessell, the ship's doctor, stepped upon the poop deck from the second cabin, unawares that Griffiths lay in

On 1 July 1866, enroute to Brisbane aboard the migrant ship Maryborough, *second mate William Griffiths bashed the ship's surgeon Dr Hessell with a heavy ship's belaying pin.*

The weapon

A belaying pin is a solid wooden bar with a curved top portion and cylindrical bottom part. The device was used on sailing vessels to secure rope lines from the masts. Normally, they were inserted into hole in a wooden pinrail, running along the inside of the bulwarks. The pins were usually left in place, but they could be removed.

Belaying pins were often used as improvised weapons (as well as a method of discipline) on both military and civilian ships. Certainly their shape and weight would make a formidable short-range club – as ship's surgeon Hessell discovered in 1866.

wait in the shadows.

There had been bad blood earlier on the voyage between the pair, leading to a push-and-shove episode. On this occasion, however, the heavily disguised Griffiths emerged from the darkness and the doctor was felled by a thunderous whack to the back of his head.

Dr Hessell was laid up for several days; Griffiths, who had been unaware that there had been a witness to the assault, spent the remainder of the voyage in irons.

In Brisbane, on 23 August, Griffiths was sentenced to two months detention on the prison hulk *Proserpine,* moored at Lytton near the mouth of the Brisbane River. ■

Fragments from the FILES of FELONS

1866. SHORTLY before midday on 13 September, William Chandler, 'a man of colour', and 19-year-old Andrew Ross entered the Australian Joint Stock Bank in Mackay. They asked for the manager… and as he drew a revolver from his coat, Chandler then said to him softly: 'Stir, and you're a dead man!"

Into a dirty leather bag the pair emptied the contents of the gold tray and bundles of notes from the counter drawer – totalling nearly £750. That done, they warned the manager and his teller: "If you stir within half an hour, we'll shoot you."

Through the window, the manager watched the pair mount their horses and head off down the street at jogging pace.

By the time the Police Magistrate was roused fifteen minutes later, the robbers had made a clean getaway.

Two months later, Ross was apprehended in Moree in New South Wales. He had £218 in his pockets. Chandler's arrest was a little more lively:

> 'The West Indian native was in the bar of a Moree public-house, and made a desperate resistance, having drawn a revolver, which was taken from him, after a severe struggle with Sergeant Doherty and two constables. In the scuffle, Chandler got some severe blows on the head, and one of Constable McDowall's arms was injured. Chandler later claimed that he did not intend using the revolver to the injury of the police, but he wanted to shoot himself…'

In Chandler's possession they found £318.

The prisoners were returned to Mackay via Goondiwindi. There they were tried for robbery under arms. Found guilty, Chandler was sentenced to 15 years penal servitude, the first year in irons. Ross joined him.

The Crocodile Creek Chinese riots

Roll up! Roll up!

ON the Queensland goldfields in the 1860-70s, the Chinese were treated just as harshly as they had been on the fields of the southern colonies during the 'roaring days' of the 1850s. Their continuous migration to the new northern fields caused much anger and resentment.

Normally, as miners, the Chinese worked poorer ground or the abandoned diggings of the Europeans, often very successfully, much to the annoyance of the diggers.

They usually built their camps well away from the Europeans, huddled together in small townships of tents and huts.

CROCODILE CREEK, 21 km west of Rockhampton produced payable gold in 1865, with over two thousand diggers soon seeking their fortune. This would also be the first goldfield in the colony where white diggers would eject the Chinese!

And here too, would be heard the increasingly common rallying cry, the same call to arms that roused the European diggers in the notorious and bloody NSW Lambing Flats riots of 1861:

"No Chinese – Roll up! Roll Up!"

Tak Lung was a Chinese medical practitioner living in Chinese Street on the Crocodile Creek diggings. It was around 2.30 p.m. on 7 January 1866.

He could hear the mob of angry diggers approaching along Chinese Street. One noisy group stopped outside his store/house.

His door was smashed in by John Stone, carrying an axe. With him was John O'Sullivan holding a pick handle. Stone took Tak Lung by the hair and dragged him into the street, throwing him towards a mob of around fifty howling diggers. Most shouted and waved weapons at him; some threw stones. With a backwards glance as he ran up the street, Tak Lung saw the mob entering his store and breaking the windows.

He returned two hours later. His store/house and everything inside, including his medicines, had been destroyed.

The same ruination was befalling his countrymen throughout the diggings.

Store-keeper Eliza Han had nailed up her door, but the mob threatened to knock the place down on top of her. She fled as Abraham Soloman set fire to her hut. When she returned, everything had been smashed or burned.

"Roll up! Roll up! Chase the bastards out! Burn their bloody places down!"

Such cries continued for over an hour. A mob of over 200 diggers had divided into groups and marched on Chinese Street, the Chinese gardens and the creek. Tents and huts were torched or knocked down, rocks were thrown, and the Chinese were threatened and driven off.

THE RIOT had begun around 2 p.m. when a European digger began an argument as he started pegging out an illegal claim in the Chinese gardens. Dozens of Chinese assembled, some with bamboo sticks; so too did dozens of diggers. An all-in brawl ensued for about 15 minutes, after which the Chinese fled, and were pursued, across the creek and into Chinese Street.

"Roll up! Roll up!", and the riot continued, fuelled by alcohol, for nearly two hours.

In the end, the ringleaders – Stone, Galvin, Soloman and O'Sullivan – were rounded up, tried in Rockhampton on 20 March 1866 for riot, unlawful assembly and affray, and found guilty. ■

Fragments from the FILES of FELONS

1867. AT 1.30 p.m. on 29 January, several new arrivals in the colony sat down for dinner at Edward Fitzgerald's boarding-house in Mary Street, Brisbane. Within moments, James Green made a few flippant remarks which John Anderson found offensive. Anderson stood up angrily and headed upstairs to his bedroom. Green followed him to apologise, but was pushed down the stairs.

Ten minutes later, Anderson re-entered the dining room. He was carrying a double-barrelled shot gun. Walking up to Fitzgerald, he put the gun to within a foot of his face, saying "You first!", and pulled the trigger. He moved towards Robert Corrie – "You next!". He fired and missed.

Anderson was quickly overpowered by the other boarders and arrested shortly afterwards for attempted murder.

It was found that Anderson had loaded his gun with studs and buttons that he had cut from his vest. Even so, the first shot had blown away Fitzgerald's lower jaw, and four of the studs, in missing Corrie, had embedded themselves two inches into the sideboard wood and window frame.

In February, Anderson was sentenced to 10 years in prison for 'wounding with intent to do grievous bodily harm'.

The Ipswich mail hold-up

It all began at 6 a.m. on 7 January 1867, when the Cobb & Co mail coach set out for Brisbane from Ipswich. On board were 10 passengers, nine men and one woman.

As the coach slowed down on the approach to Oxley Creek, a man riding a magnificent bay horse came out of the bush. He wore long boots, a pair of check trousers, a Crimea shirt and a Californian hat. Over the hat was a piece of dark cloth, which came down over the man's eyes to form a mask, with slits for eyeholes. In his hand was a double-barrelled pistol.

The man gruffly shouted for the driver to pull up.

The driver that day was John McKenzie who had been working for Cobb & Co for a little over a week. He whipped his horses into a headlong gallop but the bushranger rode alongside and fired a shot at the leading horse. At that point, McKenzie wisely decided to pull up.

At gunpoint, the masked man told the passengers to get down from the coach and forced them to empty their pockets. He then ordered the driver to hand over the mailbags, particularly the Goodna mail, which he apparently thought contained a large amount of money.

He tied the bags to his saddle and galloped off, leaving the passengers to continue their journey to Brisbane where they were able to raise the alarm.

The empty mailbags were later found at 'the Blunder' near Oxley Creek, but a thorough search of the district failed to find the bushranger although his horse was located and locked up in the police stables at Ipswich as future evidence.

But police had one important lead: the publican of the One Mile Hotel said he had seen a man called William Jenkins riding that same horse.

A Cobb & Co mail coach, carrying ten passengers and mail from Ipswich to Brisbane, would fall victim to bushranger William Jenkins in January 1867.

Trapping Jenkins

THE police knew they had the evidence they needed – Jenkins had ridden this valuable, clearly identifiable horse – but the man remained elusive.

Months passed and then the police in Brisbane devised a scheme to flush the bushranger from his hiding place. Their plot would turn the bushranger into a celebrity – and a laughing stock.

Constable Michael Burke was supplied with a horse and instructions. He rode to Ipswich and, during the night, planted his horse in the bush. At midnight, he went to the police yard and stealthily led Jenkins' horse away. Picking up his own horse, Burke rode off into the scrub and, dismounting, shot his own animal. Wood was heaped on top, leaving out the beast's hoofs, and the body was set alight. He then rode the stolen bay horse to a quiet paddock near Brisbane.

Naturally there was quite an outcry next day when the Ipswich police found their evidence gone. In the search that followed, the incinerated horse was 'discovered'. It was widely accepted that Jenkins' horse had been stolen and destroyed by a mate or sympathiser.

The news soon reached Jenkins. With the evidence gone, the bushranger, as anticipated, came into the open and was at once arrested. He felt safe, however, and ridiculed his

The Ballad of the Unfortunate Nine

THERE was little sympathy for the passengers of the Ipswich-Brisbane coach of 7 January 1867 – after all, nine men had been held up by a lone bushranger.

The *Queensland Times* led the charge: 'That nine men should have submitted in broad daylight on the Queen's Highway to the insolent behests of one solitary scoundrel is indeed humiliating...'

A few days later, the same newspaper published a satirical play on the incident and Ipswich *Punch* published a song about 'The Unfortunate Nine' *(below)*.

Unfair criticism perhaps, made by people who weren't forced that day to face a masked bushranger's loaded gun...

" So nicely our travellers were spinning along,
With the road in good order and nothing went wrong
Until they arrived at a gentle incline –
What a change in the scene for the unfortunate nine.

There a stout burly bushranger, pistol in hand,
Did swear dreadful oaths and did fiercely demand
They should quickly get out, and he made them a sign
To shell out the crowns of this unfortunate nine.

"Come, don't stand shaking there, my travellers bold,
But turn out your pockets of notes and of gold!"
And with pistol upraised drew them up in a line
So they did as he told, the unfortunate nine.

While the volunteer Captain and brave Bombadier
Were shaking and quaking with horrible fear,
They gave up revolvers with triggers so fine
For these proved no use to the unfortunate nine..."

captors—until the 'dead' horse was produced and the whole story told.

In August 1868 Jenkins was arrested and tried for mail robbery under arms.

In court, the coach driver McKenzie identified him and swore, 'I would know him anywhere', because he recalled that, while the bushranger was checking the mail bags during the hold-up, his mask fell down.

Bushranger William Jenkins was found guilty and sent to Petrie Terrace Gaol in Brisbane to serve 18 years. ■

JENKINS made two futile attempts to flee Brisbane Gaol at Petrie Terrace, being apprehended on both occasions – in 1868, by hiding a dummy in his bed ***(below)***, and in 1869, while scaling the prison walls.

Transferred to St Helena Island, he found the colony's most secure prison a harder nut to crack.

WILLIAM JENKINS *alias* John King, who was committed on Thursday last to take his trial at the next Criminal Sittings of the Supreme Court, to be holden in Brisbane, on a charge of robbing the mail coach running between Ipswich and Brisbane, made a determined and ingenious attempt to escape from gaol on Saturday last. It appears that out of the spare suit of clothes allowed him, he made up a dummy, to which he contrived to give a very natural and life-like appearance, and placed it in his bed. After breakfast a warder looked into his cell, and seeing, as he supposed, Jenkins lying on his bed, locked the door without suspicion. In the meantime Jenkins had contrived to hide himself in a closet, but before long he was espied by the warder, who was keeping guard on the wall, and was speedily secured. He said he had merely meant to have a "lark," but the gaol authorities were unable to appreciate his joke, and put him in irons as a caution not to repeat it. Had the attempt been made at night, Jenkins might have stood a slight chance of escaping, but in broad daylight it was madness for him to suppose he could get *outside* the walls. We understand that the turnkey whose duty it was to inspect the cell has been dismissed.

The letter of conscience

THE passengers on the Ipswich mail coach had included several eminent citizens. One of them was Harry Hooper, the Mayor of Ipswich (1867-1870).

Mayor Hooper later had misgivings about the justice of Jenkins's lengthy conviction. After nine years of the bushranger's sentence had been served, he petitioned the Governor for Jenkins' release.

The petition succeeded. The prisoner was released and, as a free man, he was assisted in setting up a saddlery business in Brisbane.

Jenkins proved to be more successful as a businessman than a bushranger. As his business prospered, he began having pangs of remorse about his past.

On the 14th anniversary of his crime, he despatched to Harry Hooper a letter, with money enclosed.

The letter, through a solicitor and dated 7 January 1881, read:

'Dear Sir,

I am authorised to forward and beg your acceptance of the enclosed remittance as restitution money to cover the loss sustained by you on the 7th January, 1867 (just 14 years ago) when your coach was robbed on the Ipswich Road. Any surplus you can give to the Ipswich Hospital. And I am further requested to assure you that the party concerned will never cease to remember with feelings of the deepest gratitude, the generous aid you gave him when he stood so much in need of it and which was attended with such happy results for him.'

The Clermont gold escort killings

Thomas Griffin was an Irish-born soldier who had fought in the British Army as a sergeant and had been decorated for action in the Crimean War before emigrating to Australia. He served as a policeman in Victoria and New South Wales, eventually being sent to Rockhampton to take charge of police at the time of the Canoona gold rush in 1857.

After Queensland was separated from New South Wales, Griffin became clerk of petty sessions in Rockhampton in 1862, and then police magistrate and gold commissioner at Clermont in 1863.

Griffin in trouble

IN Clermont his over-bearing manner made him unpopular. He also came close to poverty through heavy losses in Chinese gambling dens and hefty financial demands from the wife he deserted in Victoria.

Rumours that he had embezzled money entrusted to him by miners led to a public meeting in Clermont and a petition seeking his removal.

In September 1867, Griffin was instructed by telegram to take up a position in Rockhampton, as Sub-Commissioner for Goldfields. Of course, he desperately wanted to stay in Clermont, knowing that his 'fiddling of the books' would soon be discovered if he left. But his pleas were turned down – there were just too many disturbing tales regarding the man and his management practices to allow him to stay.

Griffin arrived in Rockhampton on 17 October. Shortly after his arrival, six Chinese gold-diggers, who several months earlier had entrusted him with gold and notes to the value of £252, began pestering him for their money. They even enlisted the support of the Mayor.

Griffin hatches a plan

THE situation was becoming desperate for the in-debt Griffin.

In late October, a shipment of £8000 had to be moved from Rockhampton to Clermont. This was his chance. Griffin informed the three police officers in the escort (Sargeant Julian, and troopers Power and Cahill) that he would accompany them as far as Gogango, about 40 miles from Rockhampton.

At their Rockhampton camp on 29 October, Sargeant Julian was convinced that Griffin had tried to poison the men with arsenic in their billy tea, but they had emptied the contents in the Commissioner's absence.

When the party set off for Gracemere, Griffin led them 'along a shortcut' through scrubby country, all the while looking back at the trio. Julian surmised that Griffin was expecting the troopers to be dropping off their horses, dead, from the arsenic he had put in their tea.

In the end, Griffin returned the group to town. Julian took the opportunity to re-deposit the money in the bank and to visit Police Magistrate Wiseman to report the odd goings-on.

Later that day, Griffin dismissed Sargeant Julian.

The crime committed

ON 1 November, Thomas Griffin again withdrew the £8000 from the bank for delivery to Clermont; in the process, he covertly removed £252 with which to pay his Chinese debt and dispatched the remainder with troopers Power and Cahill. Griffin once more accompanied the escort and at their camp by the Mackenzie River, around 2 a.m. on 6 November, he shot both troopers through the head, and stole the money, which he hid under a tree stump on his way back to Rockhampton.

The news of the discovery of the bodies of the two troopers and the missing money reached Rockhampton on 8 November. A large police party including sub-inspectors, detectives, blacktrackers, a doctor – and Sargeant Julian, set out for the scene of the crime. Griffin volunteered to accompany them.

It was reported that: 'About 11 a.m. on 11 November Griffin was sitting on a log near the crime scene. Detective

The Clermont gold escort, November 1867

Only one man would survive the tragic episode of 6 November 1867

The Survivor: Sargeant James Julian *(left)*, 'a most experienced and responsible officer', was aware of Gold Commissioner Thomas Griffin's dubious reputation and was suspicious of his 'odd behaviour' during the escort. At various times, Julian refused to be left alone with the £8000, especially with Griffin nearby; he questioned Griffin's continuing procrastination; on several occasions he insisted on returning the money to the bank for safe keeping – all against Griffin's wishes. In the end, he was dismissed by Griffin 'for insubordination' (although, in reality, probably for thwarting the Commissioner's continued attempts to steal the cash shipment).

The Victims: Police troopers John Power *(centre left)* and **Patrick Cahill** *(centre right)* were the first members of the Queensland Police Force to be murdered in the performance of their duties. Some 18 months after Griffin's trial, their remains were retrieved from bush graves and reburied at Rockhampton Cemetery with full military honours, and a monument erected to their memory. Their skulls, evidence in the trial, were sent from Brisbane and placed in the coffins with the rest of the remains.

The Murderer: Gold Commissioner Thomas Griffin *(right)*, according to Sargeant Julian, acted strangely during the escort. As it turned out, it was the Commissioner's intention to kill the escorting troopers, take the $8000 to cover his debts, and to blame the killings on bushrangers. But his crime was revealed and he was hanged seven months later.

Kilfeder went and sat on one side of him and engaged him in general conversation. Sub-Inspector Elliott shortly thereafter went and sat on the other side of Griffin. On a signal from Elliott, both policemen grabbed the suspect by the arms and Kilfeder handcuffed him. Elliott arrested Griffin on suspicion of murder.'

The investigating officers left no stone unturned in their efforts to tie around Griffin a chain of events, from which he could not escape. Tellingly, many of the missing notes were traced to him.

In the end the former Gold Commissioner was charged with having murdered two troopers escorting £8000 from Rockhampton to Clermont in November 1867. Griffin's position in society gave the crime a notoriety unparalleled in Queensland history to that time.

Griffin faced judge and jury in March 1868 at Rockhampton. Sixty witnesses were called. The jury took 62 minutes to return a guilty verdict and Griffin became the first person to be hanged at Rockhampton gaol.

The missing money

TWO of the prison's warders, Grant and Lee, shared the £200 reward paid by the bank for information leading to the recovery of some £7700 still unaccounted for.

While in prison, Griffin had provided them with a map showing where he had hidden the shipment, in return for poison so that he could end his life before the execution. They didn't provide the poison; nor did they tell the authorities about the map until their futile searches outside the town aroused suspicions. The money bags were later found using the map. Grant and Lee were sacked. ■

A murderer's skull

A WEEK after Griffin's execution, on the night of 8 June 1868, his grave was opened and the head removed from the body. A £20 reward for information leading to the arrest of those responsible went uncollected.

It was widely suspected that the skull was in the possession of Dr William Callaghan, a keen student of ***phrenology*** – a belief that the shape of a skull somehow determines one's mental powers and behaviour. Callaghan would have believed that by studying Griffin's skull he could discover the reason for the man's diabolical deeds.

According to historian Hugh MacMaster, when the Clermont medico Spiridion Candiottis died in 1891, an inventory of his Rockhampton house located about 20 skulls and other medical exhibits. One skull, carrying a label identifying it as Griffin's, had been given to Candiottis by Callaghan.

A few years later, a photograph of the skull was widely circulated in the form of a postcard. But whatever happened to the skull itself remains a matter for speculation. According to MacMaster, it may have come 'into the possession of a Rockhampton Lodge where it was, and may still be, used in performing rituals'.

So celebrated was this case that even the rope with which Griffin was hanged was cut into small pieces, and sold at one shilling each. It was later written that 'the genuineness of this rope is to be doubted, but the buyers seemed satisfied.'

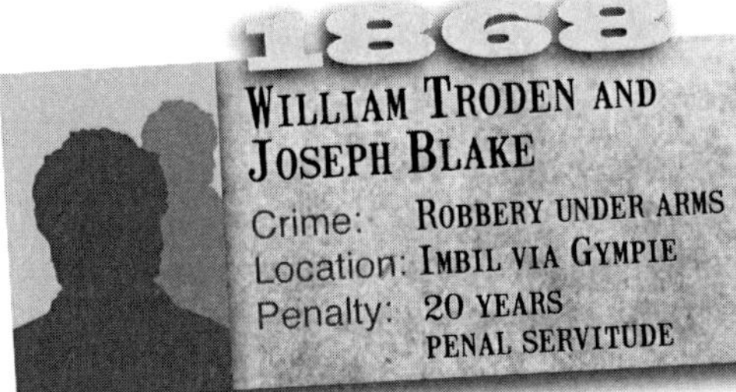

The Imbil incident

BUSHRANGING It is to be hoped no time will be lost by the police authorities in putting a stop to this sort of thing, as in the absence of any bank we must depend on private carriage for our gold and cash, to say nothing of the miners moving about with money on them. Could a couple or three of these vermin be either hung or shot it would probably put a stop to the trade for some time to come.

Brisbane Courier, 8 August 1868

The opening of the Gympie goldfields in 1867 became the catalyst for the most active bushranging period in colonial Queensland's history. The contemporary press featured a deluge of accounts reporting and decrying the latest exploits of the highway outlaws.

In the late 1860s, the out-of-the-way creeks and gullies around Imbil station, to the south-west of Gympie, were alive with gold diggers and surveyors. For those reckless enough to chance their hand with a gun, men wandering the roads could be rich pickings.

Typical of those taking advantage of isolated travellers on deserted thoroughfares between the goldfields were William ('Podgey') Troden and Joseph Blake. For Troden and his young accomplice, their moment of infamy was brief, their punishment heavy.

The crime

ON 30 JULY 1868, around 4 p.m., Ed Redman and his three fellow travellers Jack Crothers, and Tom and Jim Gill were walking towards Imbil. Four miles from Imbil station, they were approached by two masked horsemen, waving guns.

"Bail up, you bastards, or we will blow your bloody brains out!" yelled the shorter and older of the two, pointing his double-barrelled gun at the group. His face was covered by a handkerchief, with only his eyes visible beneath his distinctive hat. His companion wore a black-silk handkerchief with two eye holes cut into it.

With a wave of his gun, the older stranger signalled the group towards the scrub on the side of the road.

"No," responded Tom Gill. "If you're going to take our money, you might as well do it here."

The man shouted at them to move into the scrub – *now!* "Go on, or I'll shoot every damn one of you," he added in a very rough, raspy voice. "Walk! And the first man that looks round I'll blow his brains out."

Following on horseback, the pair marched their four victims some 150 yards off the road. At gunpoint, the travellers' hands were tied behind their backs, and the duo searched them and their swags for gold or cash.

The younger assailant then tied the four travellers together in pairs to saplings, using the saddle straps that had bound their swags.

The day before

AROUND MIDDAY on the day before the Imbil incident, a man was bailed-up on the Jimna-Imbil road by two masked men. They took their victim some distance into the scrub, and stole his horse, saddle, bridle, swag, hat, boots and £20 – all he had. Then they tied his feet together, and his hands behind him, before beating him about the head 'in a fearful manner'. He was left in the scrub all night, but managed to hop and crawl about two miles next day until found by some passing workers from Imbil station.

Almost certainly his assailants were Troden and Blake.

The older man stood over the four, waving his gun which was capped and cocked. They couldn't help but notice its quite distinctive appearance: "At the bottom of the barrel the woodwork was broken, and there was a nail through the place where the bolt usually goes, to fix the barrel to the stock." They also noted that there was something special about the bushranger's hat: it was a rare 'wide-awake' type, popular in the United States, and had a broken band.

"We will be coming back again," the rough-voiced man cautioned. "If we catch any of you trying to get loose, we will blow your bloody brains out."

With that, the bushrangers then mounted their horses and rode off.

The victims were perceptive enough to make one more observation: the older man rode a chestnut mare with a small white star on its forehead and the younger, a bay horse.

SO tightly were the captives' hands tied that it took nearly thirty minutes before any could free themselves. Tom Gill was successful 'only because he had once lost the middle finger of one hand'.

The bushranging pair was located and arrested a few weeks later at the Yabber diggings.

Both of the bushrangers' horses were identified by the victims. To confirm this, the manager of Imbil

A bushranging epidemic swept the colony in the late 1860s. The year 1868 was particularly notorious, as this selection of reports from newspapers of the day reveals.

JIMNA.

There have been several cases of stic[...]

GYMPIE.

We learn from a gentleman who came [...]

THE LATE STICKING-UP CASE.

The *Nashville Times* gives the following version of the sticking-up of Mr. Commissioner Clarke and Dr. Mason :—

It appears that on the day in question Mr. Clarke, together with Dr. Mason, was proceeding to Bonaro for the purpose of holding an inquest on the body of the man which we lately reported to have been found in the bush. Mr. Clarke left M'Taggart's station at half-past 10 a.m., and when about three miles from it, observed a man concealing himself behind a tree. Suspecting that something was wrong, he took his revolver from his holster and put it into his pocket—the man being only twenty or thirty yards in front of him, and *off* the road. He

STICKING-UP THE GYMPIE COAC[H]

We cannot say that we were greatly surpris[ed] when we heard that a case of "sticking-u[p]" had occurred on the highway between Ma[ry]borough and the diggings; though we expect[ed] the first essay would be made upon some solita[ry] wayfarer, not upon a coach laden with thirte[en] able-bodied men. There has been for some tim[e] established a well-armed escort, but many pe[r]sons were known to be in the habit of riskin[g] large quantities of gold or sums of money b[y] private hand. Coupled with which fact, it is we[ll] known our diggings have attracted a good numb[er] of the criminal classes from the other colonies the police protection being at the same tim[e] very inadequate. For these reasons we repe[at] we were not altogether unprepared to hear o[f] such an occurrence as that we now have to re[-] port. It appears that Messrs. La Barte an[d] Co.'s coach left Nashville as usual yesterda[y] morning, at about 6 o'clock, with thirteen pas[-] sengers; at about 7 o'clock, and when nearl[y] three miles on this side of the diggings, as th[e] coach was rising a hill, the driver was challenge[d] station had also seen Troden and Blake on the road the day before the hold-up, riding the same horses: "I am satisfied they are the men I met."

Troden's distinctive gun, held together with a nail, was located at Blake's tent, hidden in a nearby hollow log. The wide-awake hat with the broken band was found in the tent.

When he saw Troden handcuffed and under arrest, young Blake's manner was clearly not that of an innocent man. He trembled and said to his accomplice, "They might as well arrest me now as well."

And Troden's raspy voice was unmistakable, said the victims. As Crothers would later claim: "The short man had a rough voice. I have only heard a voice like it once since then. It was in the court house at Gympie. It was Troden."

The trial

IN his defence, Podgey Troden claimed that he had loaned the distinctive gun to a mate, that he often hired out his chestnut horse, that his peculiar gruff voice was a result of having spent many years at sea – and after all, 'scores more have gruff voices', and that the wide-awake hat simply wasn't his. The Maryborough jury was not convinced.

Crown Prosecutor Shaw's case was strong. He concluded: "This was a cold-blooded atrocity for which the prisoners are guilty of tying up their victims so that, but for a merciful Providence, they would all have died a horrible death by starvation and thirst." ■

The verdict and sentence

THE jury took only 30 minutes to find both William Troden and Joseph Blake guilty of highway robbery.

"The sentence I am about to pass," said Chief Justice Cockle, "will not be so severe as it would have been if, in the course of this outrage, the slightest wound had been made by the firearms they carried, for then it would have been my duty to sentence to be hanged both parties concerned....

That aside, it was a most cruel act to bind these men, so that they would in all probability be exposed in the bush all night; it might have led to the most serious injury – if not death.

You bound your victims with rope; I will have you bound in fetters of iron. The sentence of this Court is twenty years penal servitude – the first three years in irons."

STICKING-UP OF LA BARTE'S COACH BETWEEN NASHVILLE AND MARY-BOROUGH.

ROBBERY OF THE MACKENZIE MAIL.

(From the *Bulletin*, April 28.
ABOUT 4 o'clock on last Friday
downward mail from Peak Do
ding the Clermont, Copperfield,
wns mails, was stuck up and robb
ckenzie Scrub. The mailman—
mail-boy—for he is a youth about
rs of age, named Peter Flanag
ther to the mail contractor—was g
ter along the road through the scr
man on horseback, whom he had
rt time before following behind hi
t, galloped up beside him, drew a
l bailed up Flanagan, telling him
bush. The man had his face
h a red-colored handkerchief that

STICKING-UP OF CURRIE HOTEL BY FIVE ARMED MEN

(From the *Maryborough Chronicle*, April 21.)
ONE of the most daring cases of bushranging known in this colony occurred at Currie Hotel (Mr. Booker's) on Sunday night. Currie Hotel, we may note for the benefit of distant readers, is about twelve miles from the diggings, on the Maryborough road. The substance of the following account of what took place has been forwarded us by Mr. R. H. D. White, manager of the Bank of New South Wales, Rockhampton. It appears that Mr. White, who had been on the diggings a few weeks, opening a branch of his bank there, was returning to Rockhampton. Mr. Buckland the manager of the new

STICKING UP NEAR GAYANDAH.

INTELLIGENCE was received in Dalby on November 13 that the Boondooms public-house, known as the Old House at Home, was entered by two armed bushrangers on Wednesday night. The house, as many of our readers are aware, is situate on the road between Dalby and Gayndah, and about 18 miles from the latter town. The information to hand is to the effect that, on Sunday last, two men stole two valuable horses from Wetheron station, the property of Messrs. Moreton, and that information was given to the police in Gayndah. Constable John Kel-

1868

FRANK BOWERMAN
Crime: ASSAULT WITH INTENT TO MURDER
Location: BRISBANE
Penalty: PENAL SERVITUDE FOR LIFE

The avenging public servant

The trial was described as 'one of the most extraordinary we have ever witnessed because of the social positions of the accused and of his victim, the nature and manner of the crime, and its place of commital'.

ON 24 November 1868, an early visitor to the office of Arthur W. Manning, Under-Secretary to the Colonial Secretary, was the recently demoted Police Magistrate from Leyburn on the Darling Downs. The meeting took place in Brisbane's old colonial offices, in Queen Street.

Frank Bowerman, normally a rather shy and retiring person with a wife and four children, was furious at his recent demotion to the rank of clerk of petty sessions at Nanango and the accompanying reduction in salary and prestige.

The claim was that he had misappropriated funds. However, he had argued that the amount was insignificant, and that, although he was 'suffering a particularly impecunious period', he had always intended to replace the money, but had been prevented from doing so.

That morning in November he was intent on pressing the Under-Secretary for details of his case.

Manning told Bowerman: "I have seen documents that prove you have misappropriated public moneys and I have no other option than to place them before the Colonial Secretary."

"But that will ruin me," said an increasingly agitated Bowerman. "Can't you provide an advance in salary so that I can repay the money."

"If it were my own brother, Bowerman, I could not," replied Manning.

IN the end, a frustrated and enraged Bowerman left the building. In Queen Street, he ran into a former professional colleague to whom he related his tale and in whom he confided: "It's all that damned fellow Manning's fault. He has been the principal cause of my misfortunes. I will have it in for him yet."

Bowerman walked to Simmons General

In the 1860s, the colonial government offices (above) *were housed in the old military barracks on the site of today's Casino (formerly the Treasury Building, which was built from 1886-1928). Here, on 24 November 1868, former Police Magistrate Bowerman took a tomahawk to the head of Under-Secretary Arthur W. Manning.*

Store in Albert Street and asked for a tomahawk. The shopkeeper later said: "I wanted to wrap it up in paper when he had paid for it, but he said 'never mind' and put it under his coat."

Returning to the Under-Secretary's office in the early afternoon, Bowerman again confronted Manning.

"Have the documents been placed before the Colonial Secretary?"

"I have just shown them to him," replied Manning.

"Well, what is the result?"

"You will be suspended and a board will be appointed to investigate the matter."

At wit's end, Bowerman produced a pleading letter from his wife. Manning refused to take it.

"Such a letter cannot affect this business," he said.

Enraged, Bowerman drew the tomahawk from beneath his coat and, shouting "Well, take this!", he struck the seated Manning on the head, inflicting a frightful wound. Manning attempted, to rise.

"Murder. Murder!" he screamed. Four more heavy blows rained down upon his head and neck. He was now covered with blood.

His cries were heard throughout the building and people came running. First to Manning's office was a clerk who met Bowerman with his hand

Crossing paths

LATE on the morning of the attempted murder, John McDonald, Superintendent of Queensland's newest prison on St Helena Island, met with the Colonial Secretary's Under-Secretary Arthur W. Manning in his office in the Old Treasury Building. At the conclusion of the meeting, around midday, McDonald left Manning's office. On the way out, in the waiting room, he passed the former Police Magistrate at Leyburn, Frank Bowerman. Unbeknowns to all, Bowerman was concealing a tomahawk under his coat.

Within a few months, McDonald would have Bowerman as an inmate at St Helena, sentenced to life imprisonment for attempting to murder Manning with the hatchet – just moments after McDonald had left the Under-Secretary.

on the handle of the door, coming out. The attacker was overpowered and arrested.

AT Bowerman's trial, Manning gave his version of the attack:

'I was seated when I felt the blows, and there he was standing over me. It was so quick in motion that I had not an opportunity of rising. I remember walking across the room, with the blood pouring from me, over my face, and all down my clothes. I remember screaming. The door of my office was opened, I think by somebody from the outside. I remember seeing the Colonial Secretary opening his door from the opposite side of the passage, come out of his office, and say, 'My God, what is the matter?' I was led to the Colonial Secretary's office and seated, and I have a confused recollection of the doctors coming…'

With a background in legal affairs, Bowerman conducted his own defence, cross-examining Crown witnesses at considerable length. How galling it must have been for the incapacitated Manning, the victim, to be cross-examined by his own attacker.

Bowerman was found guilty of assault with intent to murder and sentenced to life imprisonment, a sentence that, reportedly, 'created a sensation in court'. ■

Suicide

BOWERMAN'S case was a sad one. He was described as 'a clear-headed, efficient officer, and a kind-hearted, highly respected, affable gentleman'. He had served the government for some twenty years, but was 'prone to fits of ungovernable passion'.

Following his imprisonment, his wife devoted many years seeking clemency and release for her husband. Her health deteriorated. She was on her deathbed when a telegram arrived advising of her husband's release from St Helena after nine years, on 26 February 1878, but she died before he could reach her.

In the years following his release, Bowerman slid into despair and poverty. In December 1894, his body was found in the Botanical Gardens in Sydney. At his side were two bottles of poison and a suicide note, which read in part: '... I am simply weary of the hand to mouth existence I have been compelled to endure and, while I possess the nerve, I think I had better resolve to die with my own hand...'

The victim

Under-Secretary Arthur W. Manning in retirement

IN 1869, on medical opinion that 'the victim could not long survive the effects of his injuries', parliament passed the Manning Retirement Bill, providing Arthur W. Manning with an annual pension for life of £600, the full salary of an Under-Secretary. Manning recovered and retired to Sydney. It was reported 25 years later that he was still living comfortably there – 'through the generosity of the taxpayers of Queensland'.

The lure of Halligan's gold

On Sunday 25 April 1869, Patrick Halligan, a gold-buyer and landlord of the Golden Age Hotel in Rockhampton, set out on horseback for the Morinish goldfields, thirty miles to the north-west. As usual he was well armed, for he took with him large sums in bank-notes to pay for gold which he would bring back in his saddle-bags.

He reached Morinish, obtained over seventy ounces of retorted gold, and started back for Rockhampton the same day. Having failed to return by the Tuesday, a party set out in search of him. They traced him to Morinish, and back as far as Deep Creek, fifteen miles from Rockhampton, where he was last seen, but there all trace of him was lost.

With black trackers, another search party spread out to check the country between Deep Creek and Lion Creek. There they found Halligan's hat and whip, and a torn piece from his coat. The tracks of two unshod horses were picked up, as well as those of Halligan's horse. Nearby they discovered a pool of blood, some coins, and a bullet-mark in the trunk of a tree.

The excitement in Rockhampton was now intense. A reward of £300 was offered for the discovery of the murderer, and citizens subscribed over £400 to swell the reward pool further.

On 7 May, a party again set out to search Eight Mile Island in the Fitzroy River, opposite the spot where the crime had been committed. While rowing down the passage between the island and the river bank, they found Halligan's floating decomposed body. It was attached to a bag full of bricks, anchoring it in place among the reeds.

Below: *The Alliance Gold Mining Company at Morinish, from where Patrick Halligan purchased 77 oz of gold on 25 April 1869, before setting off on the return journey to Rockhampton – and to his death.*

SUSPICION immediately fell upon 25-year-old George Palmer, who was already widely suspected of having been associated with a gang which had stuck up the Gympie-to-Brisbane stage coach. Palmer had 'taken up his quarters in the neighbourhood of the Agricultural Reserve, and established a reign of terror among the timorous near where he was camped, threatening all manner of vengeance if anyone divulged his whereabouts... He had previously made himself so obnoxious by his rowdy conduct in town, by horse-stealing, and by escaping from and defying the police,

The crime

THE ambush of gold buyer Patrick Halligan had been planned for some time by Archibald, who had a reputation as somewhat of a shady character, together with George Palmer and a no-good known as Old Jack Williams. Earlier attempts had failed because Halligan had unexpectedly returned from the goldfields by another road.

But on this occasion, on his way to Morinish, Halligan stopped at Archibald's Lion Creek Hotel where the host got him talking about his trip and his return route. Co-conspirator Jack Williams, lounging on the pub veranda, listened in on the conversation and was soon riding off to Palmer's hut on the Agricultural Reserve to finalise plans.

IT was just on dusk when Halligan crossed Deep Creek on his homeward journey. As he came into the open, Palmer rode at him with revolver levelled, caught him by the coat, and demanded the gold he was carrying. Halligan slashed Palmer with his whip.

"I know you, Palmer!" he yelled. "I will not give it to you. I won't! I won't!"

Halligan drew his gun and fired back at Palmer as he galloped off. The

AS soon as Archibald was arrested, he told where Old Jack could be captured - at a local pub. "All right. I'll go with you quietly," said Williams.

Palmer would not be so easily taken. He had headed south to Gympie. Though the police and black trackers were out after him, his superb bushmanship stood him in good stead. He stole the best horses he could find, and so traversed hundreds of miles with the police and trackers relentlessly in pursuit. But in time he was starving and in rags. His health had suffered, and he had found no way of disposing of the gold which he carried with him. But the shrewd Palmer devised a scheme to make some profit out of his surrender.

On 29 May, after evading arrest for a month, Palmer contacted Gympie solicitor, J.W. Stable, and arranged for that gentleman to secure the reward for giving him up to the police, on the proviso that he should dispense with the money 'in certain channels to be indicated'. Thus it was that, in the scrub on the Mary River, two miles from Gympie, Palmer, sick and miserable, accompanied by Stable, was handed over to the police.

At the trial, the prosecution argued that the three prisoners had clearly plotted to murder Halligan - after that he was believed to be capable of anything.'[1]

THEN, on 10 May, the police had a major breakthrough. They received a letter from a miner on the Ridgelands goldfield: he could provide information about the murderers. Soon armed with 'certain facts', police immediately arrested Alexander Archibald, the landlord of the Lion Creek Hotel.

Archibald at once volunteered to turn Queen's evidence (an immunity later denied). From his statement the story of the plotting, robbery and murder was revealed...

bullet lodged in a tree trunk.

Palmer returned fire, and Halligan fell to the ground. The pair gagged and bound him, dragged him some distance off the road, and took the gold he brought from Morinish, £14 in notes, and a ring off his finger. Then, with evil composure, they left him in the bush - gagged, bound, and bleeding to death.

Palmer and Williams rode to Archibald's hotel at Lion Creek, to tell him what had happened. There they divided the gold and money into three parts - for the ring they tossed a coin!

Later that night, at Archibald's insistence, Palmer and Old Jack rode back to the place where they had left Halligan. They found him dead. They bound up the body with rope that had been purchased in town by Old Jack, tied it on Halligan's horse, and took it to the river bank. On the way they filled a bag with bricks from the chimney of an abandoned hut, and tied this to the body. Near Eight Mile Island, they led the horse down through the reeds on the bank, and dumped the body and saddle into the deeper water.

Later they led Halligan's horse into the bush and, in a secluded spot, shot it, cut the brands out, and buried the lot. All traces of their crime, they believed, had now been removed.

all, it was still light at the time of the crime and they wore no disguises. The jury agreed, and all three men were sentenced to death by hanging.

A thunderous farewell

ON the morning of the execution, a severe tropical storm hit Rockhampton and, as Palmer and Williams came out of the gaol on their way to the scaffold, it rained heavily.

From the platform, Old Jack uttered his last words. It was recorded that 'his address was one of the most remarkable ever delivered from the scaffold. Rain fell in torrents, lightning flashed, and the thunder rolled as this man of iron will poured forth a deluge of bitter invective against those who had brought him to his doom. Palmer all this time stood silent beside his partner in crime with a despairing look on his face.'

When Old Jack concluded, the hangman drew the white caps over the faces of the two men. The final arrangements were quickly completed. At a sign from the warder the executioner drew the bolt. Death was instantaneous in each case.

One month later, on 22 December 1869, Alexander Archibald suffered the same fate. ■

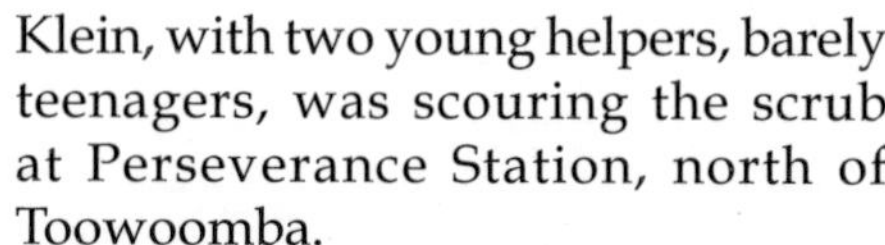

The hunt for Herrlich, the Hun

In the 1860s, the market for cedar timber had suffered a sudden decline. It just wasn't worth the effort of removing trees that had been felled in those years. Until the market recovered, the logs were simply abandoned in the forests and scrub.

By 1870, the rising price of cedar had again made hauling of the timber profitable.

On 12 February of that year, Michael Klein, with two young helpers, barely teenagers, was scouring the scrub at Perseverance Station, north of Toowoomba.

In previous weeks Klein had been pocketing good money using his bullocks to drag a number of logs to the local sawmill – much to the irritation of a German immigrant James Herrlich. Herrlich had a reputation of being fiery and short-tempered. As far as he was concerned, any cedar in this area was his. Others could look elsewhere!

Klein and the boys had just finished lunch. He was checking the harnesses on his bullock team when the German came striding into the clearing.

He looked angry, and he carried a double-barrelled shotgun.

"Are you here again, Klein?" he shouted as he levelled the gun in Klein's direction.

Before Klein could answer, Herrlich exploded: "If you take away any more timber, I will shoot you dead!"

His pent-up resentment was obvious and, as he quickly approached, Herrlich cocked the hammers of the shotgun.

By now he was only a metre from a fearful Klein, who grabbed the barrel with one hand to push it to the side.

The blast from both barrels sent Klein stumbling backwards, his chest blown open. He died instantly.

The two horror-stricken boys ran for the scrub. Herrlich waved his empty gun towards them and yelled: "I will catch you, you beggars…", but instead he checked that Klein was dead, shouldered his shotgun, and strode back into the undergrowth.

THE boys ran for help, and soon came across a bullocky who sometimes worked for Klein.

"Michael is dead! Old Herrlich has shot him," they shouted.

Returning to the scene of the shooting, they found the body drenched in blood. They covered it with blankets. Within moments a brother of the murdered man arrived. Shocked by what he found, he set off on his horse to tell his other brothers who were working some ten miles away. From there he set off for Toowoomba, arriving at sunset.

A party of police arrived at the scene of the murder around midnight but a quick search of the area could find no signs of Herrlich. The body was returned to Toowoomba.

Two days later 250 mourners attended Michael Klein's funeral. He left behind a wife and six young children.

The man-hunt begins

ONE of Queensland's most challenging and frustrating man-hunts had begun. It would take two months before they ran the culprit to ground.

There were many rumours as to Herrlich's whereabouts, but no one knew for sure. At first the search centred on the Highfields area; it proved fruitless. The weather was atrocious with bucketing rain and high winds. The initial party returned to Toowoomba; fresh men and native trackers were needed. Two weeks into the hunt a police party arrived from Brisbane. A $100 reward was posted for any information that would help in the murderer's capture.

They searched settlers' barns, huts and stables; they combed through dense thorny scrub on foot and through rocky gullies and creeks, occasionally finding evidence of a recent campfire.

Regular newspaper items reported the difficulties they encountered:

> The blacktrackers have been afraid to continue the search unless they were closely followed by the police, and at times it has been absolutely impossible for any white man to find a way through the tangled mass of vines, fern, and stinging nettles which constitute the greater portion of the scrub. The country over which the police have already gone consists of a series of scrubs, extending over about thirty miles, and divided by small belts of broken country. Deep, precipitous gullies wind throughout the scrubs, presenting some of the wildest scenes that could possibly be imagined, and forming now and

1870. ON 2 January, two men in a rowing boat at New Farm in Brisbane found a naked body half-buried in the slimy riverbank mud. Tied to the shattered skull was a large rock. Nearby, police found the murder weapon, the blood-spattered head of a tomahawk, and tell-tale rope which was traced to the home of William Pender.

Pender, clutching a crucifix, was hanged on 28 March, for the murder of Patrick Hartnett, whom he suspected of 'having blighted his matrimonial life'.

(From the D. D. Gazette of yesterday.)

MR. SUB-INSPECTOR HARRIS and the remainder of party engaged in the search for the murderer of Martin Klein returned to Toowoomba on Monday afternoon. Mr. Harris states that the police and the black trackers are completely exhausted, and require a few days rest, but he believes that if he can obtain the assistance of one or two of the native police, who would enter upon the search without that feeling of timidity and dread which has hitherto overcome the native trackers, that he will succeed in bringing the murderer to justice. Mr. Harris does not believe that Herrlich will attempt to leave the scrub, as the bunya bunya fruit will provide him with food for several months to come, and as he is intimately acquainted with the country he will find no difficulty in procuring the necessary supplies.

then an impenetrable barrier to the progress of the searchers. The murderer, Herrlich, has wandered through these scrubs for many years past, made himself perfectly acquainted with their secret places, and consequently he has been able to baffle the police in carrying out the pursuit.

Day after day through forest, scrub, mud and water they searched. On 3 April they again returned to Toowoomba, bedraggled, half-starved and exhausted, their clothes all but torn to shreds.

Fed, rested, with new uniforms and equipment, the search party returned to the man-hunt the next day.

Success at last

THREE days later they came across promising tracks which led to a barn at Highfields; clearly someone had been camping there. From there the trail led to a group of huts owned by German settlers, long suspected of assisting Herrlich and keeping him informed of police movements.

From there the police tracked a woman carrying three pounds of flour to a remote hut, where she met a man named Nuller, a known associate of the fugitive.

Later that night they surrounded a building and, with pistols drawn, they burst inside. There they found several men seated at a table. One of the men was James Herrlich.

Chained, and under heavy guard for fear his German friends might make a desperate rescue attempt, Herrlich was escorted back to Toowoomba.

On 27 July 1870, Herrlich found himself on trial for his life in Toowoomba. His defence argued that he had not set out to murder Klein with wilful intent. His case focussed on his statement that fateful day: "If you take away any more timber, I will shoot you dead!" This was but a threat, it was argued – and then the shotgun had discharged by accident, after the victim had grabbed for it.

The argument proved successful. A manslaughter verdict was returned and James Herrlich was sentenced to fifteen years in prison. Four years later, he was dead at age 59. He lies buried on St Helena Island. His autopsy report read 'senile decay'. ■

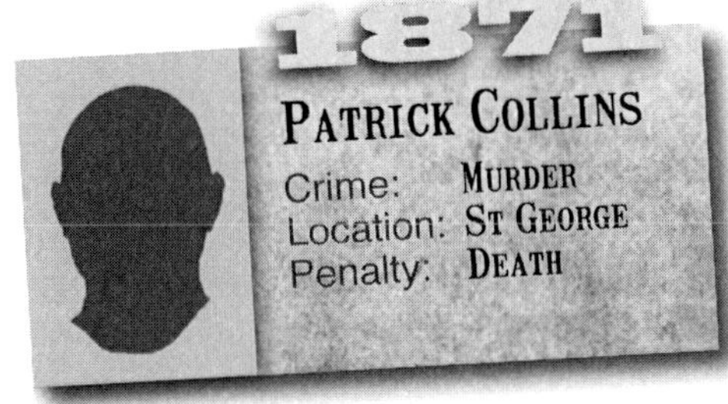

The murder of Simon Zieman

They found Simon Zieman's body floating face down in Gunde Gunda Creek about seven miles from Tartulla station, north-west of St George.

The body was dressed in a Crimean shirt and trousers, and the marks of violence to the head, mutilated to a pulp, pointed to a foul and cruel murder. A heavy log was lying across the corpse in an attempt to keep it underwater. Several footprints were found near the spot, and horse tracks led in the direction of Tartulla station.

Zieman had not been seen for nearly a week, having left Tartulla station on 21 November. The search party had been looking for him ever since his chestnut horse was chanced upon on 24 November. It appeared as though someone had clumsily attempted to hamstring the animal by cutting the sinews of its near hock.

A police search of the area found a newly dug hole in the bank about 300 yards from the murder site. There they found buried a hat, clothing, saddle cloth and money. Elsewhere they found more of Zieman's belongings – photographs, documents, letters, memo pad, and diary. They also discovered pieces of a pistol and a whip handle, and bootprints, with a distinctive triangular pattern of nails. Later Zieman's meerschaum pipe and penknife were found in a hollow log, wrapped up in an old glove.

IN partnership with his brother at St George, Simon Zieman was a young German who had been conducting a profitable business purchasing cattle in the western region of the colony.

On 20 November 1871, Zieman was visiting Tartulla station, the property of William Beckett, with whom the Zieman Brothers often had financial dealings.

On the day of Zieman's murder, Patrick Collins claimed he was 'chasing wild horses'... or 'I might have been rounding up cattle'. The police thought otherwise.

Zieman was staying at the station overnight, along with a dozen or so Beckett family members and workers. Before going to bed, he held business discussions with several of the men, during which he disclosed the fact that he had upon his person money and valuables 'to a considerable amount'.

Next day around midday, Zieman set out for Surat in the company of John McGoven, a Tartulla stockman. When police investigations began a week later, after the body was discovered, McGoven became a prime suspect – until two bullockies testified they had seen him some considerable distance from the scene at the time of the murder.

But there was another man who aroused the greatest police interest…

The man in the very fine cabbage tree hat

PATRICK Collins, the brother of Beckett's daughter-in-law, was also living at Tartulla. He was a 25-year-old of very questionable background. He had been released only a couple of months earlier from the prison on St Helena Island, where he had served five years for robbery and where he had been flogged for attempting to escape on two occasions – and for attacking the flogger.

In fact, Collins was arrested in St George, not long after Zieman's body was found. The police would focus on a number of points that convinced them of Collins' guilt, including…

- Someone from Tartulla had committed the crime because the pistol parts found at the murder scene were linked to the station. The pistol had hung in the homestead and was missing on the morning of the murder. It was readily accessible to Collins.
- The movements of every man at Tartulla station could be accounted for on the day of the murder, even the other prime suspect McGoven. Did not Collins seemed confused when asked to explain his whereabouts?
- Where *was* Collins on the day of the murder? Shortly before Zieman departed Tartulla, Collins had left the homestead. He returned that night, his horse distressed and in a lather from galloping. When asked why, he replied that he had been 'chasing wild horses in the top paddock'. Informed that there *were* no wild horses in the area, Collins replied that he was 'rounding up cattle'. What had he really been doing that day?
- And why was he wet? After all, it had not been raining at the station that day, although it had been at the murder scene Gunde Gunda Creek. Had he been struggling desperately with Zieman in the waterhole?
- The conversation between Zieman and others at the station on the night before the murder had been overheard in the next room by Collins – particularly when Zieman spoke of the money and valuables he was carrying. Did not Collins, next day, say to a fellow worker: "Zieman had a great blowing about his money last night…"?
- The tracks at the murder scene were made by boots with nails in the heels in the shape of a triangle – identical to Collins' boots. Made by a cobbler inmate on St Helena, they had been issued to Collins before he was discharged from the island prison. Only one other similar pair was made, and those boots were still on the island.
- On 26 November, Collins tried to cash

an unsigned £33 cheque in St George – the same cheque Zieman had shown during those discussions at Tartulla on the last night he was alive. The storekeeper had recognised Simon Zieman's distinctive handwriting. Collins could only have taken it from the dead man. The police were informed and they arrested 'the man in a very fine cabbage tree hat'.

- Why was Collins' saddle smeared along the side with blood and hair? He had no explanation when police found it in his hotel room in St George on the day of his arrest.

Drama in court

AT the conclusion of Collins' trial on 14 May, the jury took only 35 minutes to return a guilty verdict. The Judge was about to pronounce sentence when…

> 'The next instant Collins made a spring and, still holding onto the spikes that fringed the dock, got one foot over the front of the dock. The two stout constables, whom the wisdom of the Sheriff had stationed on either side of him during the whole trial, threw themselves upon him and, after a fierce struggle, succeeded in getting him in irons, his hands dripping blood from contact with the spikes. What his intention was, whether to kill the Judge or to make a rush for escape, is known only to himself, but the general idea is the former.'

The court was cleared and the doors locked while the Chief Justice, Sir James Cockle, sentenced Collins to death.

> 'The prisoner was then speedily removed to his cell, his face still containing the most terrible expression of rage, horror and despair. The strongest men shuddered and a positive feeling of relief was felt when the murderer was removed.' ■

Collins' confession

15 May 1872: "Overhearing the conversation of the 20th I thought he [Zieman] had a lot of money, and being only recently out of trouble and well robbed while in gaol, I determined to get money somehow, and so determined to take his, but I never intended to kill him. I met him at the end of the waterhole; I ordered him to stand, and demanded his money; he got off his horse, and I ordered him to the water's edge, where you found the bend of the whip.

He went to the water's edge and he pulled his vest and coat off. He pulled his trousers' pockets inside out. I shoved his watch in my pocket; as I did that, he said, 'Collins, it is the worst day's work you ever did.' He made a run and I ran after, and I hit him with the pistol and he fell in the water, and he caught me by the trouser leg and pulled me in, and I used the pistol there and broke it. After I murdered him I pulled the saddle off the horse and led the horse into the water to make a clean job of it, and with the penknife you found I tried to hamstring him. The horse swam over, right across.

I put the saddle and cloth and bridle into the natural hole; fetched the watch, &c., and put them in the log… I put the pocket book and cheque down the water-closet…

I alone committed the deed, and no one else knew anything about it."

The hanging

AT Brisbane Gaol, Petrie Terrace, having been found guilty of Zieman's murder, Patrick Collins was executed at 8.00 a.m. on 29 May 1872. On the scaffold, before his arms were pinioned, he shook hands with those around him, but 'refused the proffered hand of the hangman'. It is recorded that the hangman bungled the job by making the drop unusually long at twelve feet. The miscalculation resulted, before death, in Collins bleeding profusely on the gallows from a horribly lacerated neck wound. The execution was witnessed by nearly forty people.

The pure white bull

Harry Redford's crime is a tale of daring and theft on a grand scale, and of the outback's admiration for a felonious bushman whom the novelist Rolf Boldrewood featured as Captain Starlight in his famous novel *Robbery Under Arms*.

By the time Redford was a teenager he was employed as a drover and by 1870 was in Central Western Queensland as a 30-year-old working on the vast Bowen Downs cattle station which, in those days, covered 1.75 million acres.

In the early 1870s Bowen Downs was running a herd of about 70 000 cattle and Redford reasoned that the station owners wouldn't even know if they were a thousand short on muster. But he also knew that, if he stole the cattle, all of which had been branded, he couldn't sell them in Queensland or New South Wales. So he devised a plan to drove the cattle down the Cooper Creek into South Australia.

With a few accomplices, he built stockyards in a sheltered gully in an outlying part of the property, and gradually assembled a herd of about 1000 prime cattle, all without any of the station workers realising what was going on.

Among the herd, Redford included a prize pure white bull which, he believed, would help keep the cows and heifers quiet. Although he did not know it, that bull would later bring about his downfall.

In March 1870, with two associates Doudney and Brooke, he headed the herd for South Australia, through the Channel Country and the Strzelecki Desert, across land traversed a decade earlier by the ill-fated Burke and Wills expedition.

Redford was an excellent bushman and he knew that recent rains would have swelled the inland rivers and waterholes, providing plenty of feed and water for the journey.

In late June, after 1000 miles and having not lost one single beast, they reached the Walke brothers' Wallerderine station, then the farthest north of any settlement in South Australia. Using the name Henry

Collins, he told the Walkes he was a Queensland squatter and was heading to Port Augusta to sell the herd. He traded two cattle for provisions and sold the white bull to the Walkes, before setting off south once more.

Two hundred miles further on, Redford decided he'd had enough. At Blanchewater station he sold the remainder of the herd for £5000. The three duffers then pocketed the money and headed for Adelaide. Doudney and Brooke were never heard of again.

In April 1871 Redford married Elizabeth Scuthorpe at Mudgee, NSW, and had a daughter in 1872.

MEANWHILE, earlier, back at Bowen Downs in Queensland, three of Redford's former accomplices, who opted out of the long overland trek because they considered it too dangerous, had been arrested for stealing more cattle from the station. One of the men, John McKenzie, turned Queen's evidence, revealing Redford's grand scheme.

Workers at Bowen Downs discovered Redford's yards, and the tracks heading south. A party of stockmen and Aboriginal trackers set out on the trail, many weeks behind Redford. They eventually reached the Walkes' station, and found the white bull.

South Australian police took possession of the beast and it was shipped to Blackall in Queensland via Adelaide and Rockhampton. There it was put out to grass until such time as Redford could be brought to trial.

HARRY Redford was arrested in Sydney in January 1872 and brought to Roma to be tried. The charge was 'that Redford, in March 1870, at Bowen Downs station, feloniously did steal 100 bullocks, 100 cows, 100 heifers, 100 steers, and one white bull, the property of Morehead and Young.'

From the outset the trial seemed to focus on entertainment rather than justice. Locals, captivated by Redford's consummate bushcraft and daring, packed the courtroom. Forty-one of the forty-eight people called as possible jurors were dismissed because they were considered prejudiced.

The white bull, standing in a yard outside the courthouse, took part in a line-up with twenty other bulls and was immediately identified by his owner. The evidence against Redford was overwhelming – and the 'not guilty' verdict created an uproar *(see box, page 58)*.

After his acquittal, Harry Redford headed into northern Australia to work as a drover. He died while trying to swim across a flooded creek in the Northern Territory in 1901. ▶

In the main street of Aramac today stands the iconic White Bull. There, the Harry Redford Interpretive Centre reveals details of the most historically significant cattle-stealing case ever recorded in Australia. And hundreds of visitors now actively participate in a shortened version of the 'Harry Redford Cattle Drive', run annually through May and June.

The controversial verdict: An unhappy judge

THE trial of Harry Redford took place at Roma courthouse in late February 1873. Twelve hours after the trial had started, the jurymen retired to consider their verdict. They returned within the hour.

"Gentlemen of the jury, how do you find the prisoner at the bar, guilty or not guilty?"

"Not guilty," said the foreman.

A quick murmur of excitement rippled around the courtroom.

Judge Blakeney *(right)* was visibly staggered. He stared at the jurymen as though he had misheard the verdict: "Would you mind repeating your verdict please, gentlemen."

"*Not* guilty."

Those who were close enough saw the blood rush to the judge's face and his hands tremble as he fought for self-control. When he spoke he made no attempt to keep the bitterness from his voice.

"I thank God," he said deliberately, "that the verdict is yours, gentlemen, not mine."

His hard eyes raked the figure of Redford standing in the dock. "The prisoner is discharged."

And a cheering crowd led Big Harry to the nearest public house.

SQUATTERS, prevented from serving on the jury because of the defence counsel's objections, protested the verdict to the government: "We consider a more disgraceful miscarriage of justice never took place in any court of law".

Thereupon the Attorney-General asked Judge Blakeney for a report

Judge Charles W. Blakeney

– and lengthy it was – in which he concluded:

> "Although to my mind, no case could possibly be clearer for a conviction than this one, and my charge to the jury was decidedly against the prisoner, nevertheless they returned a verdict of 'not guilty'… The more respectable persons on the jury list for the Roma district are invariably set aside and the remainder are of a class whose sympathies are almost always with the prisoner."

Redford's trial was but one instance of how bushman sympathies were overwhelming justice in Roma at the time. On 5 April 1873 the governor of Queensland ordered the criminal jurisdiction of the District Court at Roma be withdrawn for two years.

The Redford verdict caused comment around the country. The *Sydney Morning Herald* observed:

> …But the saddest fact of all is the apparent indifference of the jurors to their oaths and, worst than all, the protection which they afforded by sealing the impunity of the criminal with the sanction of an acquittal, who may then laugh at the Judge – who was indignant, as well as at the prosecutors – who must have been ruined.

The downfall of a young nipper

Only a few months earlier, 12-year-old John Ruddy, after eluding police for several days, had been given the benefit of the doubt. At that time he had been arrested as the accomplice of his 12-year-old companion John Gerlee. The pair had entered Arthur Robinson's Boggo Road house in Brisbane on a Sunday afternoon in early December 1872, while Robinson was teaching at the local Sunday School. There they removed over £2 and a ring.

At their trial, Gerlee had been sentenced to five years at the Reformatory School for Boys – then located on an old hulk moored at the mouth of the Brisbane River. The case against Ruddy was inconclusive, 'resting upon the unsupported testimony of his juvenile accomplice', and countered by the statements of several character witnesses.

Police Magistrate Rawlins concluded: "While I am quite satisfied as to your guilt, instead of inflicting any punishment upon you… I shall require you to be of good behaviour for twelve months." He added: "If you get into trouble again, I will send you down to reformatory school for five years."

THREE months later, on 28 March 1873, John Ruddy was back in the Children's Court. A week earlier he entered the Boggo farmhouse of Samuel Ward, while he and his wife were working the farm.

Returning at midday, Ward found £9 in notes missing from a box on their dressing table – including a £1 note 'that had a corner torn and an ink blotch on the back' .

Police inquiries found that, about an hour after the money was missed, the young lad called at a baker's shop at the Rocky Waterholes (Rocklea), a couple of miles from Boggo (Dutton Park), where he purchased sarsaparilla and cakes – using a £1 note with a torn corner and an ink blotch on the back. He then jumped on to the Ipswich coach, which passed by shortly afterwards.

The 12-year-old was later apprehended, denying that he was the thief or that he was at Rocky Waterholes on the day. Nor did he have any money.

Despite young Ruddy's protests, PM Rawlins this time sentenced the boy to five years on the hulk. None of the £9 had been recovered, except that disfigured £1 note. Back in his cell the boy admitted to police that he had hidden the remainder of the notes in an old boot, and had buried it under the bridge at Rocky Waterholes. A mounted constable was despatched to find 'the plant'. He found the boot – but no money.

Later, back in town, it was reported that:

'the young nipper was then accused of having told a lie; but, on again being taken before Mr Rawlins, he promised to speak the truth, and to guide the constables to where the treasure was buried. He then took them to Boggo, and the money was found secreted not far from his father's paddock. The entire amount has therefore been accounted for.'

Aboard the hulk in the days that followed, no doubt Ruddy was able to share his story with his former accomplice John Gerlee. ■

The reformatory hulk

IN 1871, the old hulk *Proserpine*, moored at the mouth of the Brisbane River, became the colony's Reformatory School for Boys, housing up to 100 juvenile offenders.

Boys under the age of 18 years were sentenced to confinement at the reformatory, to segregate these youthful, convicted offenders from the poor influence of adults in prison, and to better promote their reformation and rehabilitation.

There the boys attended school three hours a day, and were taught reading, writing, arithmetic, English grammar, and geography. The remainder of the day was fully occupied – cooking, tailoring, cleaning decks, knives, brassworks, and cutting wood… Whenever the weather and duties permitted, the boys were taken out for an hour or so after 5 o'clock in the afternoon for boat exercise.

Life aboard the hulk could be tough. Shortly before Ruddy arrived, for example, the superintendent, Sub-Inspector Wassell, was investigated for mistreating Ruddy's partner in crime, John Gerlee. According to John Cockerill, a water police constable on the hulk, he (Cockerill) had taken some plum pudding from the safe, as fishing bait, and next morning the Sub-Inspector accused the boy Gerlee of having stolen the pudding. Gerlee was held on the grating while the Sub-Inspector gave him twenty stripes on the bare back with a saddle strap. The boy was then put to shot drill (carrying a 14 lb weight up and down the deck for an hour after each meal for two days), and was locked in at night in the lower hold with his blankets.

The Ipswich riot

> ONE of the most disgraceful scenes which we have ever witnessed in Ipswich occurred at the School of Arts on Thursday evening, November 5, when a violent mob took forcible possession of the hall of that institution, which had been hired by the Rev. D. Porteus, of that town, for the purpose of delivering the third and last of a series of lectures on the subject of "The Monk Who Shook the World"…
>
> – *Brisbane Courier*, 9 November 1874

They'd come from all over Ipswich and nearby districts to hear the Reverend Porteus deliver his final talk on Martin Luther, the Augustinian monk who 300 years earlier had accused the Roman Catholic church of heresy upon heresy and, in doing so, had inspired the Protestant Reformation.

As a result of the Protestant minister's earlier lectures, feelings were running high in Ipswich. Even before the 7.00 p.m. starting time, Brisbane Street was thronged with an excitable mob of men armed with walking sticks, cudgels and shillelaghs.

Admission was by ticket and the School of Arts was soon filled. Several rows of seats at the centre of the hall were closely packed with Roman Catholics, many of them well respected citizens of Ipswich.

The arrival on stage of the reverend lecturer was greeted with a growl of disrespect if not menace. Rev. Porteus began to speak amid groans and hisses, mingled with the applause of his supporters. He continued to speak, interrupted by frequent stamping feet and jeers. Women in the audience began to leave as the chairman called for order.

A fight broke out in the centre of the hall. Shouting men surged towards the stage as friends of the lecturer jumped up to protect him. Suddenly the hall erupted in violence. Chairs were smashed over heads. Cudgels, whip handles, shillelaghs, and chair legs were used as weapons. Blood flowed freely from broken heads. Stones were thrown. One man was stabbed. The lamps of some of the chandeliers were smashed and burning oil streamed down to the floor, in danger of setting the hall on fire.

A newspaper later reported: 'Men whom we have been accustomed to

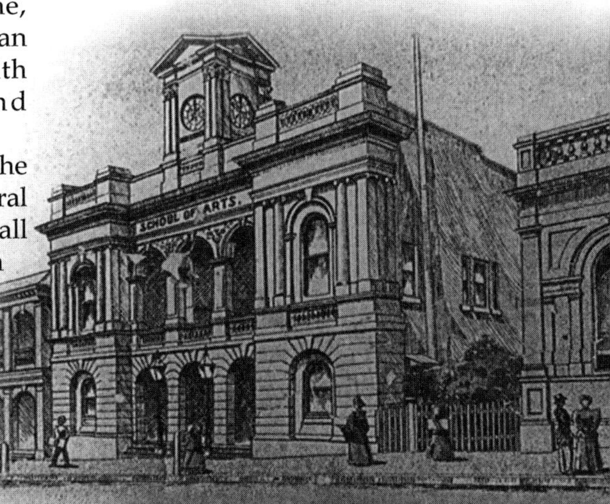

"Suddenly the hall erupted in violence. Chairs were smashed over heads. Cudgels, whip handles, shillelaghs, and chair legs were used as weapons."

look upon as rational and civilised beings were behaving like so many fiends, and the yells of some of those infuriated men were appalling.'

The Police Magistrate, who was in the audience, quickly had the speaker escorted from the building before returning to read the Riot Act. He then ordered police to clear the hall. This was done, 'with some little difficulty'.

The Roman Catholic mob left the hall in a body, and cheered as they reached the front of the School of Arts on account of the victory which they believed they had gained. Several fights, 'of a most serious character, bludgeons and palings from fences forming the weapons', broke out in different parts of the town. Police patrolled the streets, while Rev. Porteous spent the night in protective custody at the police barracks.

That weekend the colony's Roman Catholic Bishop Dr Quinn hurried to Ipswich to denounce at mass all those who had taken part in the riot. In an attempt to quell the antagonism, he attended the scheduled picnic day of Irish Protestants, travelling to the festivities in the same carriage as Rev. Porteus. There he 'addressed the assemblage with tact and geniality to soften the acerbities of the offended Protestants'.

Ipswich Police Magistrate Captain William Townley (left) *was compelled to read the Riot Act at the School of Arts meeting on the night of 5 November 1874:*

"Our Sovereign Lady the Queen doth strictly charge and command all manner of persons here assembled immediately to disperse themselves and peaceably depart to their own homes. God save the Queen!"

SEVERAL of the chief trouble-makers appeared before the crowded criminal sittings of the Circuit Court in Ipswich on 12 February 1875. Defendants Ryan, O'Sullivan, Keogh, St Ledger, Portley, Shaw and McCormack were variously fined £3-£15, and sentenced to periods of 3-6 weeks in prison.

In summing up, Judge Lilley addressed the defendants:

> 'You are now conscious of having been engaged in a very serious occurrence. By going to stop the lecture, you not only invaded the liberty of the subject, but also placed yourselves in a very dangerous situation. All history teaches that, even where a majority attempts to prevent the free expression of opinions, they end by becoming slaves themselves.' ■

The stranger who never was

Michael Whelan, a dairyman, lived on the Imbil Road outside Gympie. On the night of Saturday 1 May 1875, he was awoken around 10 o'clock. His neighbour, Mrs Pritchard, was rapping on the door. Her apron was covered with blood.

"Quickly, get up! Get a horse and go for a doctor!"

"What's up?"

"A strange man came home with son Charley and my nephew Israel – and they've just had a row at the house."

Whelan and Tom Hurley, who was staying with him, ran through the darkness to the Pritchard's two-room bush hut some 300 yards distant.

Inside they found Israel Griffiths lying dead on a stretcher to the right of the door. There were scratches to his neck, a cut under his right ear and an ugly stab wound in his chest.

Clearly there had been a violent struggle. Blood was copiously spattered over the floor and walls, and there were bloody palm and fingerprints on the doors and table.

When police arrived that night, accompanied by Dr John Benson, they detected that the victim, Israel Griffiths, when wounded, struggled violently with his back against the door; one of the hinges was partly torn off, and there were bloody handprints on the woodwork.

The Pritchards' account

THE account of events provided to police by Mrs Pritchard and son Charley (who was sporting a black eye) was along these lines:

On 1 May, Israel Griffiths and his cousin Charley Pritchard went in to

Gympie together and ordered some meat at a butcher's. Pritchard called back for it a short time afterwards.

Meanwhile Griffiths had met a strange man by the name of Jack who was with other men outside the butcher's, saying, "If you come home with us we will give you a 'doss-down' and a feed."

The three came home together and sat down at the table for dinner, Griffiths at one end and Pritchard at the other, with the strange man in the middle. The stranger was a short, stout man, very dark, with a long beard coming down from the cheek-bones, an Englishman, who wore dirty clothes, and had formerly worked in a claim with Griffiths.

In time an argument broke out about who could make the most money – a miner or a bush worker. During the dispute, Pritchard claimed he had gone out 'to refresh himself', and then came back to have another 'go in' at 'Jack', the stranger.

But when he returned, Griffiths and the stranger were 'at it', the latter with Pritchard's sheath-knife in his hand, and the mother trying to make peace. The stranger stabbed Griffiths in the chest, before jumping over the body and running out the door.

Having placed the body on the stretcher, Mrs Pritchard attempted to stem the flow of blood with her apron.

Charley Pritchard went out to look for the stranger, and was still searching when Whelan and Hurley arrived at the scene of the murder, having been aroused from bed by Mrs Pritchard.

A constable found the bloodied murder weapon on the ground outside the hut. Presumably the knife had been flung down by the stranger when making his escape.

The police apparently did not believe the Pritchards' statement, for they arrested the mother and her 25-year-old son on the following Monday, charging them with murder.

The Prosecution's account

IN the last week of October 1875, the Pritchards were brought to trial at Gympie. The prosecution put to the jury the following scenario as to what really happened that night in May:

> Griffiths and Pritchard, having been into town on 1 May, quarrelled either on the way back to the house on the Imbil Road, or on arrival there. A fight took place in the house, during which Pritchard received some blows. He stabbed or gashed Griffiths in the neck with his sheath-knife while his cousin was jammed up against the inside of the front door (a gush of blood being visible upon it at about the height of a man's chin). Griffiths fainted at the sight of his own blood (as he had frequently done before in surgical operations). While unconscious, he was stabbed in the chest. The frightful atrocity of the deliberate attempt to reach the victim's heart, was only too clearly elaborated upon in Dr Benson's evidence. He produced the heart in court, and stated:
>
> "There was only one external wound on the breast, but the knife, the blade of which was about five inches in length, had evidently been partly or wholly withdrawn after the first stab, and then pushed through the

same incision again in a slanting direction up into the heart."

Much of the evidence for the prosecution was directed at showing inconsistencies in and the improbability of the Pritchards' story. Among the points made were:

- The butcher who handed the bag of meat to one of the men swore that he gave it to Griffiths, not Pritchard; and one of two boys who met Griffiths and Pritchard going home, near the butcher's, swore that Griffiths was carrying the bag of meat.
- The boy claimed there were no men outside the butcher's and, from what he saw, no stranger was with the pair.
- A woman who spoke with them further on also said there was no 'strange man' in sight.
- Although neighbours Hurley and Whelan, upon being called by Mrs Pritchard, proceeded to the hut as promptly as possible, the stiffness of death had set in by the time they had arrived there. The Pritchards had had plenty of time to concoct their story.
- Pritchard was a left-handed man, and Dr Benson swore that in his belief the wounds to head and chest were inflicted by a left-handed man; it was only barely possible for a right-handed man to have caused the characteristic injuries.

Pritchard's demeanour in the dock was that of 'a shrewd and attentive listener'. Mrs Pritchard 'seemed simply weary and feeble'.

In the end, the mother admitted that her son had committed the murder. Mr Pring, who defended both of the accused, finally abandoned any attempt to deny that Pritchard killed his cousin, arguing that all the blows were inflicted in rapid succession during the heat of a fierce quarrel.

The jury adopted the same view – 'Jack' was the murderous stranger who never was. They brought in a verdict of manslaughter against Charles Pritchard, and acquitted his mother.

Pritchard was sentenced to twenty years penal servitude. ■

"Beyond human forgiveness..."

Dr. Benson, in his evidence at the trial, adhered to his opinion that the murderous knife had been partly withdrawn from the wounded man's lungs and then thrust upwards again into the heart...

The female accused did not deny the atrocious fact, and we can scarcely escape from the conviction that the double stab was really given.

It is this that deepens and blackens the wickedness of the inhuman crime; the hasty blow, however fatal it might have been, was as nothing, morally speaking, compared with the fiendish search for the seat of life – the heart – the horrid and dastardly desire to extinguish an already wounded and helpless man's existence. It is this that places the deed itself beyond human forgiveness, and the faintest sympathy with the perpetrator impossible. It is this that makes the verdict of "manslaughter" appear erroneous, and the sentence of twenty years' imprisonment seems a punishment lamentably inadequate to the offence.

– *Gympie Times*, 30 October 1875

The brute from the Belyando

The Queensland Native Mounted Police

THE Queensland Native Mounted Police were established prior to the colony's separation as a self-governing colony in 1859, and continued for some four decades.

Consisting of 'native' troopers under white officers, their task was to protect white settlers 'from the numerous and hostile savages', as the pioneers advanced into aboriginal territory. They were armed and authorised to use these weapons. And use them ruthlessly they did.

Remote from surveillance, the behaviour of the Native Police and their officers towards Aborigines produced many appalling incidents, massacres, beatings, abductions and shootings, including such atrocities as occurred at Fassifern near Ipswich (1861), Gladstone (1872), Irvinebank (1884) and Kimberley in the Gulf country (1887).

The Native Police operated on the fringes of colonial settlement, which meant that, because of that remoteness, and denial, cover-up and subversion of justice, the government persistently failed to enforce legal accountability. Rarely were charges laid. Over time, there were only four prosecutions, all unsuccessful.

It took many years before the government acted to stop the killings and brutality, and to bring the Native Police under control.

The arraignment of the sadistic Lieutenant Frederick Wheeler in 1876 was at least a step in the right direction.

For nearly twenty years, Lieutenant Frederick Wheeler of the Queensland Native Mounted Police led his pack of human blood-hounds, many of them Aborigines, on dozens of punitive expeditions against aboriginal people. Wherever Wheeler and his band went, they left a trail of dead and wounded victims, most of them quite innocent of any wrong-doing.

Typical was the massacre north of Rockhampton, at Cock's-comb Hill in April 1869. Here Wheeler's drunken team surrounded an aboriginal camp and forced the occupants to march up the side of the mountain. The troopers then drove the group over a cliff. Any broken bodies still breathing at the base of the cliff were later finished off, with gun-butts.

But another atrocious episode in 1876, involving a young Aborigine from a Belyando sheep station, would see a long-overdue end to Wheeler's brutal career...

EARLY in 1876, Wheeler abducted three aboriginal women from the Belyando tribe. The manager of Banchory station near Clermont, from which the women were taken, protested, pointing out the anger this caused within their people.

On 11 March Jemmy, an Aborigine in his twenties, left the station and walked to the aboriginal camp near the Belyando Native Police barracks outside Clermont. Here he was seen talking to the abducted women. The troopers apparently now regarded the women as their own personal property and dragged Jemmy to their barracks where Wheeler had him handcuffed and suspended from a rafter on the verandah.

The intruder would be taught a lesson – and a brutal lesson it would be, as police constable Thomas Baker would later testify *(see box, below)*.

Eyewitness to brutality

The account of Constable Thomas Baker,
Belyando Police Camp, 1876

I was at the Belyando police camp on March 11. I saw a strange black boy in the camp by the name of Jemmy. He was taken from the blacks' quarters to the police barracks by the native troopers at 9.30 p.m. The boy had no clothes on, but he had handcuffs on his legs. I saw Mr Wheeler assist the native troopers. They let the black boy drop on the ground whereupon Mr Wheeler kicked him, in the back I think.

They took him to the barracks and put another pair of handcuffs on his hands, through which they then passed a strap, and from there to the rafters on the verandah outside the barracks.

While Jemmy was tied up thus, with his hands above his head and his feet on the ground, a trooper flogged him with a teamster's whip, about four-feet-six-inches long, somewhat like a riding whip, giving him about eight or nine cuts on the back.

Another trooper was then told by Mr Wheeler to flog him and Jemmy received about twelve more blows when the whip broke.

Mr Wheeler then flogged Jemmy with a leather girth about six to twelve times; he had the buckles in his hand. He then called the native trooper Toby, who gave Jemmy about twelve strokes. After this, Mr Wheeler gave him a few more blows with the girth, and then told another trooper to flog the boy, and Jemmy was given another twelve blows with the girth.

I then said to Mr Wheeler, "That will do, sir, the boy has surely had enough."

WHEN the flogging of Jemmy ended, the troopers took him down from the rafters and carried him back to the nearby blacks' camp. There Wheeler called for a third pair of handcuffs which he used to connect the cuffs on Jemmy's wrists to those on his feet. There he lay for the rest of the night.

Next morning the battered Jemmy was taken back to Banchory station. Despite care, he died five days later.

Arthur Brown, the manager of Banchory, lodged a complaint with the Clermont police. This became a rare case of criminal charges being laid against an officer of the Native Police: the sadistic Wheeler's actions had been so visible and became so public that local squatters and their employees, and even local police, all joined in their condemnation of the man. Wheeler was dismissed from the force, arrested on a charge of murder, and remanded to stand trial in Rockhampton. On 10 May, he was released on £400 bail.

The trial began in the Circuit Court at Rockhampton on 2 October 1876. Frederick Wheeler failed to show up.

Passenger shipping records from Rockhampton show that, on 1 October, the day before the trial, an 'F. Wheeler' was taken down the Fitzroy River aboard the commuter boat *Bunyip*, and at Keppel Bay was transferred to the *Leichhardt*, bound for Cooktown and ports north.

The brute from the Belyando had escaped colonial justice. ■

Fragments from the FILES of FELONS

1877. AT 6 a.m. on 30 November, in a shearers' hut near Tambo, a horse handler heard, through the slab walls, groaning noises coming from the adjacent room. Looking through the slab walls, he could see a shearer, William Fitzgerald, 'sawing at his throat with a knife – blood was everywhere'. He ran in and overpowered Fitzgerald, who, it was later found, was under the influence of opium, and was later sentenced to 3 months hard labour for attempted suicide.

1877. For the manslaughter of Caspar Hahn in Toowoomba, John Hayes was sentenced to ten years penal servitude.

On St Helena Island, the prison's water supply was stored in several massive concrete-lined underground tanks. Each tank was capable of holding twenty feet of water and was accessible by means of a two-feet diameter manhole cover at ground level.

At 8.30 a.m. on 19 October 1881, Hayes asked a warder to unlock the cover of the largest tank so that he could fill his work bucket. The warder watched as Hayes began to wind a rope around the handle of his bucket before lowering it into the cavernous well below. A short while later, the prisoner could not be found.

A search was made – and his cap, and then his body, were retrieved from the dark waters of the tank.

An official investigation concluded that Hayes 'deliberately and of his own will committed suicide'. There were those who thought otherwise.

The missing bank notes

At close of trading on 6 December 1877, Benson Hall, a clerk at the Bank of New South Wales in Queen Street, Brisbane, placed £1306 in bank notes in a cash box, which he then took into the strong-room, setting it on its shelf in the normal place.

Next morning, around 9.20 when the door of the strong-room was unlocked as usual by George Lever, the bank's bill clerk, Hall proceeded to take out his box – but, on holding it by the handle of the lid, he found the lock had been forced, and inside, the bank notes were gone!

Two keys were always needed to secure the bank's money. Lever had left the bank about 10 o'clock the previous night, having locked the door of the money cage with one of the keys; the other key was then used by Alexander Archer, the bank's manager, to lock the outer strong-room door.

Between the time of Archer locking the strong-room and the discovery of the theft next morning, no one could have entered the vault. The crime must have been committed between the end of trading and closure of the bank around 10 p.m. the night before – seemingly by one of the several employees.

POLICE made little progress in finding the thief until late April the following year, when a suspicious teller at the

Top: *In the 19th century, paper currency circulating in Queensland comprised bank notes issued by many private trading banks.*

Right: *The Bank of New South Wales, corner Queen and George Streets, Brisbane*

Right: *In the Brisbane Botanical Gardens, four months after the robbery, torn fragments of the missing bank notes were collected along the river bank near The Battery*. The thief's illegal booty had been found close by.*

Union Bank informed the authorities that Victor Townsend, a clerk at the Bank of New South Wales, had been making regular bank-note deposits into his account.

How could a mere teller possess notes on various banks totalling £100 each time? And on 25 April, he had made another deposit in various notes – totalling £300. But what really attracted the clerk's attention was the fact that all the notes were damp and stained – as if they had been buried.

And how was it that Townsend purchased a beer at the bar of the European Hotel – with a £1 note, from the list of missing numbered notes? And two pairs of boots from an Elizabeth Street bootmaker using two £5 notes on the list?

Detectives began re-questioning Townsend, who said the money had been sent to him by his brother from somewhere in north Queensland. A search of Townsend's residence in Mary Street found nothing that could prove his brother's identity, location or generosity. But police confiscated several items, including two boxes – containing fragments of torn bank notes.

At 7 a.m. on 29 April, Townsend led police to the river bank in the Botanical Gardens.

"There it is," he said and, under some wood and bushes near The Battery*, they found two small damp linen bags containing bank notes and coins.

IN the days that followed, two workers found dozens of fragments of bank notes lying in the grass and rubbish near The Battery – remnants of an earlier attempt by a reckless Townsend to discard some of the evidence.

On 14 May 1878, former teller Victor Townsend pleaded guilty to the theft of £1306 from the Bank of New South Wales, and was sentenced to seven years penal servitude. ■

---

* In the 1870s, fear of a Russian invasion caused the colonial government to form a defence plan for the protection of the colony – including gunboats *Gayundah* (Lightning) and *Paluma* (Thunder), the construction of Fort Lytton at the mouth of the Brisbane River, and a series of batteries to protect the approach to Brisbane by river – including The Battery in the Botanical Gardens.

Gory goings-on at Gilbert River

The danger at Gilbert River

...But one obstacle threatens the alluvial industry of the Gilbert goldfield. That obstacle is the fine specimens of primeval man yet adorning the conglomerate of the district. One is bound to accept the existence of the savage. His present *metier* appears to be to spear miners' horses and squatters' cattle, and to give rise to retributions on the part of native police detachments.... It says a great deal for the district's gold-bearing alluvial resources that men should undertake so toilsome a journey to face dangers that are so notorious.... There is a detachment of native police in the district, which assiduously does its duty in dark defiles and broken watersheds to which both the gold and the blackfellow are confined.

– *Brisbane Courier*, 2 October 1878 (*passim*)

The untamed country of frontier Queensland could be a dangerous place in the 1870s, where aboriginal people fought to retain possession of their lands. Such were the perils for hardy (or foolhardy) prospectors who searched for gold at Gilbert River in the remote north of the colony.

Gilbert River country was characterised by rugged cliffs and narrow isolated ravines, half-starved dingoes, and Aborigines who wandered menacingly from creek to creek, gorge to gorge. Yet that precarious environment was voluntarily embraced by pioneer fossickers such as Manuel Yous and Tom Ward in 1878.

"Hour by hour, nay every second," it was written, "there is the same uneasy consciousness that bloodthirsty and vengeful eyes are upon you, and that to relinquish your gun for a minute may cost you your life."[1]

FOR protection, Yous and Ward were travelling mates. They had pitched their camp – two tents and three horses – on the Gilbert River, and had succeeded in discovering some payable gold a mile or so distant, on the opposite side of the river.

On 21 April 1878, while they were away, the blacks had pillaged their camp and, to guard against a repetition of such theft, the pair decided that they should each in turn remain at the camp while the other worked the new ground.

On 26 April, it was Manuel Yous's turn to remain at the camp and to work in a nearby ravine. His mate, Ward, left him early in the morning to work in the more distant gully.

At sundown, returning from work, Ward, crossing the Gilbert, saw that the ridge-poles of the tents were bare, the calico fluttering in the wind. He shouted for his mate, fired a gun, and loosed the dog that was on the chain. No response from his mate.

It was light enough to see tracks of blacks all round, broken spears, stores scattered and stolen, and horses missing. Ward had every reason that night to be fearful.

At daylight the following morning, he set out on foot over rough country for Georgetown, some hundred miles distant, and reached there within three days.

THE next day police-magistrate O'Brien, Ward, and two black boys (an Aborigine and a kanaka), started for the spot, arriving there on 3 May.

They found that the blacks had returned to the camp and removed many other articles – flour, tea, sugar, raisins, billies, straps, a double barrelled gun – and even caught one of the horses which they had chased up and down the sands of the river.

O'Brien's group then searched the

Pursuit and retribution, frontier-style

'THE track by which the blacks had retreated led over the conglomerate – a mass of sand, gravel, and quartz pebbles by which the high lands of the district are formed. Over this barren hard substance the leading trooper followed the trail, now at fault where some abrupt turn had been made, again recovering the trail by an upturned stone or disturbed leaf.

The four wild blacks had taken with them a horse belonging to the murdered man's mate, and had led it through gorges, ravines, and displaced boulders where no-one could have supposed it possible to go. The course kept one general direction, evidently to join by preconcerted arrangement the main tribe; but, as showing the cunning evident in the untutored savage, it was singular to notice how, whenever their path would have led them over country calculated to leave legible footprints, they diverged right or left to regain the fancied security of the conglomerate.

For three days the troopers followed these four footprints before signs were visible that a meeting with the main body had taken place. Each night the stolen horse had evidently been carefully hobbled, and the camp selected to guard as much as possible against surprise.

After joining up with the main body there had evidently been an impromptu corroboree. The horse, as was plain by the circular footprints round the camp, had been largely used for equestrian exercise, a trophy enhancing the glory of the four braves who had won it.

The chase continued. The loftiest and steepest heights of the conglomerate were selected as camps...

Doubtless it was found awkward to drag the unfortunate horse over this broken area; perhaps the fickle savages had already tired of riding; or maybe the vulgar calls of appetite could no longer be restrained. Be that as it may, on the third or fourth day the horse was killed, and a grand feast made from its carcass. Portions were carried off...

Closer and closer drew the avengers day by day. Their hopes had been fed, and their anger stimulated, by finding telling marks that they were on the right track. Now a much-worn shirt, now this or the other article, recognised as the property of the slain man or his mate, was picked ravine where the missing Yous was supposed to have been working on the day of the attack. His body was found: 'in separate portions, near his pick and shovel. In the gutter of the ravine, partially covered with burnt leaves and boughs, were the thigh-bones lying, charred by fire. On the slope of the gully was the trunk, nearly divested of flesh, and charred like the thigh bones. Still higher on the bank and a few yards further the skull, arm-bones, and lower jaw fearfully crushed by blows, and also partially consumed by fire, lay. There was no trace of flesh, features, or hair.'

As O'Brien and Ward were burying Yous's remains, a party of four native troopers, under the command of Constable Nobbs, arrived from Dunrobin, near Georgetown. Their task, as was the custom of the day, was 'to avenge the manes [spirit] of the slaughtered man'.

In less than five minutes, it was recorded, without noise, bustle, or argument, the troopers had deciphered the whole story: 'only four or five blacks, "young fellow myall", had been actually engaged in the murder, and they were detached from, and had by now probably rejoined, the main body'.

The search for the culprits began, to be recorded as follows below:

up where they had been left by the careless savage. The footprints grow clearer and clearer, the indentations have no longer had time to dull with wind strewn dust, leaving a well-defined trail...

Night is approaching. Two troopers sent ahead return with grim and significant gaze. The horses are left. The men cautiously steal towards where circling rings of smoke rise upwards. The low croon of a corroboree breaks the air. Some prophetic Cassandra sends wailing notes of mournful presage.

The night passes. Up above the horizon leaps the morning star. Circling round the camp, the troopers take post. Yard by yard they approach. A watchful dog sounds the alarm. A gin sings out in terror. A Nestor of the tribe, mounted on a rock, peers through the bursting dawn. "Come on, Mr. Policeman, come on," he seems to cry.

A sharp fire of carbines.

A scurry to every hole and cave, a trooper with a spear through his shoulder, and a stalwart constable gazing on the pieces of his broken rifle close the scene. Soon it is finished.

In this camp, hung up on a sapling, was found a pocket-book and paper. On the ground lay an adze, several axes, iron tomahawks, and wooden handles fitted with chisels and knives of every conceivable shape and size, being used for the purposes of aboriginal social life. A captured gin laid the actual spearing of Yous to a blackfellow named Jimmy....

Whatever may be the opinion in southern communities, northern residents daily exposed to like hazards are unfeignedly glad to find that the true culprits have been unmistakably caught, and "dispersed" in the time-honoured fashion.'[2] ■

1879

Joseph Mutter
Crime: **Murder**
Location: **Ravenswood**
Penalty: **Death**

Caught... down a mineshaft

W. R. O. Hill, better known as 'Willie' Hill, was one of three brothers who migrated to Queensland in 1861. After first working on station properties, he later secured a post in the Native Police, before joining the public service and becoming a police magistrate and goldfields warden.

Hill *(right)* was mainly employed in North Queensland, where his name was a household word, and where he was described as 'keen, capable and brave'.

In 1879, his arrest of the murderer Joseph Mutter at Ravenswood, under sensational circumstances, showed how committed he was.

In *Forty-five Years' Experience in North Queensland (1907)*, he described that episode as follows...

"A German named Joseph Mutter was boarding with a countryman named Steffan, and they lived in a small cottage on the main road to the Donnybrook, seven miles from Ravenswood.

One day, after dinner, when the old man was at work in his garden, Mutter insulted his wife, who retaliated by slapping his face. Mutter thereupon stormed off to Clisbett's Store, bought a big butcher's knife, and a small bottle of schnapps, which he drank to get Dutch courage, walked back to Steffan's house, and stabbed the poor old woman twice in the ribs, in the left ear and eye, twice burying the knife to the hilt. The husband hearing a scream rushed in, only to catch his wife in his arms as she was falling.

I was passing the house on duty with Vick, my black tracker, and got into the house only just in time to hear her gasp out the words, "Mutter, Mutter."

I cooeed for help, and several men arrived, one of whom I sent at once for the doctor, another for the police. In the meantime, after putting Vick on to Mutter's track, I did what I could to try and staunch the flow of blood from the wounds, but she died before the doctor arrived.

About half-an-hour later, a man came galloping up with the news that they had seen Mutter disappear down an abandoned shaft, a mile away.

I jumped on my horse and quickly got to the place to find a crowd of excited miners and two constables at the mouth of the shaft. It was at this time nearly sundown and, as I knew these shafts were connected by drives, and also that Mutter had been working in some of them, I feared he might give us the slip, so I promptly borrowed a revolver from one of the constables, and I was lowered down a shaft, eighteen feet deep, with a rope.

When I got to the bottom I noticed an underlay going down at an angle of one-in-eight and crawled in but, finding it pitch dark, returned, and sang out for a candle. Several were thrown down, so I crawled back again on my hands and knees, a candle in my right hand, and the revolver stuck in the breast of my shirt.

When about eight yards in, my hand touched something foreign... It was the knife which Mutter had buried up to the hilt in the loose earth, the blade and part of the handle thickly covered with fresh blood.

Feeling sure of capturing Mutter, I prepared by sticking part of the candle on top of the knife, crawling on my elbow, and holding the revolver in my right hand.

In a few yards I sighted the murderer, who was crouched and shaking like a man with palsy. I covered him with the revolver, and said:

"Move, you bastard, and I'll pot you."

He mumbled, "All right, I come."

Then I was in a fix, as the shaft was so narrow that we could not possibly pass each other, and up to this time I was not aware that Constable Murphy had crawled down after me to give assistance.

Seeing a glimmer of light some distance down, I made my prisoner crawl backwards and, when I got him there, found we were in a shaft fifty or sixty feet deep. I made Mutter keep his hands up, and the constable searched him.

Whilst doing so, a rope came dangling down, and I heard voices from above call out, "Let us pull him up, sir," but fearing lynching business, I got the constable to crawl back the same way we came.

Mutter followed, and I brought up the rear, and when we reached the first eighteen feet shaft, I tied a rope round Mutter's middle and, clasping my arms round his neck, we were safely landed on the top.

Then the fun began, as the crowd of infuriated miners wanted to tear our prisoner to pieces, but fortunately the Sergeant and other constables had arrived so, after a tussle with the mob, we got our man away from them, and into a cart.

When passing the scene of the murder, and before any one could prevent him, the poor half-demented old husband rushed out, clambered over the wheel and was tearing, biting, and clawing Mutter like a wild cat, so that it took three of us to remove him by force.

When I returned the revolver to the constable, I found it was empty. Nice sort of weapon to face a man like Mutter with!

MUTTER was tried and convicted by Judge Sheppard at the Circuit Court, Townsville, chiefly on my evidence.

Mutter was sentenced to death, and duly hanged in Brisbane Gaol, but a fearful bungle was made of the execution as, owing to the rope being thin, and hardened by frost on a bitterly cold night, and the hangman giving it an unusually long drop, Mutter's head was pulled off, and was rolling away until Inspector O'Driscoll put his foot on it!" ■

The very horrible scene that was enacted at the gaol last Monday morning should, we think, be made the subject of some enquiry. The official whose business it is to carry into effect the last penalty of the law should at all events understand his terrible vocation sufficiently to guard against such disgraceful accidents as the one that attended the execution of the miserable man Joseph Mutter who was done to death under such atrociously revolting circumstances. To wrench a man's head off in a clumsy attempt to hang him is—although in no sense barbarous to the condemned as adding no additional pang to his last agony—a disgusting bungle such as it is to be hoped may never occur again.

The Queenslander, 14 June 1879

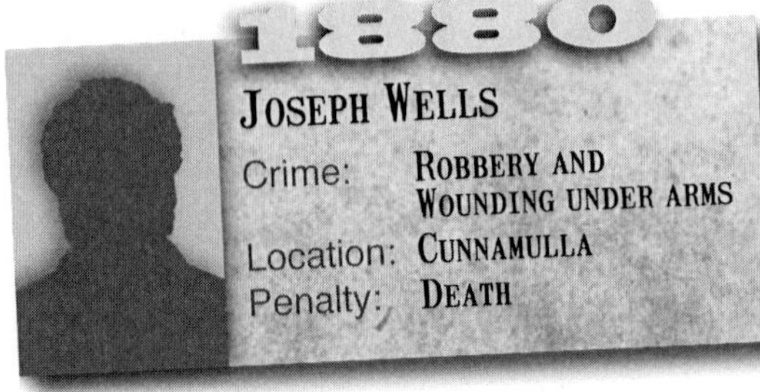

The tree-climbing bank robber

By 1880, Cunnamulla in south-western Queensland had a population of a few hundred. It also had a newspaper, a cordial maker, brewery, soap manufacturer, bakers, blacksmiths, shire offices – and a bank.

THE manager of the Queensland National Bank, Joseph Berry, had just opened the doors to his establishment. It was a little after 10 o'clock on the morning of 16 January 1880. Outside, the hot dusty street was empty, apart from a man tying his horse to a nearby hitching rail.

As he settled behind the teller's counter, Berry looked up at the sound of footsteps on the landing. In the doorway loomed the figure of the man. In his hand he held a revolver.

"I stick up the bank!"

"Well, I'll not give you any money," Berry responded without thinking.

The stranger leapt over the counter and, with the gun pointing at the manager's head, he shouted, "If you don't give me money I'll shoot you!"

Berry now took the man seriously. Backing warily down the corridor towards the back room where the safe was located, with the intruder's gun in his face, Berry slowly and clearly replied, "I'll not oppose you... just wait a minute."

In his office Berry unlocked the safe.

"Stand aside!"

The bank-robber began stuffing a parcel of notes down his shirt, along with a handful of gold and silver coins.

While the thief was thus distracted, Berry bolted through the back door, across a few metres of open space and into the rear of the shop next door. It belonged to storekeepers Warner and Murphy.

UNBEKNOWNS to Berry, William Murphy in the shop next door had

The store next door to the Queensland National Bank, Cunnamulla, 1890.

Ten years earlier, hearing raised voices and shouting, storekeeper William Murphy ran to the adjacent bank building only to be shot by the inept robber, Joseph Wells.

heard the bank-robber's shouting, had run over to the bank and entered through the front door just in time to see Berry duck out the back.

Within an instant, the bank-robber came running down the corridor towards Murphy. He jumped up on the teller's counter, waving his revolver at the storekeeper. Murphy tried unsuccessfully to wrestle the gun from the intruder's hand.

"Stand back!" screamed the robber. The gun fired and the bullet glanced off Murphy's head and into his shoulder.

Bleeding heavily, the storekeeper struggled with the thief, desperately trying to prevent him from getting off a second shot.

"Help! Help!" Murphy shouted at the top of his voice, as the pair wrestled towards the door.

All at once the intruder broke loose and ran for his horse tied up outside. But what with the suddenness of it all, and with a blood-soaked Murphy shouting as he staggered from the bank, the horse took fright, reared up, broke its reins and galloped off down the street, with the bank-robber in hot pursuit on foot.

The contemporary press continued the tale, which now took on a comical character:

> Then followed a scene of excitement that will not be forgotten for many a day… A large number of unarmed persons gave chase, raising a great noise and commotion, some men with guns [later found to be unloaded] calling on the robber to surrender, and the crowd hounding on the men to shoot the bushranger, who, poor devil, was frantically trying to catch his horse… The hunted wretch, closely pursued by a remnant of would-be capturers, turned round to get breath, and threatened to shoot anyone who should dare to come near him – a proceeding which greatly checked the impetuosity of the pursuers, who fell back and began to disperse. The man, finding himself pretty well deserted, made the best of the golden moments by putting on a desperate spurt to get out of sight…
>
> At this juncture a sheep-dog, which had joined in the hue and cry, was of great service. Being urged on by his master, the sagacious brute, with unerring instinct, was soon on the ruffian's tracks.
>
> The robber in his desperation climbed a tree of thick foliage, in the hope of avoiding detection. But the excited dog was on the trail, barking all the time his high disapproval of evildoers in general, and of this one in particular…

The frenzied barking led a mounted Sargeant Byrne to the scene. Fifty metres from the tree, the policeman shouted: "Throw down your revolver and put up your arms."

The robber, some six metres up the tree, refused. "I stuck up the bank a short time ago and I believe I have shot a man dead, and I may as well be shot now as be a lifetime in gaol," he shouted back.

The policeman, with his revolver raised, slowly advanced to within several metres. "Come down or I will shoot you dead!"

Byrne later told the tale:

> 'He soon after came down, still holding his revolver, and advanced, holding it towards me, the point inclining down. I went towards him, covering him. When I got within three paces I jumped forward and seized his right hand and took the revolver away. It was on full cock. I

The Robber's Tree – today's living reminder of the Cunnamulla Bank Robbery of 1880. The robber, Joseph Wells, hid in the tree (when it was much smaller) but he was quickly located by a yapping dog and captured by a policeman and the irate townspeople whose money he had stolen.

then arrested him and put him in the lockup.'

THE bank-robber, identified as one Joseph Wells, still had the bank notes and coins down his shirt – to the value of £175. He was charged with robbery and wounding under arms, an offence that carried a mandatory death penalty.

On 22 March 1880, at Boggo Road Gaol, the bumbling Cunnamulla bank-robber Joseph Wells dropped into history – the last person to be hanged in Queensland for armed robbery. ■

Fragments from the FILES of FELONS

1879. THE Cobb & Co. coach out of Maryborough was stopped by a calico-masked man brandishing a double-barrelled shotgun and a pistol on a Saturday morning in August. The bushranger demanded that a commercial traveller in the coach hand over a jewellery box which he knew the passenger was carrying. The bushranger turned out to be Christopher Jensen, son of a Gympie jeweller, to whom the commercial traveller had shown the jewellery, valued at £1000, the previous night. For highway robbery under arms, Jensen received 15 years penal servitude.

1880. GUIDO Antonio and William Bond were arrested on New Year's Eve 1880, after having visited several shops in Brisbane and making small purchases with half-crown coins. A confectioner in Queen Street alerted police – the coins were fake! When arrested, police found 119 dud half-crowns in the pockets of Antonio and Bond, and another 104 in Bond's house. Both were sentenced to one year hard labour for 'passing counterfeit coins'.

1881. ON a Friday afternoon in October, Job Simpson reported to police that he had just been tricked into parting with £5. While walking through the Botanical Gardens in Brisbane, Simpson had been approached by the trickster duo of Jacob Scholes and Henry Vickers. The pair had placed £5 each into a hat, and had conned Simpson into wagering a similar amount on the challenge that he could open, what turned out to be, a trick matchbox within 20 seconds. He failed, of course, and lost his money – and the tricksters lost their freedom for a month for 'playing an unlawful game'.

The tell-tale letter

The school at Tingalpa, then a small bush settlement near Brisbane comprising a few dozen farmer inhabitants, was less than a decade old when Michael Minnis was appointed as its resident teacher.

The school had been built on a block of land owned by a local farmer named William Pillinger, whose house was less than a mile away. There he lived with his wife Elizabeth and four orphan children for whom they received a small allowance from the Brisbane orphanage.

For some time, Minnis had boarded with the Pillingers but by mid-1881 was taking his meals at the farmhouse and was sleeping at the school.

Tingalpa was first settled in the 1860s. By 1870, the area boasted a post office, church, and the Royal Mail Hotel (above). *In 1873 a primary school – a shed made of bark and sapling – was opened. Michael Minnis was appointed to the school in 1881.*

ON the morning of 30 September 1881, Pillinger set out for Brisbane in his dray, loaded with posts and rails for sale. At daylight next morning, John Evans, a shingle splitter who worked on the farm, found the dray and horses standing unattended near the farmhouse, and no sight of Pillinger. He called out for the farmer's eldest son John. On the dray they found supplies from Brisbane - meat, bread and a bag of chaff - also Pillinger's hat. In the hat was a handwritten note on a slip of paper.

John pocketed the note, saddled his horse and set off down the track towards the school. About half a mile from the farmhouse by the road, he discovered his father's body, face covered in blood.

He then ran a few hundred yards to the school.

"Minnis! Minnis! Father is dead!" he shouted as he approached.

The school teacher ran from the school - and said, oddly, "Never mind."

"But he's been murdered!"

"Never!" replied Minnis.

The pair returned to the body by the road, and thence back to the farmhouse, where they reported the news to Evans.

They examined the dray and found blood smears on the side.

Minnis, the most literate of the three, read the letter *(below)* aloud.

The trio returned to the body, and covered it with bags. John Pillinger, with the note in his pocket, then set off on horseback for Brisbane to report the crime.

The investigation

TWO detectives and two constables were immediately despatched to Tingalpa, and their investigation was thorough and extensive. Dozens of relatives, friends and residents were questioned.

From the start it became clear that the relationship between school teacher Michael Minnis and farmer William Pillinger was a bitter one.

It seems that Minnis respected, perhaps even loved, Mrs Elizabeth Pillinger; and she thought him to be a kind and considerate young gentleman. Such mutual respect, even attraction, allowed Mrs Pillinger to reveal that all was not well with her marriage: her husband was mentally cruel and abusive, if not physically abusive.

The result was that both men frequently argued, with the hot-tempered Pillinger often flying into a rage. Michael moved out of the house, returning only for evening meals – at which time the rows over the wife and orphans grew even more furious.

The situation was made worse when Minnis began sending letters to friends and acquaintances, accusing the farmer of transgressions and brutality – beating a naked child with a bunch of stinging nettles, 'inhumane, nefarious, and diabolical treatment of his wife', stuffing bedclothes into her mouth to stop her screaming, taking money provided by the orphanage for the children's upkeep without allowing Mrs Phillinger access, driving his wife in fear into the bush at night, causing her through his actions to suffer fits…

Phillinger was, in Minnis's written words: 'the lowest specimen of degraded humanity I have known or

Bury the bastard hell-hound in a water-hole, or hang him on a tree.

Know all that this bastard and villain, upon whom is found this paper, is hatching an infernal plot intending to suffocate his wife to death this very night, and say she died in a fit he says she's subject to. We have watched him for months past, and we know all his plots. He determined, after doing away with his wife, to get a son of his at home to help him to kick out a young gentleman who he got to teach his school, who he has robbed of his money. We have heard that young man spoken well of everywhere he goes, and has been highly esteemed and respected by all classes. We have been keeping our eye on this old hound for months, and watching all his dodges, and we have just overtaken him this time. Let this be a warning to those who are left, and all who are like him, lest they meet with the same end. By the time his corpse reaches home, we shall be far away, and shall watch others like him; so, horses, take him home. We sign ourselves

No Professors
No.2

Tucked into the band of farmer John Pillinger's hat, they found a note. It appeared to have been written by a group of vigilantes – but had it really? Later the farmer's bloodied body was located.

met with', 'for all his ostentation and religion, the veriest hypocrite that ever lived', 'a low, mean scoundrel and vulgar malicious miscreant'...

Then things came to a head in late September at the farmhouse. Pillinger was angry. He had heard that Minnis had written an accusing letter to the inspector of orphanages. A scuffle turned into an all-in brawl.

Pillinger soon gained the upper hand, knocked the school teacher to the floor, dragged him from the house by his ankles, and threw him into the yard. Minnis got to his feet, shaking with anger.

"Get off my property!" shouted the farmer.

"No, you old brute!"

Pillinger again attacked Minnis, grabbing him by the shoulders and pushed him out of the yard towards the school.

Minnis, clothes torn and incensed, set off for the school, but glanced back and called, threateningly, "You'll suffer for that!"

That was the night before William Pillinger was murdered.

Trials and punishment

WHEN the 25-year-old Minnis was arrested on 2 October, his response seemed to be one of inevitability: "All right," he said as he hung his head.

The school teacher's murder trial began in Brisbane before Mr Justice Harding on 22 November 1881. The Crown's case focused on the hatred that existed between Minnis and Pillinger, and the belief that Minnis was the writer of the note found in the victim's hat.

Had not the detectives discovered in the school a bottle of ink that seemed to be the same colour as that used in the murderer's letter?

Mr Justice Harding to the jury: *"Are you convinced that the man who killed Pillinger was the man who wrote Exhibit No.1* [the letter in the hat], *as identified by other letters, and who used the language and knowledge contained in that paper?"*

And there too, had they had not also found note paper identical to that on which the letter was written? Did not the government chemist's tests prove this to be so? Did not the Crown's handwriting 'experts' attest to similarities between the murderer's note and the many notes written earlier by Minnis to his friends? And did not that letter in the hat appear a little too obvious: clearly its purpose was to cast suspicion *away* from the school teacher?

But after discussion lasting several days, the jury could not agree on a verdict.

Minnis went on trial for a second time, on 24 February 1882. The trial lasted another eleven days.

The judge pointed out that in his view there was room for a lesser verdict of manslaughter. After all, perhaps there had been no premeditation; perhaps the pair had again exchanged angry words on the farmer's return from Brisbane and had come once more to blows, resulting in Pillinger's death. In which case, manslaughter might be a consideration for the jury.

After six hours deliberation, manslaughter was indeed the verdict returned. School teacher Minnis had escaped the hangman's noose and was sentenced to life imprisonment. ■

Murder in the fowl house

Michael Irwin and his wife Honora lived on a small dairy farm in West Street, near the newly established Toowoomba Hospital.

At 10 o'clock on the morning of Monday 5 June 1882, Michael set out on foot for town to pay a few bills and to buy meat. By midnight, his wife and daughter were still awaiting his return. Where was he? Close to 2 a.m. they heard a distant scream – it sounded like Michael. Now they were really concerned.

A CHECK by police the following day revealed that Michael had purchased from Smith's butcher's shop blade-bone steak, wrapped in the pages of the *Toowoomba Chronicle*. By the time he visited his tailor friend John Davis in James Street later that afternoon, he was carrying his meat in a large white handkerchief. He left for home around 9.30 p.m. Davis claimed they'd had a few drinks and Irwin was probably 'under the influence'.

The tell-tale trail

ON the Wednesday afternoon, a mounted constable located Michael Irwin… "I found him in the hospital paddock near thick bushes, dead. His body was in a corn sack down to the waist… I pulled the sack off. His face was splattered with blood and dirt, his hair covered in blood and clay mixed… His head was battered in and the body was quite stiff… I found him down towards the swamp, near a fence running up to West Street. That fence divides the hospital paddock from Timothy Spillane's farm…"

Two native troopers were in town and they were called in to search the area for clues. By nightfall, they had followed tracks – as if a body had been dragged – from where the body was found, up the hospital paddock, to a panel of fencing about fifty yards from West Street. Here the ground was covered in blood, traces of which were also on the fence and nearby palings. An attempt had been made to conceal the blood-drenched turf with tufts of grass and timber.

Next morning the trail was taken up again. It led them from the bloodied fence panel into Spillane's farm, through their barley field for about 80 yards, and to the gate of their milking yard. There they found Mrs Spillane, milking.

Damning evidence

"I saw you and the other fellows coming through the barley," she said.

"Have you heard yet that Michael

Irwin has been found dead?" asked Senior Constable McCusker. "And that he was murdered near your fence? Could a man be murdered near your place without you hearing?"

"No, I think I would hear a thing of that sort."

"My good woman, I think you *must* know something about this."

"Surely you don't think *I'd* do a thing of that sort," she responded.

The police followed her into the house. Inside they found two pieces of steak hanging on a wallplate near the back door; there were pieces of the *Toowoomba Chronicle* clinging to the meat. (Yes, butcher Smith later confirmed, that is blade steak cut my way.) In a bedroom they found a large handkerchief, recently washed. (Yes, said the Irwins, that was Michael's.) In the fireplace, they found a half-burned branch with blood stains on it. The blood, and blood on the cuff of one of Mrs Spillane's dresses, proved to be human. The police had enough evidence to arrest Margaret Spillane.

In court a month later, it was claimed that she bashed Irwin in the fowl house and followed him as he stumbled over 80 yards through the green barley field to the slip rails where she gave him the final battering. Her 11-year-old son Timothy had admitted to police that she had woken him during the night to help her drag the limp body from the slip-rails murder scene, down through the hospital paddock, to the swamp. Say nothing to anyone, she told him, or it will mean seven years in gaol for you. And all this happened while her husband was working a selection at Westbrook.

At Margaret Spillane's trial in Toowoomba, a first jury failed to agree on a verdict, 'possibly they believed the woman's story about her supposing that it was only a thieving Chinaman whom she was assailing'. A second jury found her guilty – and she was sentenced to die, later commuted to life imprisonment. ■

Margaret Spillane confesses

Before the police magistrate on 13 June, on suspicion of having murdered her neighbour Michael Irwin, Margaret Spillane suddenly fell on her knees and, with hands clasped and eyes raised to heaven, cried out: "I murdered him!" Often rambling and repetitious, at times almost incoherent, for nearly thirty minutes she agonised loudly *inter alia* —

My bad murdering hands did it; no one but God witnessed it; my child was in bed; my child was asleep. Lord have mercy on his soul! I did it. Oh, God have mercy! I did it at 11 o'clock at night, and dragged him before day. I did it, I did it, and dragged him in the morning by the legs; he was dead. My murdering hands! I thought I was dragging a Chinaman. Oh, Lord have mercy on his soul! I would not think, Michael, that you would come into my fowl house. The man lay from 11 till 2 o'clock, and I know he died in agony, he died in agony. I hit him five blows with a stick, and murdered him; with a round stick I murdered him; and I did it; I did it. Oh, Michael, I didn't think you so mean as to get to my fowl house for the sake of a few fowls. And you never spoke to me, never spoke to me at all. I sat up by the fireplace, and I heard the man moan from 11 till 2 o'clock. I then chased him as far as the top fence, where he threw himself down because he did not wish me to see him; and I thought he was a Chinaman; and he lay on his face, and I hit him with a round stick; and I gave him five heavy blows, and I came home. But he died at 2 o'clock. Later I got up and dragged him by the leg, and the devil helped me to drag him and I thought I had a Chinaman. Fifty times I rested when dragging him. I put a bag over him to gather the blood; I did not mean to kill him, but gave him too much. Oh, don't I have always a wild temper! But let my body suffer anything at all. Oh, that I should do that to poor Michael, the father of a family. Great God have mercy on your soul! I did murder him, cruelly....

The Mackay Racecourse riot

The Mackay Boxing Day racecourse riot of 1883 was the largest racial disturbance between Pacific Island labourers and Europeans on the sugar plantations of 19th century Queensland.

By 1883 the Mackay district was at the heart of the booming sugar industry, with 31 major plantations and 26 mills.

Over one-third of the 6000 inhabitants were Pacific Islander workers. Most worked for at least five and a half days a week. On any Saturday afternoon several hundred Islanders would stream into Mackay for their big outing of the week; they visited China Town for gambling and drinking, and many attended the Mackay races.

IN THE 1880s, the Boxing Day race meeting was an important event on Mackay's social calendar.

Fashionably attired, many of the white population – the plantation owners, town trades people, mill workers, ploughmen and overseers – would come to town from all over the district to attend.

So too would hundreds of the district's large Islander labour force. For the Kanakas, it was an occasion to buy alcohol, gamble and seek out women.

Alcohol was the favourite vice of all groups in Mackay – Europeans, Asians and Islanders alike. By law Islanders were forbidden to consume alcohol, but they rarely had any difficulty in obtaining it.

And alcohol would be the root cause of the 1883 Mackay Racecourse riot.

ON 26 December 1883 a riot erupted at the race meeting when a sly grog dealer called Dimmock refused to serve a New Hebridean Islander by the name of Boslem. A quarrel began among the already drunken Islanders, one of whom threw an empty bottle at others in the group. Within moments, a bottle-throwing skirmish broke out among the Melanesians.

Some of the many Europeans standing around the liquor booth were hit by ill-directed bottles. They joined in the fight. None too sober themselves, they began returning fire with empty bottles and by the time the police arrived, fighting had got out of hand.

To this point the fighting had been among Islanders; now the Melanesians united in a common cause against the

Europeans.

The Islanders, armed with bottles, forced the Europeans to retreat for a hundred yards. For some time the two sides retreated and advanced, attacking each other, until white reinforcements arrived from the nearby Caledonian hotel. The wire fence surrounding the course was cut, and fifty or sixty horsemen charged, the riders using stirrup irons and riding crops as their weapons.

> The white men, excited and quite without control, galloped about in all directions where ever a black head was to be seen and pounced upon the wretched Kanakas, knocking them down, riding over them, and kicking, and brutally ill-using them.[1]

Women and children fled to the grandstand or to the safety of their homes. Islanders who were still on their feet fled the racecourse. Four of them, panic-stricken, hid in a nearby house. There pursuing police found several white men surrounding an Islander named Medetoo who was lying on the floor, while a European George Goyner repeatedly struck him with a large piece of wood.

Medetoo later described his beating thus:

> one fellow take him stick and hammer me along head – he hit me a good many times... Blood come all over face... Me no throw him bottle at all. I see some fellow throw bottles – when they started fighting, me run away – some white fellow hit me along head in several places and on hand when I put up hand to save my head.

The riot was over within the hour. Two Islanders had died, but legend suggests a greater number. Many of those involved from both sides received serious wounds, although the most intense injuries were to the Islanders, inflicted during the ferocity of the mounted charge.

While many feared that the Boxing Day riot would lead to a wider uprising of the Islanders in the district, life in Mackay soon returned to normal.

GEORGE Goyner was found guilty of assault and battery and sentenced to two months imprisonment. Many Europeans around Mackay were outraged at the sentence passed on Goyner, whom they saw as having acted in the interests of public safety. About thirty Islanders were imprisoned, some of them later sent back in chains to the New Hebrides. ■

1881. IN June, police raided Henry Watchorn's residence in Wickham Street, Fortitude Valley, where they found in the backyard hayloft a boiler capable of producing 20 gallons of illegal brew a day and equipment under a mattress. His next door neighbour William Thornhill owned a saddlers shop. Under the counter in the shop police discovered the remaining utensils – connecting pipe, cock, worm and still-head. Both received 3 months hard labour for possession of an illicit still.

1881. ABRAHAM Cutsy was a lodger at the Maryvale Hotel near Blackall. Being considerably behind in the payment of his rent, he was in time issued with an eviction notice. On the night of 21 September, with a flaming torch and buckets of fat, Cutsey set fire to the weatherboard building and sat on a chair in the doorway of the blazing hotel, brandishing an axe, and preventing anyone from extinguishing the flames. He received a seven-year sentence for arson.

1884

NEIL MCNEIL AND BERNARD WILLIAMS

Crime: MURDER
Location: INGHAM
Penalty: DEATH COMMUTED TO LIFE IN PRISON

SHAW, SCHOFIELD, FREEMAN, PRESTON AND ROGERS

Crime: KIDNAPPING
Location: INGHAM
Penalty: 7 - 10 YEARS IMPRISONMENT

The South Sea slavers

Blackbirding

FOR over forty years from 1860, thousands of indentured labourers recruited from the South Sea Islands worked Queensland's cotton and sugar plantations – the probity of which divided the colony. In essence, this was an era of cheap labour, bordering on slavery.

Many of these kanakas, as they were called (Polynesian for 'human beings'), had been lured by false promises and bribes of cheap trade goods. Others were taken by force – or, as a Royal Commission in 1885 discovered, through a process of 'deceit, cruelty, treachery, deliberate kidnapping, and cold-blooded murder'.

The blackbirders – the tough adventurers who often 'recruited' these islanders at gunpoint – were sometimes callous and brutal individuals who thought nothing of raiding island villages and herding men, women and children on to luggers for shipment to Queensland.

In the 1880s, there was a government crackdown on the practice. Determined to begin demolishing the system, in March 1884 Premier Samuel Griffith legislated to restrict kanaka labour to field-work on plantations, and to introduce more stringent controls on recruiting practices.

The battle between the kanaka and the anti-kanaka factions became increasingly bitter at this time.

Then came the *Hopeful* case...

The schooner *Hopeful* arrived at the mouth of the Herbert River in north Queensland on 17 June 1884. On board were over 120 South Sea Islanders, recruited from the Bismarck Archipelago off New Guinea. The kanakas were landed and distributed among the surrounding plantations.

Before long, rumours began to circulate about the health of the recruits and the method by which they had been recruited, and these were eagerly seized upon by the anti-kanaka faction.

The outcome of their investigations was the arrest of the crew of the *Hopeful* on grave charges – captain Lewis Shaw, the mate Thomas Freeman, government agent Harry Schofield, and seamen James Preston and Edward Rogers, all on kidnapping charges. Recruiter Neil McNeil and

In theory, kanakas were 'contracted' workers. In truth, many had been press-ganged – rounded up by force and virtually sold to plantation owners.

boatswain Bernard Williams were charged with murder.

THE trial of the seven men took place in Brisbane in November 1884. All seven were convicted of kidnapping, and received terms of imprisonment ranging from seven to ten years. McNeil and Williams were found guilty of murder and sentenced to death but, because of widespread agitation and petitioning, this was later commuted to life imprisonment.

Public clamour had risen to a crescendo by the time the sentences were passed. The pro-kanaka faction drew attention to irregularities in the trial and claimed it was no more than a political farce designed to create public support for Premier Griffith's plan to do away with kanaka labour; the anti-kanaka group demanded a Royal Commission into the whole affair so that the evils of the labour trade could be exposed for all to see.

Trial reports and the 1885 Royal Commission disclosures *(below)* revealed the nature of the crimes committed by the *Hopeful*'s crew…

Mayhem and murder

'THE history of the cruise of the *Hopeful* is one long record of deceit, cruelty, treachery, deliberate kidnapping, and cold-blooded murder,' said the Royal Commission. 'The number of human beings whose lives were sacrificed during the recruiting can never be accurately known.'

In addition to the men killed at Sennaroa, for which McNeil and Williams were tried and condemned, there was abundant evidence of many other murders, the Commission continued.

At Warari the crew began forcible kidnapping, seizing natives who came alongside to trade, and dragging them on board. At Bentley Bay they went ashore, kidnapped natives and burnt their huts.

And then an even more tragic episode. At Ferguson Island they began chasing canoes in the two *Hopeful*'s boats.

The first boat, under McNeil, was unable to overtake one canoe containing eight natives. McNeil stood up and fired at it. The native who was steering was struck in the back of the neck; the bullet came out at his throat and struck the man next to him. The latter fell overboard and sank. The steersman fell into the canoe, dead. All the other occupants leapt into the water as McNeil began to hack at the canoe with a tomahawk. He then directed the crew to pick up the natives and to tie them beneath the seats of the boat to prevent their escape.

The other boat, under Williams, overtook a second canoe which he stove in with his tomahawk. The natives took to the water – one was shot and the other five men, and a small boy, were hauled into the boat.

One of the captured islanders jumped overboard, whereupon Williams swam after him with a large knife in his hand. He caught the native as he was crawling up onto the reef, cut the poor wretch's throat, and let the body slip back into deep water.

The two boats then joined company. The small boy, being of no use as a recruit, was cast adrift on two coconuts which were tied together and placed under his arms. The little fellow was seen to slip from the coconuts and was drowned in the surf.

The canoe which McNeil had earlier slashed with his tomahawk had not sunk. It contained the body of the steersman. Williams cut off the head and the mutilated remains were thrown overboard.

In all, eight islanders were taken on board the *Hopeful* that day and kept below deck.

On the next island at which the *Hopeful* called, three more men were shot as natives were rounded up. That night two men escaped on shore and McNeil said that if they were not handed over, the village would suffer. He burned down two houses. Angry natives rushed out, throwing spears and stones at the boat's crew. Another two islanders were shot…

After outlining many other instances of kidnapping, the Commission's report went on to say that, when the *Hopeful* had 149 islanders on board in the hold, twenty-eight of them escaped and swam about two miles to shore. The rest rioted. The *Hopeful*'s crew were sent into the hold with rope ends to flog the defiant kanakas into submission.

On the return voyage to Queensland, the interpreter was told to say nothing about the shootings or kidnappings, and to report that all the recruits had come willingly for three years.

From cell to celebration

DESPITE the enormity of the crimes and however guilty the *Hopeful*'s crew might have been, public opinion continued to strongly favour the kidnappers in the years after their trial, denouncing in particular the severity of their sentences.

An enormous petition was later organised and signed by 28 000 Queensland supporters of the kanaka trade. It was 750 feet long and mounted on linen with rollers at either end.

When Samuel Griffith's government lost office in 1888, the petition was presented to the new government which ordered the release of McNeil and Williams and the other four kidnappers (Schofield had died in prison). The released men were carried shoulder-high by cheering crowds through the streets of Brisbane, shouted drinks in the hotels, and, that night, treated to a public dinner by politicians and planters.

As former Premier Griffith reflected at the time: 'This is a disgrace to the colony, and it can only be excused on the suggestion of sympathy with the crimes which were committed'. He added that he had never heard of a voyage of such murderous atrocity as that of the *Hopeful*: at least 38 natives had been shot by different members of the crew. He would have preferred to have seen 'every one of them hanged from their own yard-arm'! ■

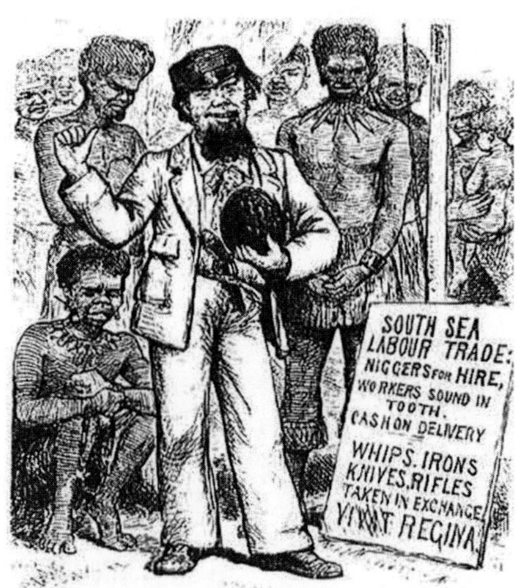

It took another decade or more before humanitarian lobby groups eventually turned the tide against the blackbirding trade. In the end, Commonwealth legislation laid down that no Islander could enter Australia after 31 March 1904.

The Muttaburra murder

Walter Gordon had been employed on Darr River Station, outside Muttaburra, for the past three weeks as a wool-washer.

He had not been feeling too well and had twice complained to the overseer that he was suffering from a fever that was sweeping the district at that time.

On a third occasion, on 1 May 1885, he approached the station manager Walter Bunning.

"Boss, I really am quite ill. Can you get me to the hospital in Muttaburra for treatment?"

Bunning knocked back the request and instead gave Gordon some medicine to take.

The wool-washer was not happy. That night, talking to the other workers, he threatened to get even with Bunning. 'Bitterness and malice were exhibited in his manner and expressions', but the men took it as the man 'talking tough'.

EARLY next morning, a worker from the station arrived at the washpool.

"Is the boss sending over a buggy for me?" asked Gordon.

No.

It was reported that Gordon then 'turned round and made use of the most insulting and malicious remarks concerning Bunning' before storming off.

Nothing more was seen of Gordon until around 11 a.m. when he was observed walking from the washpool towards the station building.

He strode to the door of the store, looked in, and then walked to the window of the office where Bunning was working at his desk.

He went back to the door and entered. Walking past three other men in the room, who took little notice of him, Gordon strode up to Bunning writing at a desk, his back to the door. From his sleeve he withdrew a Colt

In 1885 Walter Gordon was employed on Darr River Station as a wool-washer. After washing, the wool was spread on a clearing, to dry in the sun, prior to baling.

revolver and, placing the muzzle to the back of the station manager, fired.

'The bullet passed through poor Bunning's body and hit the rail of the table in front of him…The murdered man fell dead.'

The revolver was taken from Gordon. He offered no resistance as he said, 'with an expression of satisfaction on his face': "The dog would not take me to Muttaburra!"

AT some time that morning, Gordon had removed the revolver from the tent of a fellow worker. In his defence, it was argued that Gordon was, at the time, delirious and weakened by the fever. But two doctors ascertained that 'he was shamming to a very great extent, and informed the magistrates that he *was* in a fit state to be brought before the bench on a charge of murder'.

Walter Gordon, 28, was tried in Rockhampton in September 1885 and sentenced to death by hanging. His execution took place at Boggo Road in Brisbane. ■

1885. HAVING just returned from a funeral, the horse-drawn cab pulled up outside the Waterloo Hotel in Brisbane's Fortitude Valley around 4.00 p.m. on 11 January. The pub was closed on Sundays, so the cabman, who knew the landlady, entered the building via the rear entrance. His five passengers were keen to 'have a drink at the Waterloo'.

On the back step, the cabman passed a stranger; near the bar inside he saw another man. Neither man knew where Mrs Wheeler, the landlady, was. Odd, thought the cabman. He heard a noise upstairs. Along the passage, in Mrs Wheeler's private bedroom, he came across two men rummaging through her wardrobes.

The cabman shouted to his passengers downstairs to help him – "There are robbers in the house!"

The two upstairs intruders darted through the outside bedroom door, on to the balcony, jumped the rail, and dropped to the pavement 14 feet below into Ann Street. They headed off down the Bulimba ferry road, pursued by two local residents who had heard the shouting. One of the fugitives was overpowered waist-deep in a creek, and escorted back to the hotel. The other had joined up with the remaining two fleeing burglars – all three of whom were caught after a brief chase by the five cab passengers.

Robert Boulton, James Murray, Thomas Irwin and Arthur Clint faced the court later in January, charged with breaking and entering with intent to commit a felony.

During the trial, as they were being returned to Boggo Road gaol for the night, the four handcuffed men flung open the door of the police wagon and took to their heels, pursued by the two escorting constables. Irwin and Clint were caught after a chase; Boulton and Murray vanished. Some days later Murray was retaken at Pimpama, heading for NSW, as was Boulton, who was captured further south while trying to cross the Coomera River.

All four received sentences of up to five years in prison.

Left: Waterloo Hotel, a few years later during a flood in 1890.

A brotherly bullet?

Wong Tong worked on Seaview plantation near Bundaberg as a Chinese gardener.

On 25 April 1886 he arrived at the door of the hut belonging to a fellow worker Cock Tow and demanded money owed to him.

Again, as was the case on previous occasions, Cock Tow offered yet another worthless assurance: "When the boss pays me, I pay you."

Wong Tong was angry. He had been fed too many of Cock Tow's flimsy brush-offs. This time, he burst into the hut, screaming: "I want it now. You don't give now, I kill you!"

As the infuriated Wong Tong approached, Cock Tow ran from the hut with the other calling after him: "How you run now!"

Wong Tong grabbed a rifle and ran after him. Witnesses watched as they saw him raise the gun and fire a single shot at the fleeing man. Cock Tow fell to the ground with blood oozing from a bullet hole behind his left ear. Within fifteen minutes he was dead.

BY nightfall a warrant had been issued for the arrest of Wong Tong. An alert police constable spotted him casually walking down Bourbong Street in Bundaberg around 7 o'clock that night. He had the loaded rifle over his shoulder.

The policeman approached to apprehend him and, no doubt to his great relief, Wong Tong simply shrugged and handed over the weapon, saying: "All right, me no care. I shoot him, suppose he die. I go 'long to Brisbane and die too."

AT his trial for murder in Maryborough two weeks later, Wong Tong gave another version of the crime.

As background, he claimed that Cock Tow was his brother, whom he detested. He said that Cock Tow had written to their mother in China informing her that Wong Tong was suffering from leprosy. Apparently the news had so upset her that she died of shock.

On the fateful day, he had been out shooting birds with Fun Chong and had inadvertently ended up near Cock Tow's hut, where his brother started to shout abuse, calling him 'a dirty leper' amongst other things. Maddened with rage, Wong Tong raised his rifle and shot his brother.

Whatever the true account of events that day, both were hanging offences. The jury took but twenty minutes to find Wong Tong guilty of murder and Judge Harding passed sentence: death by hanging.

Wong Tong faced the hangman on 21 June 1886. It is recorded that he 'betrayed no emotions until he left his cell to go on to the scaffold. He twice nearly fell on his knees while walking there. While the arrangements were being made, he sobbed and trembled'. ■

A woman on the gallows

Billy Thompson was a cranky old farmer who owned a property on the Mossman River in north-eastern Queensland.

Old Billy quarrelled with everyone. He believed the whole world was against him. In particular, he loathed the local Chinese, illogically blaming them for his financial worries. Poor health darkened his outlook even further.

Then one day in the late 1870s, Billy surprised everyone by finding himself a wife.

Ellen Thompson arrived from Ireland as an 11-year-old in 1847. By the time she was in her 30s and moved to north Queensland, she was the mother of five illegitimate children. The one child she and Billy produced was found later to be the fruit of an extra-marital affair as well.

Ellen was no angel. She had a sharp tongue and could swear profusely. She was certainly no beauty, with plain features, and grey eyes to match her greying hair. But somehow Ellen managed to attract the attention of a local labourer, John Harrison.

Harrison, a strapping royal marine, had earlier deserted from *HMS Myrmidon* when it called into an Australian port.

Disagreeable as old Billy was, he reserved his bitterest feelings for the 26-year-old John Harrison. He was furious at the obvious friendship that had sprung up between the 41-year-old Ellen and this labourer from a nearby property. On several occasions he warned the young man to stay away from his wife.

Harrison took little notice and treated his older neighbour with disdain.

"Look here, Billy," sneered the former marine, "you needn't think I'm frightened of you. I've made away with better men than you."

Old Billy's dead

IN October 1886, Harrison's employment contract in the district expired and late on the afternoon of 22 October, he told his co-worker Edward Marshall that he was setting off in search of new work.

He returned to the house a couple of hours later: "It's too dark to travel tonight. I'll set off again in the morning."

Minutes later, a breathless Ellen Thompson entered the house: "For God's sake, come quickly," she urged. "Something's happened to Billy back home."

After taking a few nips of rum, which Ellen had resourcefully brought with her to settle the nerves, the trio set out for the Thompson residence.

They arrived in time to find Billy gasping his last remaining breaths. He had been shot in the head. On the floor near his legs was a revolver.

To Marshall it seemed likely that

old Billy had chosen an easy exit from his miserable existence.

A few more nips of rum. Ellen asked Harrison and Marshall to stay the night with her in the house and they would call in the police the following morning.

The police make their move

TO the police Billy Thompson's death at first appeared to be suicide, although in the days that followed, their suspicions that this case involved something more sinister were aroused.

Ellen hired Harrison to come and work for her at £1 a week, and he moved into the house of his new employer. Local gossips soon noted that the recently-hired worker was providing much more than cursory consolation to the widow Thompson, a point also noted by police who were keeping a close eye on them as well. It was clear that the couple showed considerable affection for each other, laughing and cuddling when they thought no one was watching.

And when the couple decided to go off together on a holiday cruise off Townsville, a detective assigned to shadow them arrested them both for murder. Harrison's response was a resigned "All right". Thompson protested her innocence: "Who's going to prove this?"

The authorities took up her challenge. Billy's remains were exhumed and a Port Douglas chemist boiled the flesh off the skull. Upon examination, surgeons found that the two holes in Billy Thompson's skull were not the entry and exit wounds made by the same bullet, as had previously been assumed, but rather two separate wounds. Either old Billy had shot himself *twice* in the head – or it was murder.

The trial

THE Townsville jury found the pair guilty of old Billy's murder and Justice Cooper sentenced them to death.

When the judge asked if Ellen had anything to say, she responded, "Yes, I have a lot to say…", and for more than 45 minutes she treated the judge and jury to a barrage of abuse. Justice

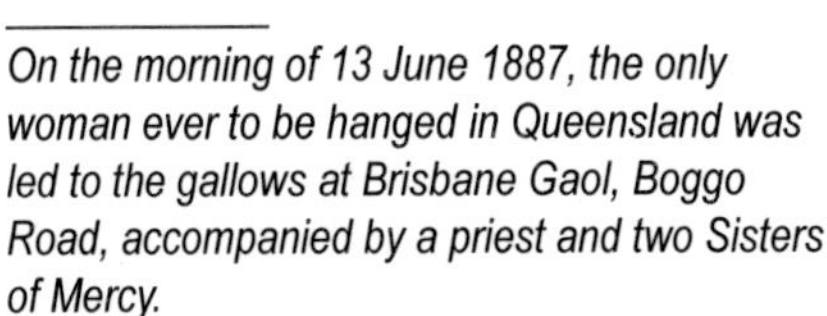

On the morning of 13 June 1887, the only woman ever to be hanged in Queensland was led to the gallows at Brisbane Gaol, Boggo Road, accompanied by a priest and two Sisters of Mercy.

The trapdoor was on the first floor walkway (in front of the middle gateway); the gallows beam was just underneath the upper walkway (below the top gateway); the victim's body would be lowered into a coffin, on the ground floor (in front of the bottom gateway)

Cooper, mindful of his judicial dignity, sat through the tirade without comment. Others in the courtroom forgot the gravity of the occasion and were hard pressed to conceal their amusement at the unusual entertainment furnished by Ellen's screechings.

As convicted felons, the two prisoners were taken to Brisbane Gaol at Boggo Road to await their execution.

WHAT really happened on the night of the old man's death can never be known. It seems, however, that Harrison hoped to benefit from the money that Ellen would receive after her husband's death, and Ellen sought release from the grumpy old man.

But we do know that the ex-sailor later confessed the crime to a fellow inmate. He had fired at old Billy and wounded him. Ellen laughed and said, "Jack, go at him again."

"So I then sent another bullet through his head," John Harrison concluded. ■

The horror hangings

ON 13 June 1887, with a white cap over her head, Ellen Thompson, the first and only woman to be legally hanged in Queensland, appeared calm when led to the scaffold. She was accompanied by a priest and two Sisters of Mercy. Grasping a crucifix, her last words were: "Goodbye everybody. I forgive everybody. I never shot my husband, and I will die like an injured angel..."

The hangman cut short her utterances. He sprung the trapdoor and the woman fell to her death.

It was a sickening sight for the witnesses. The hangman had miscalculated the length of the drop and the rope severed Thomson's jugular vein. Fresh blood spurted everywhere: the body was covered with blood and a pool formed below. Horrified officials rushed to cover it with sawdust.

Harrison then walked, soldier-like, calm and self-possessed, to the scaffold. He spoke no audible word. To the dismay of spectators, the hangman had again miscalculated. Like his lover, Harrison also died above a pool of his own blood.

Fragments from the FILES of FELONS

1885. ON a Saturday morning in June, William Potts had a drink or two with John Holberg at the Clarence Hotel in South Brisbane. The pair subsequently went shopping, with Holberg buying some powder and shot, and afterwards at Sinclair's drapery, two white shirts and half-a-dozen white handkerchiefs. Later, at the nearby Plough Inn, Holberg asked the landlady to take charge of a box containing his purchases.

Potts returned shortly afterwards and demanded the box, claiming it was really his, and it was given to him.

On the following day Holberg, finding that Potts had taken the property, informed the police, who subsequently recovered the items and arrested Potts. Potts was later found guilty in court, and sentenced to six months' imprisonment with hard labour on St Helena.

On his arrival at the island, however, Potts had to be carried from the jetty to the prison hospital where the 31-year-old remained – until he died within two months of a cancerous growth. He was buried on the island.

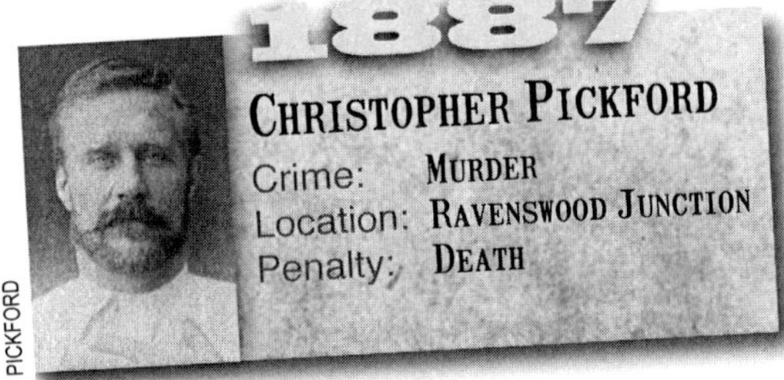

PICKFORD

1887

CHRISTOPHER PICKFORD
Crime: MURDER
Location: RAVENSWOOD JUNCTION
Penalty: DEATH

The American killer

When sober, the good-looking American Christopher Pickford was handsome, good-natured, at peace with the world, keen to make friends, and always anxious to do the right thing. When drunk, he was the opposite: a vile-mouthed, unreasoning brute who stormed and cursed, and brawled with anyone – even his mate.

Which is what happened on the night of 20 February 1887.

PICKFORD was one of a gang of navvies working on the railway line outside Ravenswood Junction.* His particular friend was Martin Emmerson, also in his early thirties.

At the camp almost every night, the navvies would play cards by the light of hurricane lamps. On Saturday nights they would take a quick trip on their trollies into the little village for drinks.

On 20 February the cheerful group arrived at Ravenswood Junction for their weekly party around 6.30 p.m. Three hours later Pickford and Emmerson were very drunk. They staggered about the bar singing and

* The gold-mining town of Ravenswood in North Queensland was serviced from 1884 by a spur-line, which broke away from the main east-west line from Townsville to Charters Towers at a place called Ravenswood Junction.

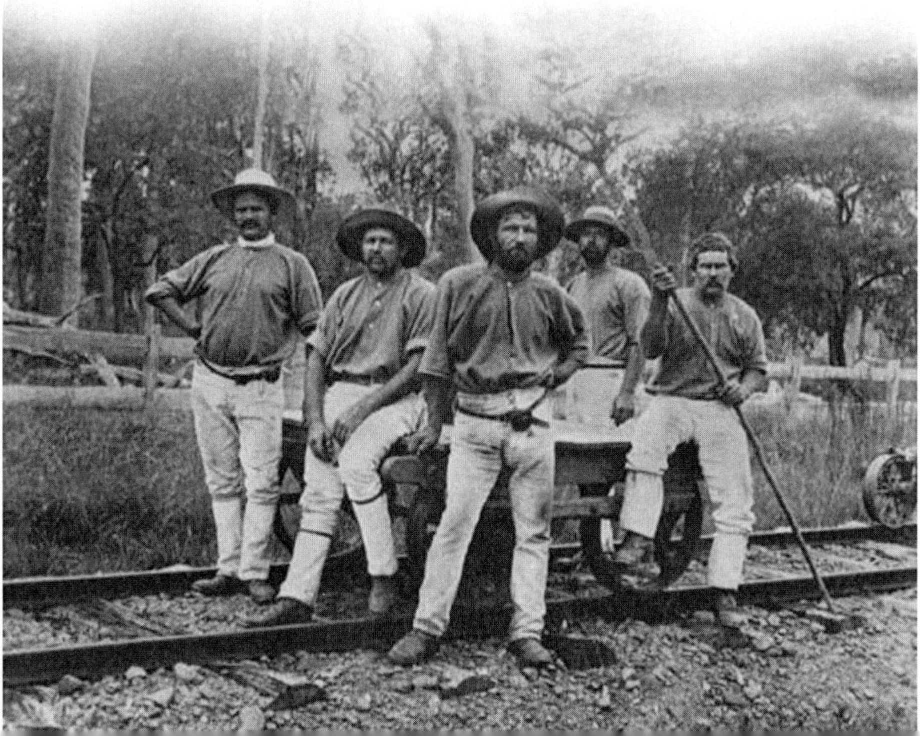

affectionately locked in each other's arms.

At closing time, bidding the rest of the party good night, the pair departed into the darkness with a bottle of whisky.

The two friends staggered about in the dark until they came to a bank near the railway, where they sat down and promptly consumed the liquor.

Then they quarrelled. Pickford lost his temper and argued fiercely with Emmerson. Quickly his rage increased until finally he was more maniac than man.

Picking up a crowbar that lay beside the track, he swung it wildly and hit Emmerson on the head, fracturing the man's skull with the heavy blow. Then, with his brain clouded in a drunken stupour, he fell down the bank and was soon in a deep sleep.

NEXT morning at dawn, some of the other men from the camp came upon Emmerson groaning painfully, and bleeding from the ugly gash on his head. Then they saw Pickford, still fast asleep, his trousers splattered with blood, and the bloodied crowbar nearby.

When woken, Pickford ran to his mate's side and wept as his friends explained what they thought had happened.

Pickford helped carry the injured Emmerson to the police station and was at his side when he died moments later. Whereupon the constable laid his hand on Pickford's shoulder and said: "I arrest you on a charge of murder."

CHRIS Pickford was tried at Charters Towers before Justice Pope Cooper in April 1887. During his testimony from the witness-box, he vehemently protested his innocence and told a lie for which many of his navvy friends never forgave him.

He claimed that a co-worker named Jensen had done the deed, a statement that the jury promptly discarded when, after only a few minutes' consideration, they returned with a verdict of guilty.

Pickford arrived at Boggo Road gaol in Brisbane on 15 May. His day of execution was set for a fortnight later.

An almost constant companion in the death cell was Archdeacon Dawes who, it was recorded, 'was able to bring the prisoner complete peace of mind by spiritual aid'. Under the churchman's guidance, Pickford became devoutly religious, and penned the following confession:

> 'I, Christopher Pickford, do hereby confess to the charge of murder against me, and say that my statement about Jensen is false, and that he had nothing to do with it. I am very sorry that I mentioned his name and ask for his forgiveness as I pray God for my own. I had no ill-feeling against Martin Emmerson, nor did I want his money. Drink alone was the cause of it all. I'll say good-bye to all my mates, and I hope they all keep away from drink.'

Pickford blamed what he alleged was adulterated liquor for his crime. "The first few drinks they give you are all right," he told the Archdeacon. "But after that they deal out villainous stuff that makes a man stark mad."

The condemned man was hanged on 30 May 1887. Until the final snap of the rope he was calmly murmuring prayers to himself. His remains were later lowered into the earth in unconsecrated ground at the nearby South Brisbane cemetery at Dutton Park.

Archdeacon Dawes officiated. ■

The condemned man views his own coffin

'OF the last minutes of Chris Pickford's earthly life, there is recorded an episode of an amazing situation the like of which has never been experienced before or since. It was a situation so bizarre, yet so strangely brimming with pathos.

With studied deference to the feelings of the doomed man, warders, having ascertained that Pickford had expressed the wish for "a last walk with his thoughts" in the prison yard, escorted him there from his condemned cell by a devious route that would avoid his viewing of the waiting scaffold.

It was a few minutes after 7.30 a.m. when Pickford arrived in the exercise yard and, at his express wish, was allowed to wander about alone, having given the promise that he would not try anything rash...

As he strolled about the yard on that crisp, exhilarating early morning, Pickford no doubt felt as much mental tranquillity as is possible to be experienced by a man who knows he will die before 30 more minutes have ticked by.

It so happened that Pickford was near the gate at the end of the yard when there drew up a black-painted hearse. The condemned man, stunned and immobile, his face deathly white, stood as the vehicle rumbled through the gate and drew up at the entrance to the prison proper about thirty yards distant.

Pickford, like a man hypnotised, watched two undertaker's assistants jump from the hearse and lift out a black-painted coffin of pine.

He was still standing like a petrified person when one of the warders approached and asked him if there was anything wrong. The doomed man gulped. "Naw," the American drawled, "nothing especially wrong... but is that what they're gonna bury me in?"

"Yes," answered the guard sympathetically. "I'm sorry you had to see this. It was all a mistake. I didn't think it would happen like that."

Answered Pickford: "Don't let it worry you, buddy. After all, it's not every guy who gets the chance to see his own coffin arrive! I guess this is mighty unusual."

Pickford laughed. It is on record that he was still seemingly amused when, ten minutes later, he was told he would have to return to his cell. He knew then that the end was near."

Back in the cell Pickford related the weird experience to his friend and comforter Archdeacon Dawes.

"Will ***you*** please bury me when they put me in that coffin?" he asked.

"I will, son," replied the Archdeacon.

Ten minutes later Pickford was led to the scaffold.'[1]

A right royal ruckus over stolen boots

In 1887, newly-married Benjamin Kitt worked as a shop assistant in a Townsville drapery store. After he relocated early in 1888 to Brisbane with his wife, it was discovered that he had stolen a couple of pairs of boots, valued at £2, before he left.

He was arrested and taken back to Townsville. On 28 March, a jury took ten minutes to find him guilty of theft and Judge Noel sentenced him to three years in gaol.

Kitt made a final plea to the Court. He said that he was certain that, if he were kept in prison, his young pregnant wife would 'become insane'. He asked to be given the benefit of the recently enacted First Offenders' Probation Act, which would provide him with a period of supervisory probation instead of a gaol sentence.

In sentencing Benjamin Kitt to three years in prison, Judge Arthur Noel unwittingly lit the fuse to a constitutional crisis that brought Queenslanders into the streets.

When Benjamin Kitt stole two pairs of boots, valued at £2, he could not have foreseen the trouble he would cause: A few months later, the Government of the day resigned!

Kitt was sent to the prison on St Helena Island. In the meantime, Judge Noel forwarded his application for mercy under the new First Offenders' Act to the Government for consideration.

The stalemate

KITT's passionate appeal in the courtroom had apparently been made with awareness. Before he had spent but three months on St Helena, and as the period of his wife's confinement drew closer, her mind *did* in fact break, so completely that she had to be sent to the old Woogaroo Asylum. There she died shortly afterwards.

Perhaps it was this melancholy fulfilment of Kitt's courtroom prophecy that impacted upon the consciences of the members of Premier McIlwraith's Cabinet when they finally considered the prisoner's request: they would extend clemency to the man who had stolen the shoes and recommended to the Governor-in-Council in June 1888 that Kitt should be released on probation.

Governor Musgrave, who had had clashes on previous occasions with the Premier, refused to sign the order of release.

Over coming weeks, several letters were passed from the Government to the Governor telling him that his veto on the constitutional advice of his Ministers was neither expected nor desirable.

In mid-August McIlwraith sent yet another angry memorandum down George Street to nearby Government House. In it he set out clearly to the Governor the reasons why the Ministry considered Kitt should be released.

But Governor Musgrave was adamant: the prerogative of mercy was vested in himself as Queen Victoria's representative - not in the Government. He would not budge on his decision regarding Kitt's release.

So it was that, while Benjamin Kitt was biding his time on St Helena Island completely unaware that he had become the pawn in a major constitutional battle, McIlwraith had to consider his next move - and, when it came, it was a bombshell.

The combatants

The Governor Sir Anthony Musgrave *(left)* and Premier Sir Thomas McIlwraith *(right)* were at loggerheads over the imprisonment of Benjamin Kitt for stealing boots.

MAYBE the stress of battle in July-September 1888 over Benjamin Kitt and his boots had weighed just a little too heavily on these two adversaries. Governor Musgrave died at his desk in Brisbane on 9 October. In November, McIlwraith was forced to resign the premiership through ill health.

The bombshell

ON 3 September, the Premier curtly informed the Governor that, if he persisted in adhering to his decision, which constitutionally was not his to make, Cabinet would resign immediately.

No word from the Governor.

The following day the members of the McIlwraith Ministry resigned - and the resignations were accepted!

Musgrave was determined to fight on. He sent a courier off to the Supreme Court where Sir Samuel Griffith, the Leader of the Opposition, was arguing a case. Sir Samuel dashed off to Government House in a hansom cab and was asked by the Governor to form a Ministry.

If Musgrave imagined he would receive an immediate and favourable response, he was mistaken. At best, Griffith advised the Governor, he would consider the matter - but in the end declined to form a Ministry, advising the Governor that he did not have a leg to stand on. After all, as McIlwraith had informed the Governor, instructions given by the Colonial Office in London to the representative of the Crown in Canada applied equally to the Governor in Queensland: that 'in all cases of a purely local nature the advice of his Ministers with respect to the exercise of the prerogative of mercy should not only be taken, but must prevail'.

But still Musgrave refused to budge. As he would again tell the Premier, "I refuse to prostitute my convictions at the direction of any man or body of men."

To the streets

BY now, crowds were gathering on street corners in Brisbane condemning the Governor. Thousands of Queenslanders attended mass meetings around the colony. At one stage 8000 protesters gathered outside Parliament and Government House; speakers quoted everything from Magna Carta to the Bill of Rights. The self-governing colony of Queensland would *not* be dictated to by a 'foreign' Governor, was the cry.

Meanwhile, Benjamin Kitt, unaware of all the fuss on the mainland, continued life as a prisoner on St Helena Island.

Queensland was now without a Government, but McIlwraith moved decisively. He cabled the Agent-General in London and instructed him to place all the relevant facts before the Secretary for the Colonies.

While a reply from Downing Street was awaited, mass meetings condemning the Governor poured their resolutions into Brisbane – from Rockhampton, Toowoomba, Warwick, Townsville, Bundaberg, Roma, Dalby, Winton, Ingham, Hughenden, and elsewhere, even from the remote gold-mining town of Normanton.

Men who had never heard of Benjamin Kitt now demanded his release from prison.

Suddenly the crisis was over.

When a cable was received from Downing Street instructing Musgrave to sign Kitt's release, McIllwraith and his Ministers withdrew their resignations. Premier McIlwraith had 'vindicated the most cherished right of free people – the right to govern themselves'.

The constitutional crisis had ended – and Benjamin Kitt made the journey back from St Helena, a free man. ■

At one stage 8000 protesters gathered outside Parliament and Government House...

Murder – and the Normanton riot

Racial unrest

IN the wake of anti-Chinese riots and protests throughout the country, the Australian colonies met in Sydney in 1888 to formally consider a unified, legislative response to growing racial tensions. Sir Henry Parkes's fear was that Australia could be 'overrun by alien races... incapable of assimilation with the body politic, strangers to our civilisation, out of sympathy with our aspirations, and unfitted for our free institutions, to which their presence in any number would be a source of constant danger.'

In Queensland alone there had been racial riots in Brisbane, Croydon, Clermont, Etheridge, Georgetown and Bundaberg.

In the northern Gulf town of Normanton, the *Chronicle* had for some time been agitating for the removal of all Malays and Chinese, who together comprised one-sixth of the local population. Then, in June 1888, a grisly triple murder triggered more mob violence in the frontier town…

Tolerance was a rare commodity in Normanton in the 1880s. By the end of the decade, the Gulf town was populated by nearly 1100 people – white miners, fishermen and merchants and a large community of 'coloured aliens', Chinese, Malays and Indians.

The whites were fearful of the growing Asian immigration and the aliens regarded the white population with contempt for their superior attitude.

The Malays had confined themselves to a shanty settlement on the outskirts of town, where they were better able to protect themselves from the continued abuse they had to endure on an almost daily basis.

Tensions were high. The Europeans resented the Malays parading 'arrogantly' around in their robes and red cummerbunds, a fashion statement

The frontier town of Normanton in the 1880s – the gulf port for the nearby goldfield at Croydon and hotbed of racial violence in 1888

normally associated with the colonial planter class. As well, they keenly competed for jobs with the whites as labourers, stevedores and fishermen.

ON 14 June, the Malays in the camp were celebrating a religious festival, feasting that would continue into the night.

By 9 p.m. a young Malayan man, known as Sedin, had worked himself into a frenzy over the way his people were being treated by the white community.

Brandishing two Malay kris daggers, he stormed from the festive gathering, shouting that he would punish Europeans.

CARPENTER John Fitzgerald and his labourer mate Christian Meriga lived in a tent not far from the Malay camp. Their mutilated corpses were discovered later that night. Both men were somehow stabbed to death, from the outside, through the canvas of their tent.

The body of a third man, J.P. Davis, was found at daylight - covered with twenty stab wounds and nearly decapitated. Claw marks in the dirt suggested a frantic struggle. It was assumed that Davis, in running to the aid of Fitzgerald and Meriga, was cut down in the dark some twenty metres from their tent.

When the police arrived next morning, Sedin was arrested. He surrendered 'with resignation and passivity'.

Retribution

AS word of the murders spread, there was angry and bitter talk about what the whites should do by way of taking revenge upon the 'murderous heathens'.

That night a 'monster meeting' was held at the School of Arts. Over 500 angry residents jostled to have their views heard; Chinese and other coloureds, concerned enough to attend, were grabbed, dragged from the hall and thrown into the street; the police were abused for not arresting Sedin's countrymen; resolutions were passed; vengeance was loudly advocated; and the threat of a lynch mob moving to the town lock-up where Sedin was being held became a major concern for the authorities.

By midnight, tempers were at fever pitch. More than 200 noisy men assembled and, armed with ropes, kerosene and tarred fire sticks, marched on the Malay camp. They tore down most of the aliens' houses or burnt them to the ground. Furniture was smashed. They torched fishing boats and nets. Pleas from the police for calm were ignored. Terrified Malays fled for miles into the inhospitable darkness of the surrounding scrub.

Next day, 15 June, businesses were closed. A hearse carrying the bodies of the three slain men passed slowly through town to the cemetery. A cortege over half a mile long followed, containing nearly every European in Normanton.

After the funeral, it was found that forty Malays had returned to the settlement. Again a large mob of whites assembled and proceeded to the Malay camp. Once more the inhabitants scattered into the bush while their remaining houses were destroyed, totalling 22 in all.

In an attempt to keep the peace, forty special constables had been sworn in earlier that day - but the majority of them joined in the fracas.

The angry crowd then scoured the countryside on horseback, flushing out the Malays from the surrounding scrub. They were herded back to the town landing, where they were detained aboard the hulk *Rapido* by the Police Magistrate for their own safety.

While anti-Asian feelings continued to run hot for some time, at least the rioting ceased and life in Normanton slowly returned to normal.

For nearly two weeks, 84 aliens, mainly Malays, were kept on the hulk *Rapido* until the regular steamer *Birksgate* arrived to deport them from the agitated township to Thursday Island.

ALL the time, the prisoner Sedin was secure under heavy guard in Normanton lock-up. In all this racial turmoil, why was it that he was not forcibly removed by the fired-up mob and dealt with?

Perhaps it was because of the rapidly circulating view that the arrested man, who 'had been caught red-handed', had *not* undertaken the brutal killings alone – even though in the end, it was he who would pay the full penalty for the triple murder.

On 15 October 1888, the Circuit Court met at Normanton under Mr Justice Cooper. Amid 'cheers and excitement', the four arrested white ringleaders of the riot were exonerated for their part in the episode. Not so Sedin; after a six-hour trial, the Malay fisherman was found guilty of wilful murder and sentenced to death.

He was hanged at Brisbane's Boggo Road on 12 November 1888. ■

Sedin: Unanswered questions

RECENT analysis of the murders and the subsequent rioting at Normanton in 1888 has raised some interesting questions.[1]

- Was Sedin *really* the triple murderer?
- How could he, a slightly-built man, have *singly* inflicted scores of terrible wounds upon three large European men, virtually decapitating one of them in the process?
- How could one man outside a tent stab two men inside, who were purportedly awake, with 'one reading to the other', ostensibly upon their own stretchers or sleeping bags against opposite sides of the tent?
- So was Sedin the *lone* perpetrator, or had there been, as rumoured around the town, a 'band of assassins'?
- Why was it that, soon after the triple-murder, nine or ten Malays were known to have decamped in a whaleboat and sailed to Thursday Island? Could these men have been Sedin's co-conspirators, involved in a sacred slaughter following the Malay festival? Could their outburst have been fuelled by collective outrage over their recent mass dismissal as workers on the Normanton wharves?
- Why was it that, having run amok that night, a calm Sedin was arrested without difficulty or resistance?

Perhaps Sedin was indeed a sacrificial lamb.

The strychnine scones

In September 1889, Albert Hyde was employed as a sawyer on Thomas Abell's small farm at Dugandan, near Boonah.

Hyde lived five miles away at Treviotville with his wife Elizabeth and two young children but had arrived at Abell's the night before, to stay the night and begin work early the next morning, 11 September. He brought with him a box of food, prepared by his wife, comprising meat, bread, butter, jam, cake and scones.

At breakfast, he was eating from his food box when he was joined by Thomas Abell, who later recalled that Hyde was in good spirits and ready for the day's work. He remembered that Hyde had commented on the bitterness of one of his scones, but had said that his wife had probably just used too much horehound in her recipe.

At 8.30 a.m. Hyde went to his work, having finished his breakfast, but at 9 o'clock, hearing his agonised cries for help, the Abells found him lying on his side by the log he had been splitting. He was clearly in great pain and vomiting. A salt and water emetic was given to him, after which he vomited again.

He was at times calm and then convulsing, fighting and grasping at the air. Sometimes he would straighten up his body, and then arch it backwards. In the convulsions he was sometimes dark and sallow, and his lips were a dark purple.

His employer sent for the local chemist, Henry Downing, who administered another emetic, with no effect, and Hyde died about five minutes later.

Abell had a large black dog there that morning. The dog ate about half of the first vomit, and within half-an-hour it too began convulsing. It died shortly afterwards.

Albert Hyde's body was carried into the farmhouse and the police were called. Within hours, mounted constable Dunn had examined the body, taken statements and impounded Hyde's box of food which was soon on its way to the government chemist for analysis.

Within minutes of starting work, sawyer Albert Hyde would be convulsing and gasping for air...

Later that day, Dunn rode to Teviotville to speak with Mrs Hyde. He found her visiting her sister a few miles away…

"WHERE is your husband, Mrs Hyde?" asked Dunn.

"At Abell's working."

"Do you know Mr Downing, the chemist at Boonah? He told me that your husband bought some strychnine from him some time ago to kill dingoes. Do you know if there is any of it left?"

"Yes," she said.

"Where is it?"

"Mr Hyde put it in a small money-box, and locked it, and then put it in a large box, and locked that, and I have not seen it since."

"I suppose, Mrs Hyde, you know your husband is dead?" said Dunn.

"No indeed, I don't. Is he?" she replied matter-of-factly.

"Yes, it seems that he has been poisoned," Dunn said. "When did your husband leave home?"

"Last night. "

"What did he take with him?'

"Some cakes which I made him."

"Mrs Hyde, perhaps you have put this strychnine in the bread through mistake for soda?"

"No fear, I never done anything like that."

"Will you come with me, and see if we can find the poison?" asked Dunn.

She made no reply, nor did she return to the Hyde house with the policeman.

Constable Dunn returned to the Hyde residence, entered the bedroom, and found the small money-box containing a packet marked "Strychnine" in red ink. This, along with bread, flour, baking soda and scones, he parcelled up and took for analysis.

Murder or suicide?

ON 13 September, Constable Dunn was given two unopened letters, the first seemingly addressed by Albert to Elizabeth, the second to the local school teacher. Elizabeth claimed she found one in her daughter's bonnet, and the other in her own dress pocket.

Odd, thought Dunn, since I had found no trace of these in my search of the house on 11 September.

In both letters, supposedly written a couple of days before his death, Albert Hyde claimed that he would be taking his life because he could no longer tolerate the pain he was experiencing from a chronic ear disease.

Dunn asked to see samples of Albert's handwriting.

Elizabeth produced a box containing a marriage certificate, letters, and sundry other papers. Albert's handwriting in these just didn't match the letters.

The constable then arrested Elizabeth Hyde 'on a charge of wilfully murdering your husband, by administering strychnine to him'.

She made no reply to the charge whatever, he later said, adding also that "despite losing her husband, she never cried in my presence at any stage… I thought her conduct suspicious".

The trial

THE trial of Elizabeth Hyde was held at the Ipswich Circuit Court in February 1890.

Neighbours testified that she and her husband had never been on the

The old Ipswich court house, where Elizabeth Hyde stood trial for the poisoning of her husband Albert in 1889

best of terms, she had often complained about him, and he had once thrown soapy water over her.

Post mortem analysis had shown that Hyde's stomach and liver certainly contained sufficient strychnine to cause death, and that the remaining scone from Hyde's food box had minute crystals of the poison baked into it.

A handwriting expert revealed that the handwriting on the two letters was that of Hyde's wife – that she herself had written the supposed suicide notes, presumably to divert public focus from her own actions.

In summing up, Judge Mein reminded the jury that the Hydes' married life had been a wretched one and that they would have to decide, on the basis of the evidence provided, was this a case of murder or suicide?

After lengthy deliberation, the jury returned a verdict of guilty, but with a strong recommendation for mercy on account of Elizabeth's two children.

Judge Mein then sentenced Elizabeth Hyde to death, adding that the jury's recommendation for mercy must reside with the Executive Council. She showed no emotion as she was led away, apart from a few dabs to her mouth with a small white handkerchief.

In time, Executive Council commuted the death sentence to life imprisonment. ■

Escaping the scaffold

There is now being taken round the town for signature a petition to the Executive, praying for the commutation of the sentence of death passed on Elizabeth Rebecca Hyde, who was found guilty at the Circuit Court here recently of having poisoned her husband at Dugandan, on the 11th of September last. The petition, I hear, has already been numerously signed, and it is intended to forward it to the proper quarter in the course of a few days.

Brisbane Courier, 2 March 1890

Elizabeth Rebecca Hyde, who was sentenced to death for the murder of her husband, but whose sentence has been commuted to imprisonment for life, had news of the reprieve conveyed to her in Toowoomba Gaol, but showed no trace of emotion. She admitted her guilt to a clergyman a fortnight since, saying, "I did it right enough, but others put me up to it, saying I would not be found out."

The Argus, 22 March 1890

1890

MAURICE LONERGAN AND PERCY MATTHEWS

Crime: THEFT
Location: BRISBANE
Penalty: RELEASED WITH WARNING

It's only a pumpkin I found

> At the City Police Court yesterday, much astonishment was created when two little boys named Maurice Lonergan, aged 9 years, and Percy Matthews, aged 8 years, were charged with having broken into the Roma Street markets and stolen a number of articles.

Brisbane Courier, 11 September 1890

It was early on Sunday morning, 31 August 1890, when Mr Tooth, a shop-owner at Brisbane's Roma Street markets, reported to the nearby police barracks: His shop had been broken into the night before. Indeed, it was one of a series of such thefts from the markets in recent times.

Detective Dickenson investigated. He found that entry had been gained via boxes and empty kerosene tins that had been stacked up against a back wall, with a small ladder on top.

Acting on information provided by Tooth's son, Dickenson went to the Spring Hill home of a 9-year-old boy, Maurice Lonergan, who arrived shortly afterwards with a sugar bag containing a pumpkin.

"I found it at the train station," the boy responded when asked.

Later, at the markets, the boy broke down: "If you don't lock me up I will show you where the things are that Percy Matthews and I took..."

He took police to several stashes throughout the markets and to a nearby gully, where the loot from several offices and shops was revealed, including a packet of envelopes, a book, a small ink bottle, oranges, bananas, some small pictures, and a long silk sash.

Lonergan and Matthews faced court on 10 September 1890, where PM Pinnock passed judgement... ■

Police Magistrate Philip Pinnock:

"The law requires that I should go through the whole case, but I think it would be an utter waste of time.

To you parents, I say take your children home. I fancy I am a great judge of character – from the features of the boys I am quite sure if they ever are criminals it is because they are not looked after properly.

Mrs Lonergan, go home and ask Maurice's father to give him a proper thrashing, but not a cruel thrashing. If you find you cannot manage that, bring him to me and I'll have him sent to the Industrial School for boys."

The law would show no mercy

Rockhampton bridge carpenter Michael Barry married Mary, twelve years younger than he, in 1878 and over the next decade, they were happy and had four children.

By the late 1880s, the hard-working, sober Barry found that his job was causing him to spend much of his time on the roads, away from home.

With her husband absent most of the time, Mary began to drink heavily and to take secret lovers. When he became aware of this, Barry left his well paid job and returned to his West Street home. He was determined to save his marriage.

Unfortunately, around this time Michael Barry also turned to drink. Apart from her infidelity, what was particularly upsetting as well was that Mary had been accessing their bank account and his hard-earned savings were disappearing fast.

ON the morning of 25 February 1890, Michael Barry was offered a supervisor's job out-of-town, but reluctantly turned it down in favour of keeping the family together. He spent the rest of that day drinking heavily. At 11.00 that night, Barry was taken home, after being found drunk in the gutter.

At 5.30 next morning, a major argument erupted over his missing wallet, which he accused his wife of hiding. He dragged Mary by the hair through the house, struck her repeatedly with a cross-saw handle and, when it broke, he used an axe handle. He paused to smoke his pipe for a few minutes in the kitchen before returning – only to find his wife dead. He then walked off down the street to give himself up.

AT the end of Michael Barry's trial, a sympathetic jury, on more than one occasion after retiring, sought clarification as to the difference between murder and manslaughter. In the end, Justice Mein coercively stated: "It is your plain and manifest duty – your manifest duty, gentlemen, – to find the prisoner guilty of wilful murder with which he is charged!"

Found guilty, although with the jury's 'strong recommendation for mercy', Barry was sentenced to death.

Local community committees and petitions supported the jury's plea for mercy – Mary's actions had driven him to the point of insanity. Moreover, it was revealed, surprisingly for the first time, that Mary had 'engaged in the greatest possible immorality', and that Barry was suffering from a disease that was sending him blind, and had been affecting his brain.

All pleas fell upon deaf ears.

On the Sunday before the execution, Barry's four children, now living at the Neercoll Orphanage, visited him in prison; nearby, the Sherriff and hangman were disembarking the steamer from Brisbane.

Next day, 2 May 1890, Michael Barry became the last man to be hanged at Rockhampton Gaol. ■

1891

William Hamilton and others

Crime: Conspiracy

Location: Barcaldine, Clermont, Hughenden, Blackall

Penalty: 3 years hard labour

The Union conspirators

THE year 1891 will long be remembered as the year of the Great Shearers' Strike.

In a time of economic decline, bush workers and shearers banded together to protest against falling wages and conditions.

Failed negotiations between the pastoralists and unionists led to sporadic strikes and unrest around the country. In early 1891, strikers massed and marched in strength at Barcaldine, Clermont and Hughenden.

With unionists, soldiers and strike-breaking labour pouring into Barcaldine and surrounds, the situation became critical. By mid-March some 4500 people were in Barcaldine or camped nearby. The threat of a bloodbath was real.

The introduction of non-union labour from Victoria had fuelled the

The Argus, 16 June 1891

THE END OF THE SHEARERS' STRIKE.

THE BREAKING UP OF THE CAMPS.

BLACKALL, MONDAY.

The strike is over here, and a number of men have been passing through the town for the last two days *en route* to various stations seeking employment. There is no difficulty in engaging any number of men for various descriptions of work.

Above: *Striking shearers at the Barcaldine camp, 1891*

Right: *The infantrymen who arrested the striking shearers were from Queensland's colonial army and were on their first active service.*

Left: *For three years, these political prisoners – leaders of the Great Shearer's Strike of 1891 – were among the most celebrated inmates to be confined in the colonial prison on St Helena Island.* Left to right from back row: *Smith-Barry, Fothergill, Forrester, Stuart, Taylor, Griffin, Murphy G., Blackwell, Brown, Prince, Bennett, Murphy D., and Hamilton.*

On their release several again took up the struggle for the rights of workers in various ways. In Queensland, William Hamilton became Labour MLA for Gregory (1899), Minister for Mines and President of the Leglislative Council (1915-1917), and William Fothergill, from 1919, the Barcaldine Shire Chairman. In Western Australia, George Taylor became the Labor MLA for Mount Magnet (1901-1917), Colonial Secretary in Australia's first elected Labor government (1904-1905), and speaker of the Legislative Assembly (1917-1924). Julian Stuart became a union secretary, Labor MLA for Leonora (1906-1908), and journalist for workers newspapers. Blackwell, Forrester, Smith-Barry reportedly left to join William Lane's ill-fated utopian experiment to establish a commune based on socialist principles in the Paraguayan jungle.

antagonism to the point that central Queensland was on the verge of civil war. With scab labour protected by police and colonial troops, frustrated union hotheads resorted to burning down shearing sheds, starting grass fires, setting alight to loaded wool wagons, derailing troop trains, rioting, kidnapping, and beating up police.

On 25 March 1891, in a move intended to break the back of the strike, the Colonial Secretary ordered the arrest of the union leaders. 120 mounted infantry surrounded the union office at Barcaldine and arrested the Queensland strike committee while infantrymen with fixed bayonets guarded the police station. Similar arrests of union leaders were made in Clermont and elsewhere.

The union leaders were charged under an act of George IV (which had been repealed in Britain but was still operative in Queensland) with unlawful assemblage, riot and tumult, sedition and conspiracy. Some unionists were released but the leaders were sent to Rockhampton to stand trial.

The legitimacy of the arrests and fairness of the trial has been heavily debated by historians over the years.

A reluctant jury had sat before Mr Justice Harding who, on 18 May, took seven hours to sum up. After retiring at 7.15 p.m., the jury returned at 9.30, the foreman announcing that they would be unable to agree on a verdict. Next day the judge addressed them: 'Perhaps there is some person on the jury who does not know his duty… Probably you have not understood me. I have already told you that there is sufficient evidence to convict all the defendants on all the counts."

At 5 p.m. on the second day, the foreman again advised Harding that they were not in the least likely to agree. The judge again: "I see no reason to discharge the jury, the case being the simplest I have ever tried." Back they went.

In the end, the jury returned a guilty verdict – and thirteen of the strike leaders were despatched in chains from Rockhampton to serve three years hard labour on St Helena Island in Moreton Bay. In all, the names of over twenty shearer-strikers appear on the St Helena prisoner registers.

With the arrests and imprisonment of the union leaders and dwindling funds, the 1891 strike collapsed. Within six months the tumult had died down, and the voices of thousands of strikers faded. But the failure of union militancy to achieve the desired outcome prompted the union movement to turn its attention to the pursuit of *political* power as a means of advancing the interests of working people. The Great Shearers' Strike had laid the foundation for the formation of the Australian Labor Party, and a political wave at the turn of the century washed a number of Labor men into parliaments around Australia, among them a few of the St Helena prisoners *(see page 110)*.

WHILE the union prisoners were on St Helena, a huge public campaign for their release was undertaken.

The Government expressed a willingness to free the men, provided that they themselves petitioned for clemency and admitted that their actions had been unlawful and unjustified. This, however, they declined to do. As a group, they held firm to union principles and refused to compromise.

In October 1892, for example, when the men were visited on St Helena by two of their union colleagues, Andrew Fisher, a future Prime Minister of Australia, and T.J. Ryan, later a Premier of Queensland, they agreed, according to the Chief Warder who sat in on the conversation, 'to stay in gaol rather than crawl for mercy'.[1] And as conspirator William Hamilton declared, 'I will see you in Hell before I'll scab on my mates.'

They were released in 1893, after having worked out their sentences in full. ■

William Hamilton

FOLLOWING his release from St Helena, William Hamilton returned to western Queensland and in June 1896 married Mary Ann Mitchell, daughter of a Longreach grazier, who in his youth had participated in the Eureka rebellion.

Interviewed in 1991, Hamilton's 91-year-old daughter Ida Welsh recalled that, after a lengthy courtship, 'he married Mum and they went back out west. He was shearing in Winton and he decided to run for parliament. He was so popular that nobody ran against him. He just walked in and he was in for 23 years. He was only opposed once, and that man lost his deposit.'

She recollected that, 'because he was a good gardener, he often did the garden at St Helena. They'd always put a beautiful bunch of flowers on board the boat for Mum and these came out of the garden that Dad had made when he was there.'[2]

'Big Bill' Hamilton, over six feet and more than 15 stone, was in the 'housemaids' gang' on St Helena. He had to go down on his knees to pipeclay the steps and climb ladders to clean windows. At times he complained of housemaid's knee, but they kept him at it.

He delighted in re-telling the stories of his St Helena past.... When President of the Legislative Council, he made a visit of inspection with a party to St Helena. The Chief Warder was careful to lavish much attention upon the honoured guest. Coming to a short flight of steps, he took the President by the arm, remarking, 'Mind the steps, Mr Hamilton.'

'The steps be buggered!' came the instant retort, 'Many's the time I've scrubbed the bloody things!'[3]

Bones in his bed

The crime for which the Chilean Leonardo Moncardo paid the supreme penalty in 1892 was of a most atrocious type, of such a nature that the judge allowed none of the evidence taken at his trial to be published at the time.

No one saw the deed committed and it was only with some difficulty that sufficient evidence was gathered on which to convict the prisoner.

Indeed, the murderer left no body - only a few bones, so chopped and smashed by axe blows that they could not be positively identified as any particular part of the human anatomy.

But what made this crime even more grisly was the fact that the murderer took his victim's bones to bed!

FOR a number of years, Leonardo Moncardo had been employed as a deck-hand on board the sailing ship *Sketty Belle*, which traded along the Queensland coast. He was 41 years of age, a tough and seasoned seaman and, as the events of April 1892 were to reveal, a paedophilic villain of the most callous order.

In the months leading up to April 1892, Moncardo had made unwanted advances towards another crewman, a 14-year-old aboriginal lad named Bob. The relationship became bitter, they often quarrelled, even fought.

The other crew members were well aware that bad blood existed between the two, but none on board would have dreamt it would end one night with one violent episode.

At about 10 o'clock on that mid-April night in 1892, as the *Sketty Belle* made her way through the coral seas towards Thursday Island, Moncardo and Bob were on deck quarrelling once more.

The rest of the crew were in bed or asleep and were taking little notice of the commotion on deck, so used were they to the sight and sound of the pair's altercations.

But on this occasion, Moncardo had become a raging devil, possessed by an all-consuming passion that finally exploded into primeval violence.

During the fight, he produced

a long-bladed knife and, as the combatants struggled, there was an agonised cry as the blade found its mark deep in the Aborigine's back.

As the wounded youth lay groaning on the deck, the Chilean ran to the nearby cookhouse, returning with an axe. With the first blow of the weapon, he severed Bob's head. A second blow shattered his victim's chest, a third chopped off one of his legs. Blow after blow rained down upon the pathetic Aborigine until his frame was hacked into small pieces.

Moncardo now threw the blood-dripping mass and loose pieces over the side of the ship. The grisly remains fell into the ocean to be lost forever. And so animal-like had the blood-thirsty butcher become that, when he retired shortly afterwards, he took several of his victim's bones and body parts with him to bed!

Some of the crew later recalled hearing groans in the night and had seen the Chilean moving about in the dark, but they did not discover the gruesome deed until next morning.

An immediate search for a missing Bob found signs of a crime most horrible. At the stern of the ship, they found fragments of human flesh and bone, and the side and deck of the vessel were liberally splattered with blood. A trail of blood led from the scene to Moncardo's bunk, where the man was sound asleep. The nauseated sailors hauled him to the floor and, in throwing back the blankets on his bunk, found several pieces of bone and blood-stained flesh.

The captain returned the *Sketty Belle* to the spot where he calculated the incident had occurred and sent divers down to search the reefs for remains. Nothing was found.

Moncardo, in irons, was handed over to the authorities in Cooktown. There, in his cell, he confessed his crime to a fellow prisoner, describing the episode in graphic detail, which his cellmate relayed to the jury some weeks later.

Moncardo was hanged on the scaffold at Boggo Road gaol in Brisbane on 24 October 1892. ■

1892. THE youngest person to be legally executed in Queensland was Frank Horrocks *(left)*, aged just 17 years 6 months and 23 days. He was hanged on 26 September for having murdered a 20-year-old German, Rudolf Weissmuller, in bushland near Murrarie railway station. The murder weapon was found near the body, a tomahawk that Horrocks had bought earlier at a Queen Street ironmongers.

Both men had left their South Brisbane boarding house on 5 April and took the train to Murrarie, where Weissmuller had an appointment with a pastoralists' agent about a job on a sheep station. The pair disembarked at the station – and the German was never seen alive again.

Horrock's motive was robbery.

Some time later police located the runaway Horrocks at Tallebudgera and arrested him for the murder.

A few days before his execution, Horrocks confessed his guilt in writing.

1892

GLEESON

George Gleeson

Crime: Murder
Location: Torres Strait
Penalty: Death

Death among the pearl divers

George Gleeson, aged 26 years, worked for the Cussen brothers who owned a pearling station on Prince of Wales Island (Muralag) in the Torres Strait. He was one of the company's best divers and was happiest when, with a rope tied around his waist, he was twisting about among the coral at the bottom of the ocean.

The month of May in 1892 was a quiet time for the pearling fleet in the Torres Strait, for the men were busy preparing rigging and boats for the coming season, the kind of activity that Gleeson found monotonous. The delay frustrated him.

On the morning of 10 May, Gleeson stood at the entrance of the hut that the Cussens used as their office and asked for permission to borrow a boat so that he might visit nearby Thursday Island for a few days.

"Aren't you happy here with this job?" he was asked.

"No, boss," stammered the Indian. "Too slow here now. I come back when boats ready again."

Gleeson's request was turned down. He was reprimanded for trying to avoid doing his share of the work and told that he would simply have to be patient for a few weeks longer.

Obviously annoyed at his treatment, the diver went among the men of the settlement cadging liquor. By nightfall, he was much the worse for drink.

After dark, Gleeson broke into the supply shed and stole several bottles of rum, all of which he consumed before morning. By sunrise on 11 May, he was very drunk - and in a particularly ugly mood.

Pearl divers of the Torres Strait, at the time when Paddy McKiernan was murdered by Indian-born George Gleeson in 1892

At about 11 o'clock he once more staggered into the Cussen's hut and demanded to be allowed to go to Thursday Island. Permission refused once more, Gleeson ran through the settlement shouting, "White men pigs. They are no-goods."

Then he remembered that, in his rummaging through the supply shed the night before, he had seen a double-barrelled shot gun and cartridges. Moments later he was running from the shed, waving the gun, screaming vile curses to all men with white skins, and shrieking vengeance on the Cussens in particular.

On the way to the brothers' hut he had to pass the shanty occupied by Paddy McKiernan, a good-natured Irishman who, at that moment, was stretched out on the small veranda reading extracts from *The History of the Old and New Testaments* to the company's sailmaker Charles Irvine. Both of them retreated into the hut when they saw the approaching Gleeson's nasty disposition. McKiernan, more in jest than threatening, returned with an old unloaded revolver, confronting the Indian outside his hut, telling him to 'clear off'.

Gleeson fired two shots.

McKiernan fell to the floor with the side of his neck blown away. The Irishman's chest received the full blast of the second shot.

Every man in the settlement came running and Gleeson was soon overpowered. So violently did he struggle that the Cussen brothers ordered he be secured to a tree with thick chains from one of the luggers.

It was only then that the murderer became aware of what he had done: "Poor Paddy, the best man on the station," he wept. Indeed, it became clear that, whatever feelings he harboured against anyone else at the station, he had no animosity towards the man he had killed.

At his trial in Cooktown he was found guilty, sentenced to death, and was hanged on the Boggo Road gallows alongside the bones-in-the-bed killer Moncardo on 24 October 1892. ■

1892. IN the 1880s Frederick Vosper took up a career in journalism at Charters Towers in the north Queensland goldfields, where he soon developed a reputation as a radical writer with a fiery, flamboyant public speaking style and a strong sympathy for trade unionism. By 1890 he had become the editor of the *Australian Republican*.

During the Great Shearers' Strike of 1891, in an inflammatory 'Bread or Blood' editorial, he denounced the proclamation issued by Sir Arthur Palmer's government calling upon the shearers to disperse; Vosper encouraged revolution. He was arraigned for seditious libel. The jury failed to agree, and a fresh trial was held some six months later, when he skilfully defended himself and, after a five-day hearing, was acquitted.

Then followed a miners' strike at Charters Towers in 1892, when Vosper became the elected leader. This strike culminated in a riot involving several hundred miners. Vosper assumed responsibility for the violence in which he assisted in pulling an engine-driver at Day Dawn mine from his train and carrying him off. He surrendered himself to the police, but later, crowds surrounded the lock-up and threatened to demolish it; in time, the men were pacified and were induced to disperse. At the conclusion of the subsequent trial before Judge Noel, Vosper was sentenced to three months in prison for inciting a riot and molestation of the train driver.

Legend has it that when in gaol he received the usual prison haircut and, on his release, he vowed that he 'would never have his hair cut again'. He moved to Western Australia in 1893 and made a name for himself as a vitriolic long-haired journalist, unionist and politician.

BLANTERN

1893

GEORGE BLANTERN

Crime: MURDER
Location: MARLBOROUGH
Penalty: DEATH

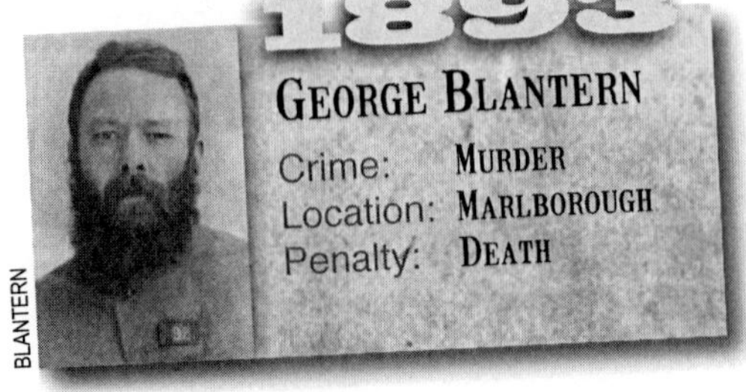

The burning body

Joseph Barnett, manager of Marlborough Station 100km north-west of Rockhampton, awoke to the pungent smell of suffocating smoke entering his bedroom. It was just before 1.00 a.m. on 8 May 1893.

In the darkness he dashed from the station residence to the servants' quarters, some 12 metres from the house, where smoke was billowing from the windows. He arrived just as stockman Walter Lunn came running from the male workers' sleeping quarters, fifty metres distant.

Together, the two men forced their way into the bedroom of Flora McDonald, the only female servant on the property at that time. They found her lying on her back on a smouldering heap of burning and bloodied bedding and clothing. Her body was badly scorched and her skull and face had been smashed in.

The men threw a dozen or more buckets of water over the bedding and walls. Initially, Flora was still alive, but she died within 15 minutes.

Lunn rode off in the darkness to notify police at Marlborough. A mounted constable, Michael Cavanagh, arrived within the hour, examined the scene of the crime and, on Lunn's advice, arrested the station handyman George Blantern, who freely admitted to having murdered the 20-year-old domestic.

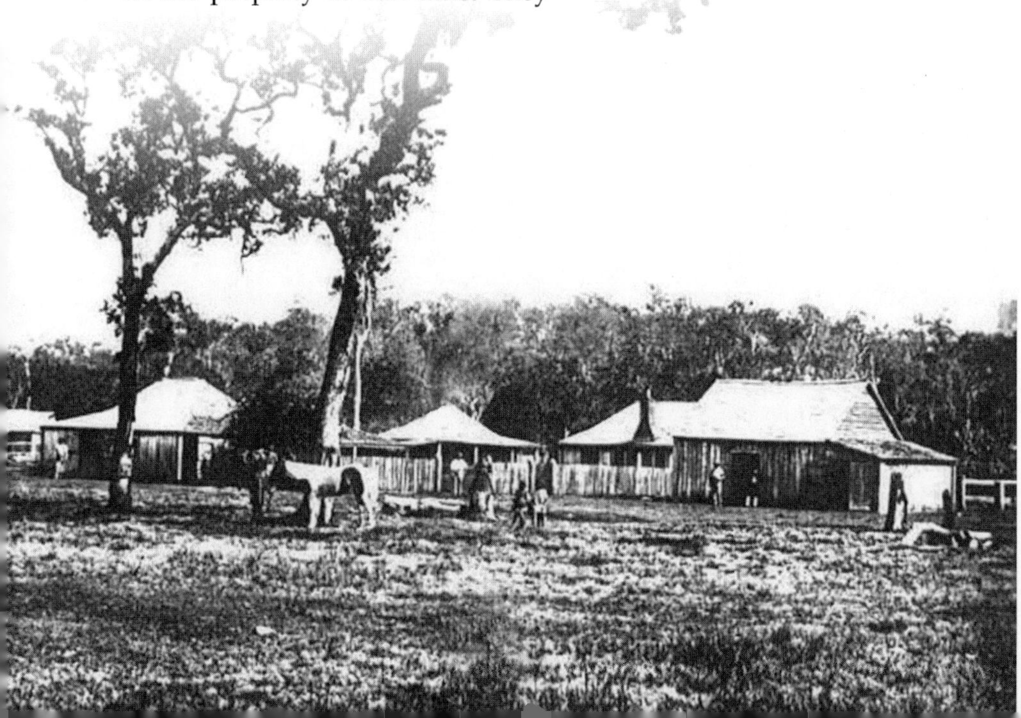

The crime

THE prisoner had been courting Flora for several months and, with the unspoken approval of Barnett, Blantern often spent the night with Flora McDonald in the servants' quarters.

Blantern was expecting a substantial amount of money to arrive for him from England in late July and Flora had agreed that, when the money arrived, the couple would marry.

Sundays were free days on Marlborough Station. On Sunday 7 May, Blantern and Flora had enjoyed a day's riding and picnicking. They returned late in the afternoon and ate the evening meal together. Flora then went to the main house for Sunday prayers before returning to join George in her servants' quarters.

Blantern later told what happened next:

> "We spent a pleasant evening and I am sure neither of us were the least apprehensive of approaching danger.
>
> About half an hour before Flora went to bed – about ten o'clock – we quarrelled when I proposed to buy an engagement ring for her. Hot words were exchanged between us and she said, 'Go to bed, George, and try to forget all about me'."

Blantern was shattered. Flora was breaking up with him. He continued:

> "I did not go to bed but wandered about for about two hours. I worked myself up into a state of desperation, all inward resistance seemed to be gone from me and I was urged on in some inexplicable way to take the life of one I dearly loved."

IT was a little before 1.00 a.m. when Walter Lunn, asleep in the male workers' building was awoken.

"Walter. Walter."

Lunn sat up in bed.

"George. What's the matter?"

"I have murdered Flora," Blantern said. "She had promised to marry me when my money came through. She told me tonight she wouldn't. I've murdered her so that no one else should have her."

A shocked Lunn, as he stood up and moved to the door, asked, "How did you kill her?"

"I chopped her up with an axe I found in the blacksmith's shop and burnt her."

The trial

AT Blantern's murder trial, held in the Rockhampton Circuit Court on 20 September 1893, Barnett, Lunn and Constable Cavanagh gave evidence relating to the events of the night Flora McDonald died. All said that Blantern openly admitted to the killing and then attempting to conceal the crime by burning down the building in which the victim's broken body lay.

In his defence the accused said:

> "When I was about thirteen years old I received a very bad wound on my left temple – a kick from a horse. About two years ago, whilst on a heavy spree in Maryborough, I was arrested by police and charged with being of unsound mind. I received medical treatment from Dr Garde, to whom I showed the cut on my forehead. He told me if I was not careful I should probably end my days in a lunatic asylum…
>
> I committed that horrible deed when insanely enraged with jealousy, preying upon a mind un-

hinged… I am of an over-sensitive and excitable temperament and was at the time temporarily insane."

If Blantern had thus hoped to avoid the hangman's noose, he had failed. He was found guilty of murder and sentenced to death. ■

Blantern's last requests

IN his last days, while awaiting execution at Boggo Road gaol, George Blantern made two requests.

First, with his anticipated money arriving from England, he asked that this be bequeathed to his victim's only sister, Charlotte.

Second, he sought permission to create for himself a wreath, comprising a cross of white flowers mounted upon cardboard and bearing his own handwritten inscription. He asked that this be placed on his coffin.

And it was, shortly after 8.00 a.m. on 23 October 1893.

Mr Justice Harding
21 September 1893

"George Thomas Blantern, after a trial by a jury of your countrymen, you have been convicted of the awful crime of murdering Flora McDonald. I do not think the jury could have come to any other conclusion. The only redeeming feature in the case is your expression of regret at the deed you have committed. May such regret meet with that reward in the future life which we are led to believe a beneficent Creator gives us. …My duty – a painful one – is to pronounce sentence upon you. The sentence is that you be taken hence to the place from whence you came and on a day, at such hour as the Governor, with the advice of the Executive Council, shall appoint, you be hanged by the neck until you be dead. And may the Lord have mercy upon your soul."

Fragments from the FILES of FELONS

1893. FOR over five years, a syndicate of clever thieves was able to steal some £30,000 worth of gold from their employer, the Mount Morgan Gold Mining Company.

In a secret operation to unearth the felons, the company sought the services of a Sydney-based private detective, Frederick Gabriel. Gabriel, working undercover, was employed on the site using the name F.W. Edmunds.

Over several weeks, Gabriel was able to provide names and evidence to the company directors, sufficient for them to seek arrests. But the suspects lived in Mount Morgan and scattered throughout nearby settlements, so it was imperative that all suspects be arrested simultaneously. This strategy would require a large number of police, however – which is why a bus-load of ten additional constables was sent from Brisbane. The authorities swooped on 23 September, and nine of 38 suspects were formally arrested.

Unfortunately, the cases against most of the men fell apart through lack of concrete evidence – the possession of gold was insufficient proof; nor was the possession of gold-smelting dishes, pipes, tools… after all, they were gold miners. In the end, only three men were sentenced to gaol terms of up to two years.

The Mount Morgan episode was but one of many similar gold-theft cases in Queensland mines at that time.

Death of a swagman

An old and unknown swagman trudged into the small township of Avondale, 16 miles north of Bundaberg, on the last weekend of December 1894. Entering Atwell's store, he asked for some water, then made camp beside the nearby railway station, and boiled his billy.

Two of the Atwell children approached and purchased from him some matches, which he apparently sold to make a meagre living.

Nearby, loafing around the station, was a group of South Sea Islanders, indentured to work at the local sugar plantation. 'Would any of you also like to buy some matches?' asked the swaggie.

One of their number, Narasemai, agreed and handed over a half sovereign. In providing change, the old man fumbled in his purse, revealing that he was not as poverty-stricken as he looked. His purse contained several guineas in gold coins, a fact that did not go unnoticed by Narasemai.

The Crime

THE lure of that old man's gold was just too enticing for the kanakas.

Next morning, Narasemai and several others set out for the station with the intention of robbing him – but they would have to wait until he decamped because he was in full view of the townsfolk.

In the early afternoon, the swagman packed up and left town accompanied by a fellow itinerant. As the pair walked into the bush, the islanders followed, armed with an array of weapons.

It was a few miles down Baffle Creek Road before the pair went their separate ways. But just as the group were about to make their move, a rider by the name of Webster galloped past.

When the islanders were sure they had the old man to themselves, they quickly surrounded him, demanding he hand over his purse.

In an instant the swagman was set upon – struck on the chest with an iron bar, clubbed with a length of log, then hacked at with butcher's knives.

They dragged the lifeless body into an adjoining paddock, where it lay decomposing for several days, until a settler's wife, drawn to the powerful smell of death and decomposition, discovered it hidden in the thick wattle under-scrub.

Initially the police had no clues other than the body of a penniless and unknown swagman. But as news of the crime circulated, Webster, who had seen kanakas following the lone traveller, and other witnesses helped them piece the events together.

A dawn raid by police on Avondale plantation enabled them to arrest the suspects while still in their bunks.

To teach a lesson

FOURTEEN kanaka labourers from Queensland canefields were escorted to Boggo Road prison to witness the execution of Mi Ori and Narasemai on 20 May 1895. From Childers, Mackay, Maryborough and Bundaberg they came to observe what they might expect if they too decided to take the life of a fellow man.

As the *Brisbane Courier* reported: 'They were arranged in a line two deep in front of the scaffold and watched every movement with extreme anxiety and horror.'

A little after 8.00 a.m., both condemned men, standing a metre apart, with one pull of the hangman's lever dropped into eternity.

AT the Bundaberg Circuit Court in April 1895, six islanders were charged with the swagman's murder, found guilty, and sentenced to death.

In time, the sentences of all but two of the men were commuted to imprisonment. For the ring-leaders and chief offenders, Narasemai and Mi Orie, the death penalty would stand. ■

Fragments from the FILES of FELONS

1894. IT was not the first time John Townsend had threatened his Blackall neighbour – twice previously he had done so with a hammer, but had been restrained by friends. However, on 6 February, he ended the long and bitter feud by battering his neighbour to death with an axe handle, following a noisy, running battle through both houses. He spent eight years of his 15-year sentence on St Helena – as the prison butcher.

1895. ON the 2 July Senior Constable William Conroy, stationed at Thursday Island, was called to attend a domestic disturbance at the home of Frank and Amelia Tinyana in Douglas Street. Frank Tinyana had armed himself with a knife and was hiding in the house. As Conroy began searching for Tinyana in the yard of the house, the man attacked his wife, stabbing her several times. Conroy ran and placed himself between Tinyana and the wife in an attempt to protect her. He was stabbed a number of times and, although bleeding profusely from his wounds, Conroy managed to restrain Tinyana until he could be assisted by the arrival of Constable Clines.

Senior Constable Conroy died shortly after Tinyana was taken into custody. The killer was executed on 4 November.

Following his death, members of the Queensland Police Force took up a collection for a memorial monument that still stands today over Conroy's grave on Thursday Island.

The hallucinating husband

Helen Gibson was frightened. On the night of 17 June 1895, she found her husband, Charles, under the kitchen table, hiding from people who, he said, wanted to kill them both, and their baby. This was yet another example of his odd behaviour over recent weeks.

She hurried next door to the Priors, in Short Street in Kangaroo Point, Brisbane. James Prior set off after Charles Gibson who had now left the house.

Some time later, at the nearby intersection of Wellington Road and Mobray Terrace, he heard cries of 'Murder!' and 'Help!' and found Gibson, clad only in a shirt, remonstrating with two men who, he claimed, were trying to kill him.

Gibson agreed to return home with Prior, but he refused to go near his own house – after all, men were trying to get in through the windows to kill his family!

He stayed the night with the Priors, who spent a distressing time with the hallucinating Gibson. Crawling under their kitchen table, armed with knives, he was again ready to kill all those phantoms who dared pursue him.

Next morning, around 7.30, Gibson rejoined his wife in the house next-door.

THIRTY minutes later, screams from the Gibson house had James Prior running to investigate. There he found Gibson on the floor, bleeding profusely from a slash to his throat. Nearby lay a razor.

"Where's Helen?" shouted Prior.

Unable to speak Gibson pointed to the bedroom, where Prior found

Helen hiding under a bed, her windpipe severed by a deep five-inch gash. There was blood everywhere. The baby, untouched, lay on the floor.

Police were called and an ambulance cab rushed the pair to hospital for emergency treatment. Both husband and wife survived the ordeal.

Charles Gibson was later arrested and tried on a charge of wounding with intent to commit murder and attempted suicide.

Chief Justice
Sir Samuel Griffith
22 August 1895

"If, when a man commits an act and his mind is so enfeebled either by mental or physical disease, or natural defect, that he has no control over himself, he ought not to be held responsible any more than a ship which has lost its rudder and was drifting by wind and tide could be held responsible for a collision."

The turning point for Gibson

GIBSON had earlier witnessed an accident, on 24 May 1895, which had greatly affected his mental stability. A young woman had been thrown from her horse, landing at Gibson's feet. Her head had struck the pavement heavily and blood from the wound splashed over his clothes. He had carried the woman to a nearby hotel and summoned a doctor.

The incident continually played on his mind: from that day he avoided strangers and suspected detectives were stalking him because they believed he had killed the woman by knocking out her brains with a rock. In reality, the woman had quickly recovered from the injuries she had received in the fall.

But since that day, Gibson had become noticeably morose, depressed, delusional.

AT HIS TRIAL in August, witnesses gave evidence to the effect that, since the incident of 24 May, Gibson claimed he had also seen 'black men running after milk carts'. He thought he was the Duke of Buckingham. He would speak wildly about men trying to kill him, of detectives pursuing him, of men who were coming to take Mrs Gibson and the baby away from him, of Magistrate Pinnock threatening to gaol him 'for six months for not giving him a proper military salute', and of having killed several people who lived nearby.

According to medical witnesses, the accused was showing clear 'symptoms of incipient insanity'; he did not know the difference between right and wrong; and Mrs Gibson's life had in truth 'been in danger for a period of from a fortnight to three weeks'.

Indeed, his defence argued that 'at the time of the commission of the crime, Gibson was a raving maniac'.

The jury agreed, returning a verdict of not guilty on the grounds of insanity. Gibson was ordered 'to be kept in strict custody until Her Majesty's pleasure was known regarding him'. ■

The Snob

From the 1860s to the turn of the century, Edward 'The Snob'* Hartigan led a remarkable criminal career in central Queensland as a forger – that is, when he was not paying for these crimes as a guest of Her Majesty at St Helena Island or Boggo Road prisons.

Shrewd, bold and uneducated, his powers of imitation, particularly when it came to forging signatures, were unequalled in an age when financial business of all kinds was done with cheques.

EDWARD Hartigan had learnt the bootmaking trade in England as a lad. Arriving in Australia in 1856 as a 21-year-old, he settled in Rockhampton and soon found work as a bootmaker, a trade he soon tired of.

Instead, writing and cashing other people cheques was to become his speciality. Historian Hugh MacMaster explained how Hartigan found this new career path:

> The Snob started his cheque-scamming interest by firstly acquiring – honestly it seems – a cheque made out by a squatter in favour of another person, for the amount of *eight* pounds, seventeen shillings and six pence (£8.17.6). This cheque was soon to read, *eighty* pounds, seventeen shillings and sixpence (£80.17.6).
>
> Hartigan cashed this cheque at a town more than 100 km from where he had received it. In change, he received a bundle of cheques of lesser value, a few bank notes and

* 19th century slang for a cobbler or boot-maker. When on the road, on the run, or in prison, Hartigan was known as 'The Snob'.

A cheque economy

IN the early years of the colony, coins were in short supply, and bank and treasury notes were not distributed in sufficient numbers for a cash economy to flourish.

For this reason, commercial firms would mint their own coins, using their own crests and face value, for exchange within the locality.

So too with cheques. Cheques drawn on such establishments as the Union Bank of Australia or the Bank of New South Wales, were often kept in circulation for months, before they were eventually presented to the relevant bank for clearance.

It was within this setting that Edward Hartigan would thrive as a forger – though not without a few risks and major setbacks.

Left: *The bootmakers workshop at the St Helena Island prison, where the young Edward 'The Snob' Hartigan* (pictured in 1875) *would spend many years of his life for forging cheques*

several coins, all to the value of £80.17.6.

He set aside for later any of the cheques he could easily 'adjust' whilst living on the proceeds of the remainder. [1]

In this way, Hartigan was able to maintain a fine lifestyle for over 45 years, from the time of his arrival in Australia to his 'retirement' in an old people's home in 1902 – although, of course, for over 31 of those years, he was in government residence in the colony's gaols.

NO doubt many of Hartigan's successful forgeries went undetected; others brought to the attention of police lacked adequate detail for

Hartigan. . . a murderer?

IN July 1896, Edward Hartigan and his travelling companion John Ackroyd had made camp at Greyrock on the Clermont-Aramac Road.

Twelve months later a kangaroo shooter found a number of human bones in the ashes of a fireplace in that same camping spot. The bones had seemingly been cut into smaller pieces with a sharp tool.

Police investigations revealed that this was indeed the old Hartigan-Ackroyd campsite. Ackroyd had not been seen since July and, when a metal money-purse clasp identified as Ackroyd's was found in the ashes, suspicion immediately fell on Hartigan. Had he disposed of his companion and tried to destroy his remains in the fire?

Further inquiries disclosed that, during one night in July the previous year, witnesses recalled hearing shots and next morning saw Hartigan riding off with Ackroyd's horse and dog.

A warrant was taken out for The Snob's arrest – except that Hartigan was once more in gaol for forging cheques. On his release, he was taken into custody, committed to stand trial for the murder of Ackroyd, and held in remand.

But in the weeks that followed police were unable to gather sufficient evidence to convince the Attorney-General that a guilty verdict was possible.

Hartigan was released – only to find himself back in custody a few months later on more forgery charges.

charges to be laid. On other occasions, the full force of the law was brought to bear, with The Snob's file recording convictions of 10 years (1869), 15 years (1875), 21 months (1888), 23 months (1894), 17 months (1896), 23 months (1898), and 22 months (1901).

By 1902, Hartigan had had enough and, at the age of 69, took up residence across Moreton Bay at the Dunwich Benevolent Asylum for the aged and destitute, from where on a clear day and at low tide he no doubt could catch a distant glimpse, across the Bay, of his former home of many years – the St Helena Penal Establishment. ■

Fragments from the FILES of FELONS

1896. 58-year-old Jonathan Longland returned to his Brisbane home at Morningside around 8 o'clock on the night of Saturday 2 May. As usual, the postmaster/storekeeper was somewhat the worse for liquor and went into the bedroom to sleep it off.

An hour later, by the light of a kerosene lamp, his wife was sitting quietly sewing in the sitting-room with two of the couple's 13 children when Longland came into the room. Without a word of warning, he raised a revolver, shot his wife in the chest, and walked out through the back door.

Mrs Longland staggered to the front garden gate where she fell into the arms of her son-in-law who lived nearby and had come running, having heard the shot. The 51-year-old Mary Longland was taken by ambulance cab to hospital (where she would die on the following Monday).

By midnight, several mounted constables were searching the scrub for Longland. He was still wearing slippers and his tracks led to nearby Belmont. Around midday, police found Longland at the house of a friend, John Samuels. A short while earlier, the fugitive had arrived at Samuels' house where he said he intended to return to the bush and shoot himself, having just shot his wife. Samuels persuaded him to hand over his gun, which was given to the police when they appeared thirty minutes later.

"I shot her. I meant to do it," he admitted.

The jury heard that Longland had been drinking heavily for some months, being insanely jealous – he falsely believed that Mary was 'improperly intimate' with 73-year-old grazier Ezra Firth who lived on a nearby hill with his wife. Mary did paid housework for the Firths.

The Longlands *(pictured)* often quarrelled loudly and violently over the issue – invariably when Jonathan was drunk. Indeed, the husband had only three months earlier tried to cut Mary's throat, but was prevented from doing so by the children who had wrestled the knife from his grasp.

The jury found the prisoner guilty of murder, but strongly recommended mercy on the grounds that, although they believed he was not sufficiently insane to be ignorant of what he was doing, they thought his mind was unhinged by his excessive drinking.

Longland's death sentence was later commuted to life in prison. He died on St Helena Island in 1904, from 'senile decay' – and is recorded as being the last prisoner to be buried on the island.

1896

MARIE CHRISTENSEN

Crime: MANSLAUGHTER
Location: MYORA
Penalty: TWO YEARS IN PRISON (SUSPENDED)

Marie, the mission matron

IN 1893, Myora Mission Station on North Stradbroke Island, 4km north of Dunwich, was designated an industrial and reformatory school, 'to detain and train aboriginal boys and girls and make them useful and profitable to the mission and society'.

In 1894, when Archibald Meston was commissioned to investigate the conditions of Aborigines in Queensland, he found the mission to be poorly managed and, under Matron Marie Christensen and Supervisor Edwin Renshaw, conditions 'were deteriorating rapidly'.

Things came to a head in September 1896, when Christensen found herself on trial for the manslaughter of an aboriginal child, Cassey.

The school was immediately closed and the children sent to mainland institutions.

On the morning of 14 September 1896, Matron Marie Christensen, took several children down to the beach at Myora Mission to bathe them. Cassey, a five-year-old who had been sickly from the time of her placement in June, was singled out, Christensen ignoring her ill-health.

Christensen plunged Cassey roughly into the sea. When they left the water, the girl collapsed and balked at walking up a steep hill. The matron insisted that Cassey walk, but Cassey wanted to sit. Christensen snapped off a green switch, and whipped the child. Over the next few minutes, Cassey suffered a series of attacks.

When whippings failed to budge the child, the matron seized her arm, and dragged her. Reaching the top of the hill, she insisted that Cassey walk. The emaciated child was unable to comply. Christensen found another switch, again thrashed the girl, then hurried to her quarters to retrieve a cane. In a few minutes she was back, beating Cassey's legs and kicking her.

Christensen's shouts attracted the attention of several people. From her humpy on the edge of the settlement, Budlo Lefu saw the disturbance on the hill. She hastened to the scene and picked up Cassey. Christensen told her to put the girl down: this was none of her business! Christensen took Cassey into the dormitory where the caning resumed.

Cassey died a couple of days later. A doctor found 'thirty contusions on the posterior aspect of the lower extremities, also extending from the buttocks to the heels of the body'.

Judge Real sentenced Christensen, found guilty of manslaughter, to two years hard labour, suspended on the condition that the woman be taken into the care of the Salvation Army. As he concluded: 'the woman did not seem to possess a very large amount of intelligence', and he added: 'I think the committee of the Myora Mission is as much to blame as the prisoner'. ■

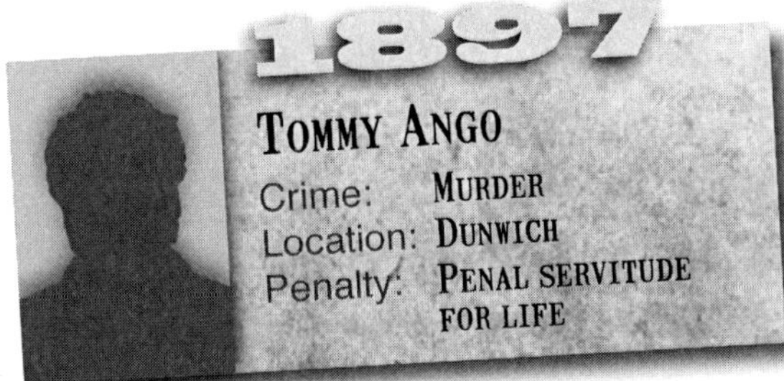

Double death at the asylum

The Dunwich Benevolent Asylum

THE Dunwich Benevolent Asylum was established in 1865 when inmates were first transferred to North Stradbroke Island from the Benevolent Ward at Brisbane Hospital.

Unwanted by the hospital – and the colonial government, the colony's rejected were sent to Dunwich because of the availability of vacant quarantine buildings.

For the next eighty years, almost every type of person who was unable to fit in with society was admitted. The blind, crippled, mentally deficient, terminally ill, cancerous, tuberculosis and leprosy patients, inebriates and others were shipped indiscriminately to the asylum. Most were old. All but a handful accepted their fate uncomplainingly, not because they were happy but because they became 'institutionally dependent'.

The asylum was isolated, but that physical isolation was only a symptom of social abandonment. In housing the unwanted members of society who were embarrassments and liabilities, the asylum's function was not to help the weak and crippled but to hide them in isolation, the outcasts 'whom nobody owned'.[1]

The asylum continued to operate until it was officially closed in 1946, when inmates were transferred to Eventide at Sandgate.

Early in 1897, See Ong, a Chinese inmate of the Dunwich Benevolent Asylum, began taunting his roommate Tommy Ango, a South Sea Islander, about his bad breath, to such an extent that Ango was forced to sleep by himself in the washroom. He even ate alone. The antagonism continued for several weeks until Ango could bear the taunts no longer…

Each morning, the mocking See Ong would follow Ango to the beach where the Islander would take a daily stroll, fish, and cook his catch on an open fire.

On the morning of 26 January, however, Tommy Ango was prepared; he had with him an iron bar wrapped in white calico. As See Ong started his daily abuse, Tommy produced the weapon and began striking Ong brutally about the head.

Another inmate Andrew Thompson saw what was happening and came running to help the fallen Chinaman - but he too was set upon and soon both victims lay dead on the beach, heads broken and bloodied.

Three other men, attracted by the distant cries of Thompson, soon appeared, overpowering Ango as he was dragging his victims into the sea.

On 22 March Ango was found guilty of murder, and the jury's plea for mercy, on account of Ango's distressing illness and the aggressive taunting, was heeded. His death penalty was later reduced to life imprisonment. ■

1898

William Archer

Crime: Murder

Location: St Helena Island

Penalty: Trial aborted

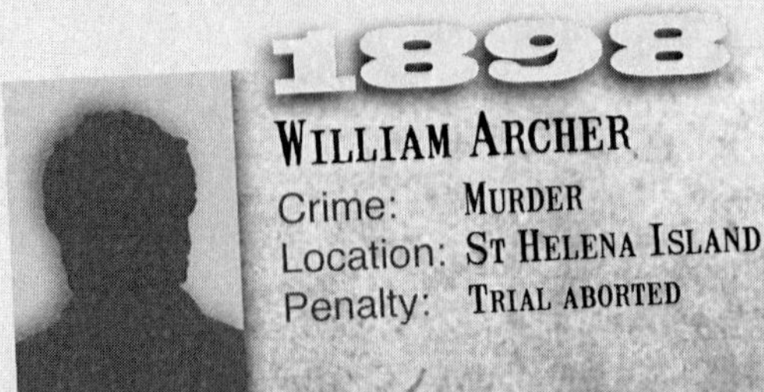

The murder of Warder Dodd

In 1897, William Archer, 'a man of pale, cadaverous appearance', about 37 years old and suffering from consumption, was sent to St Helena Island prison to serve out a severe sentence of ten years for stealing a quantity of cloth to the value of £35.

Archer was put to work in the prison tailors workshop but, arguing that the indoor work did not agree with his delicate disposition, he sought permission from the Superintendent to be allocated outdoor activities. This privilege, which he requested more than once, was refused.

On 13 February 1898, as a last resort, Archer asked the Visiting Surgeon to recommend that he work in the open air, adding that, unless he was granted this request, he could end up injuring someone in a fit of temper. Again his request was refused.

That same afternoon in the cutting room of the tailors workshop, the trade instructor was stopped by Archer.

'I say, boss, can't *you* get me out of this shop? It's injuring my health and affecting my mind. I've seen the doctor

The tailors workshop at the St Helena Island prison, where Warder Dodd was knifed by prisoner William Archer in 1898

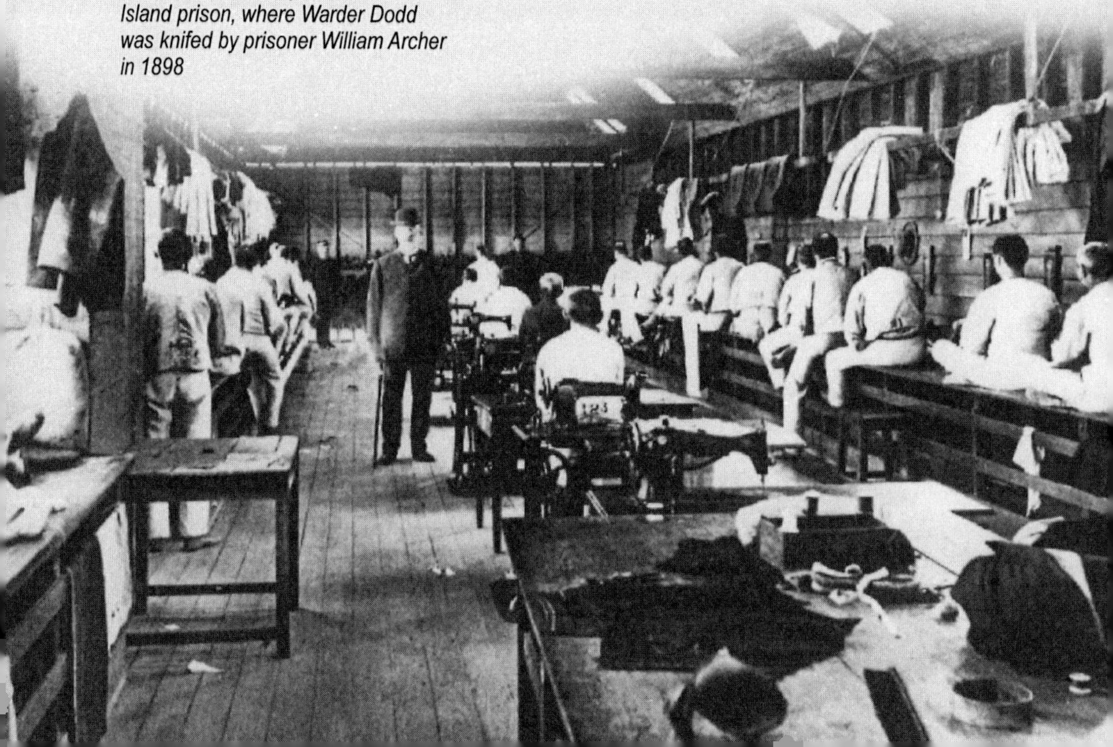

and he'll do nothing for me.' The disgruntled prisoner was told to go back to his place, his frustration now further inflamed because, earlier that day, he had already been reprimanded by Warder Downie over a minor rule infraction.

On duty by the door of the tailors shop that afternoon was Henry Dodd, who had been rostered that day as the roving 'shopwalker' in the workshops. Warder William Downie had asked Dodd to relieve him at the door for a short time while he visited the toilet.

While Downie was absent from the workshop, a seething Archer walked up to an unsuspecting Dodd at the door and, without warning, savagely drove a knife several times into the warder's stomach. As Dodd staggered towards the workshop gate holding his bleeding abdomen, the prisoner turned and shouted to the trade instructor, 'I'm taking myself out of this b---- shop now, you b---- b----s!'

As Archer reached the barred gate separating the workshops from the main building, still carrying the blood-stained knife in his hand, a returning Warder Downie confronted him.

'Downie!' exclaimed the surprised prisoner. 'It's you, you white-livered b----! You're the b---- that I intended it for!', and he put his arm through the bars and threw the knife at the approaching warder. He then ran to the nearby saddlers bench where he grabbed another knife to throw at Downie. It hit the wired partition and fell to the floor.

Archer ran back into the tailors workshop with the warder in pursuit. Prisoners dived for cover. He picked up a pair of large tailors scissors and yelled at Downie, 'It's you I wanted!' and, holding the scissors above his head with both hands, he approached the warder.

When about four paces from Downie, Archer threw the scissors, which the officer dodged by ducking down behind a table. The warder then jumped on the table in the direction of the prisoner who hurled a galvanised iron pot full of water at him. Downie warded off the projectile with his arm and, leaping from the table, he crash-tackled Archer.

The screaming prisoner was carried through the workshop, struggling violently, and, with the assistance of other warders arriving on the scene, Downie took him off to the cells.

Warder Dodd was taken by the Visiting Surgeon to Brisbane Hospital where an emergency operation failed

The memorial gravestone for murdered warder Henry Dodd, Toowong Cemetery, Brisbane, funded by his fellow officers

to save his life.

On the day of the funeral, as many warders as could be spared journeyed up to Brisbane to pay tribute to their late colleague who was laid to rest at Toowong Cemetery in heavy rain.

Archer was taken to Brisbane Gaol on 19 February 1898 and later brought before the criminal sittings of the Supreme Court, under committal for trial for the murder of Warder Dodd. But the case was adjourned on medical grounds after three days, for Archer was now at the mercy of frightful coughing fits which forced him on numerous occasions to cling to the dock for support.

He was returned to Brisbane Gaol to recover but at 6.30 a.m. on 8 May 1898 was found dead in his bed, the post-mortem report quaintly recording that 'the cause of death was failure of the heart's action'.

In dying, Archer had managed to escape the full penalty of the law which, in those days, meant the hangman's rope. ■

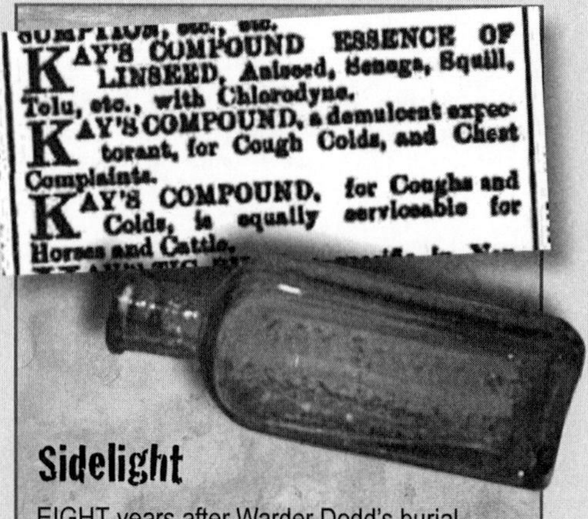

KAY'S COMPOUND ESSENCE OF LINSEED, Aniseed, Senega, Squill, Tolu, etc., with Chlorodyne.

KAY'S COMPOUND, a demulcent expectorant, for Cough Colds, and Chest Complaints.

KAY'S COMPOUND, for Coughs and Colds, is equally serviceable for Horses and Cattle.

Sidelight

EIGHT years after Warder Dodd's burial in Toowong Cemetery, his sister Elizabeth Dale, who had just visited her late husband's grave nearby, took a shortcut across a small dam wall in the cemetery grounds to visit her murdered brother's grave.

Crossing the wall, Mrs Dale slipped, fell in, and drowned, a tragedy that later prompted the authorities to fill in the dam.

Curiously, Mrs Dale was found to be high on morphine at the time. Like many middle-aged ladies of the day, she was a regular user of Kay's Compound, a morphine-loaded cough medicine.[1]

Fragments from the FILES of FELONS

1898. 15-year-old Alfred Hill left his Nundah home on 10 December to visit his uncle at Redbank Plains near Ipswich. He never arrived. Several weeks later his decomposed body and the carcass of his piebald horse were found in the bush at Oxley, 350 metres off the Brisbane-Ipswich Road. Both decapitated boy and his horse had been shot through the head.

Edward Wilson *(left)*, previously a master at Ipswich Boys Grammar, with a record of sexually abusing young boys, became the prime suspect.

In evidence, Wilson's 11-year-old son said that, as he and his father approached Oxley on the afternoon of 10 December 1898, he saw a boy riding a piebald horse in the bush beside the road. He said that his father left him sitting in the cart while he climbed through a fence and went into the bush. After some time he heard revolver shots and soon afterwards his father came out of the trees and told him he had shot a hawk.

The evidence against Wilson seemed damning but, with the discovery that there had been 'no true bill' against Wilson, the case failed to proceed. Wilson was later convicted of unrelated sexual offences and spent five years at St Helena. The murder of Alfred Hill remained unsolved.

1898

UNKNOWN
Crime: MURDER
Location: GATTON
Penalty: —

The Gatton Mystery

MURDER.

A HORRIBLE OUTRAGE.

ONE OF THE MURDERS OF THE CENTURY.

BROTHER AND TWO SISTERS KILLED.

MURDERERS STILL AT LARGE.

NO CLUES TO BE FOUND.

On Boxing Day 1898, the sisters Norah and Ellen Murphy and their brother Michael were murdered in particularly strange circumstances.

For 20 years the Murphys had lived and farmed at Tent Hill, nearly 10 km from Gatton. The parents, the four sisters and six brothers, along with sister Polly's husband William McNeil, had spent a carefree Christmas together. On the night of 26 December, following a day at the Mt Sylvia races, after dinner Michael took his sisters Norah and Ellen to a dance at nearby Gatton.

They left their parents' farm in a sulky at about 8.00 p.m. and arrived at the hall at 9.00 p.m. They found that the dance had been cancelled due to a lack of young women, so Michael turned the sulky round and headed for home.

A TERRIBLE DISCOVERY.

Early next morning, finding that the trio had not returned, brother-in-law William McNeil set out to look for them.

On the Gatton Road, about 3 km from town, McNeil saw the distinctive tracks of the sulky, a result of one wobbly wheel, heading off the road, through the sliprail opening in a fence at Moran's paddock. Some 800m from the fence he found the carnage.

Michael and Ellen lay back to back, bludgeoned, with their hands tied behind. Beside them was a heavy stick, 'covered in blood and brains'.

A few metres away, under a gum tree, Norah's body lay on a neatly spread blanket. Her head was also smashed, her hands were bound behind her back, and a leather strap was tied tightly around her neck.

Nearby, the horse was still attached to the sulky, but it was dead, slumped against the broken shaft, with a bullet hole in its head.

Curiously, the siblings had been laid out so their legs crossed over their bodies with the feet pointing west.

McNeil set off for Gatton to notify the police.

INVESTIGATING THE CRIME.

Sergeant Arrell, accompanied by a couple of townsmen, was soon on the spot, and at once took charge of the bodies, which were removed to a hotel.

Later that afternoon the Government Medical Officer arrived from Ipswich to conduct a post-mortem examination. It

Murder Victims
Ellen Murphy, 18 years;
Norah Murphy, 27 years;
Michael Murphy, 29 years

was clear from the appearance of the bodies, fingernail scratches, and their torn and stained clothes that both sisters had been sexually violated, before being bludgeoned to death and their bodies mutilated.

Michael had been bound, bashed, and shot behind the ear. The horse had been shot and had its throat cut.

Police officers of the highest level were put on the case. Over 100 possible suspects were interviewed in the early weeks. With little progress being made in finding the murderer, a Magisterial Inquiry into the murders was held in late January 1899, examining 45 witnesses and creating 835 pages of depositions.

Several months later, following widespread dissatisfaction and doubts concerning the efficiency of the Queensland Police Force, a lengthy Royal Commission [see page 136] was conducted focusing on the unsolved murders at Gatton and at Oxley, which had been committed two weeks before the Murphy atrocity [see page 130]. Again hundreds of pages of evidence were accumulated from scores of witnesses.

Investigators remained baffled, the crime stayed unsolved, and the Gatton murders of 1898 remain a mystery to this day.

▲ **Scene of the outrage.** The sulky that carried the three siblings to their death; the remains of the horse, butchered by authorities for boiling down, in their search for bullets; a kneeling blacktracker surveying the spot where the bodies of Ellen and Michael Murphy were found; and the tree *(right)* in the shadow of which sister Norah's body lay.

▶ The prime suspects

Several books[1] and countless articles have been written about this triple murder and various theories offered as to who was the perpetrator of arguably Queensland's most baffling crime…

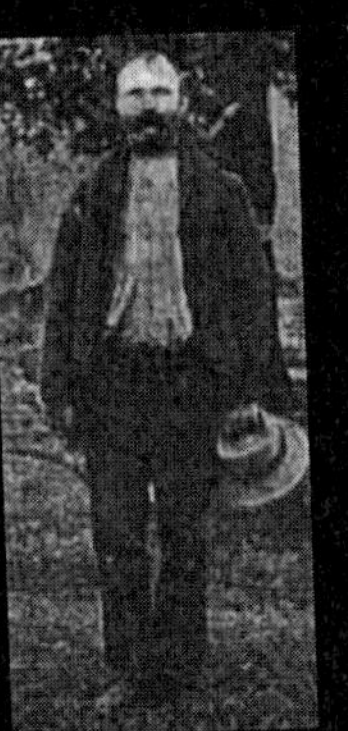

Was it Richard Burgess, a swagman in the district at the time, with a long criminal and gaol record as a thief, bully, and sexual pervert? Had he not said that 'the eldest Murphy girl was a great flirt, and that it was time she was put out of the road'?

Was it Thomas Ryan, a local labourer, who some months earlier had feuded with Mrs Murphy over his association with eldest daughter Polly?

Was it Thomas Day, 'a shadowy figure' who worked for the local butcher? All the evidence pointed towards Day. He was living near the scene of the crime. He claimed he had been asleep in bed that night by 7.00 p.m., despite a noisy fireworks display on the property where he was staying. Was he the man seen standing by the sliprails of the paddock that night by several people? It was claimed that he had washed blood from his pullover a few days after the murder. The evidence seemed strong, but police weren't convinced. Then, claiming that he didn't like his employer's food, he simply packed up his swag two weeks after the murders – and was never seen again.

Was it William McNeil, brother-in-law of the victims? At least there were locals who thought so at the time, suggesting he hadn't even visited the murder scene that morning, but had, knowingly gone straight to the police.

Was it William Lilley, sadist and sex pervert, whose

author-son Merv claims his father was near Gatton at the time and was a worthy suspect?

Or was it someone else?

▶ What makes the Gatton mystery so mysterious?

Among unanswered questions…

What possessed the Murphys to drive into the paddock that night, where they were brutally slain?

Why were there no signs on the ground of a struggle, despite obvious violence, fingernail scratches and marks on the girls' ravished bodies?

Or, although there was no blood on the sulky, were they killed elsewhere?

Why were the bodies so carefully laid out – feet all pointing due west?

Why had Norah's body been left on a rug that was so neatly arranged?

Why were there no tracks in the soft earth surrounding the scene?

Why was there an empty purse in Michael's hand?

Why had the horse been shot?

What gun was used – and what became of it?

Could there have been more than one murderer?

What was the significance of the screams of "Father" from the paddock that night?

Could a member of the Murphy family have been involved?

Was there any significance in the 'In Memoriam' notice, cut from a newspaper and found hidden, along with a strap from the horse's harness, in a tree several hundred metres from the scene – the same clipping that Norah had kept in her room for months prior to the murders?

Who was the unidentified man near the sliprail, seen by five of eight people on the road that might?

Why did the police handle the case in so slip-shod a manner?

After more than a century, so many unanswerable questions.

▶ A botched investigation?

History records that the investigation into the Gatton murders became a catalogue of bungling by virtually everyone involved. For example:

- Police investigators took a day to arrive from Brisbane. By that time up to forty sightseers had trampled across Moran's paddock and the murder scene, destroying whatever evidence there might have been. Even blacktrackers were left with nothing to go on.
- The first doctor failed to find a bullet in the head of Michael Murphy; it was only found later when his body was exhumed and a second postmortem carried out.
- Police focused valuable time exploring the whereabouts of suspect Richard Burgess, only to conclude he had an ironclad alibi – while they allowed a prime suspect, the itinerant worker Thomas Day, to simply walk out of the town, untraceable.

Memorial grave of the Murphy victims, erected by public subscription in Gatton Cemetery

Now, over 100 years later, it is clear that the murderer took the long sought-after answers with him to the grave. ■

The Woolloongabba murder

At about 4.45 on the morning of Thursday, 8 June 1899, Sam Stanford left his home in Wilton Street, Wooloongabba, for the short walk along Ipswich Road to the Fiveways, to go to work at the local butcher's shop. On the way, while passing old Mrs Weaber's house, he noticed the glow of a fire under the floorboards.

He ran to the Poulton house next door, and raised the alarm. James Poulton and Stanford forced the front door of the small four-roomed cottage. The house was full of smoke, which they discovered was coming from a bedroom.

Inside they discovered a fire burning beneath the bed. The bedding and bedclothes were on fire, and also a number of Austrian bentwood chairs, which had been piled on top of the bed. They removed the burning chairs and the smouldering bedclothes, and these were carried outside, where Mrs Poulton and her children extinguished them.

Traces of blood were to be seen about, but at first they found nothing of the aged occupant. When the room had been sufficiently cleared and the smoke dissipated, the body of the old lady was seen lying beside the bed, with a number of ghastly wounds laying open the back of her skull from one ear to the other.

By now a crowd was beginning to gather.

"Go for Bonnor," said Poulton. William Bonnor was the husband of one of Mrs Weaber's step-granddaughters. He lived just across the street with his ailing wife.

The police take over

BY 5.20 a.m. the police turned up. They found no evidence of the place having been ransacked, with drawers, cupboards and boxes being untouched and £22 in a small tin trunk.

All day, it was written, 'crowds of morbid people gathered, all anxious to catch a glimpse of anything connected with the tragedy which, yet again, has convulsed the public with horror… Crowds of young and old, young men and their sweethearts, husbands and wives, nursemaids with children in

A HORRIBLE CRIME.

MURDER AT WOOLLOONGABBA.

AN OLD WOMAN KILLED.

Yesterday information was received at an early hour of a tragedy said to have occurred at Woolloongabba, and full inquiries have resulted in confirming the intelligence in all its ghastly details. It

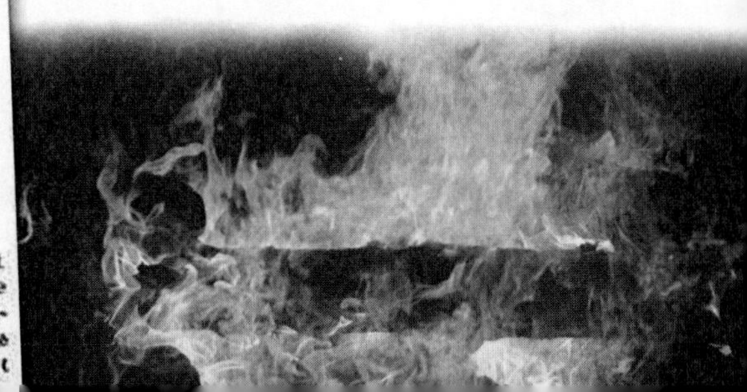

arms and perambulators, gathered round, conversing in hushed whispers of the horror, while troops of cyclists, people on horseback, and others in vehicles came careering along and pulled up before the spot…"

In the meantime, police were already searching nearby premises and backyards, and several axes, tomahawks and other items were confiscated. It was clear that Sarah Weaber had been murdered before an attempt was made to incinerate her in her bed. Nearby waterholes and watercourses were checked in search of the possible weapon, as were wells in adjoining streets. A blacktracker was called in. The movements of many people were traced. And documents were removed from the house.

An arrest – and release

POLICE made an arrest at 11.45 that night at the hospital morgue, within 24 hours of the crime. William Bonnor, husband of old Sarah Weaber's step-granddaughter and described as 'a man of most inoffensive appearance', was charged 'on suspicion of being concerned in the murder'.

Police were keen to make an arrest in the light of their failure in recent months to solve the well-publicised murders of the three Murphy siblings at Gatton and the Hill boy at Oxley.

In the Weaber case, the police were following several lines of inquiry.

They were convinced that a hole had been cut in Mrs Weaber's front door panel next to the keyhole, enabling the intruder's hand to pass through and turn the key inside to gain access. After the crime, he again locked the door from outside, and stuffed the hole with red cloth – and similar red cloth was found in the Bonnor house.

Mrs Weaber had recently sold two houses at Highgate Hill and had an interest in a small farm in the Logan district. Her will favoured Bonnor's wife, but here was talk that she intended to change her will and that the Bonnor children would be the beneficiaries – no longer Bonnor and his wife, who were described as 'being in poor circumstances'.

As well, the police argued that Mrs Weaber 'did not appear to have looked with any degree of favour upon the marriage' of the Bonnors – and that she 'was trying to come between the pair'.

But Bonnor's ailing wife, 'kept awake by a pain in her heart', had been unable to sleep on the night of the murder. She gave evidence that her husband, a sound sleeper, did not leave the bed from the time they retired until he received the urgent call at 5.00 the next morning.

Despite William Bonnor being in custody for several weeks, the police could mount no credible case against him and he was released on 20 June. Not only did the police fail to produce a solid motive for the murder, they had no clue as to the identity of the murderer, in spite of a reward of £1000 being offered by the government.

AND so it was that yet another unsolved crime was added to accusations of police incompetence, for the murder of Sarah Weaber was not the only unsolved murder on police books – a Royal Commission later that year into the effectiveness of the police force [see page 136] would reveal that there had been a further 20 unsolved murders committed during the preceding five years, representing the deaths of 24 victims. ■

Royal Commission into the Queensland Police 1899

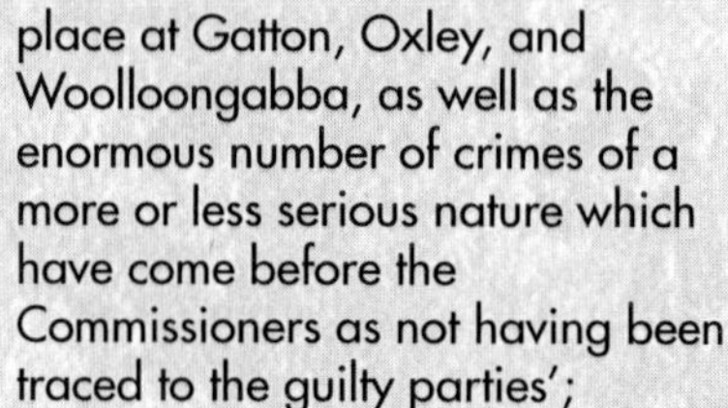

AS a consequence of the failure of police to solve the Oxley murder of 10 December 1898 [page 130], the Gatton murders of 27 December 1898 [page 131], and the Wooloongabba murder of 8 June 1899 [page 134], a Royal Commission, headed by Judge Arthur Noel, was established to investigate the shortcomings of the Queensland police force, particularly the Criminal Investigation Branch.

In December 1899, the Commissioners submitted their report to Parliament: 'We have inquired into the three several murders which struck consternation into the community at the latter end of last year and the beginning of this, but restricted ourselves to such evidence as would tend to show whether the Police Force was in such a state of organised efficiency as to successfully cope with heinous crimes following in quick succession.'

In a nutshell, they concluded that the Police Force was not.

Among their many comments and findings, the Commissioners concluded that:

- Inexperienced officers and men were 'responsible to a very great extent for the absolute and apparently helpless inability of the force to discover the perpetrators of the diabolical outrages that have lately taken place at Gatton, Oxley, and Woolloongabba, as well as the enormous number of crimes of a more or less serious nature which have come before the Commissioners as not having been traced to the guilty parties';
- 'Sufficiently exhaustive inquiry and investigation were not made in every instance as regards suspects';
- There was 'an appalling lack of action at Gatton and Oxley because it was holiday time';
- 'Some members of the police have a very imperfect comprehension of their duty to the public';
- The Chief Inspector was 'out of touch with his duties' and had 'outlasted his usefulness'…

The Commission also addressed such matters as superannuation, pay and allowances, promotion and transfer, barracks accommodation, defaulters' sheets, inquiries into misconduct, fines and punishments, and a range of issues to attract men to the service. They proposed a substantial increase in the number of officers and men in the police force; and the removal of certain officers and the promotion of certain others.

In summary, the Commissioners had some strong things to say about police red tape, incompetence, and the way the force was being run, and particularly they condemned the 'lack of cohesion and efficient organisation in coping with serious crimes'.

And they ended: 'If this Commission did nothing more than remove some of the stumbling blocks, which have so interfered with the discovery of crime, it would deserve well of the Country.'

The Queensland Criminal Code 1899

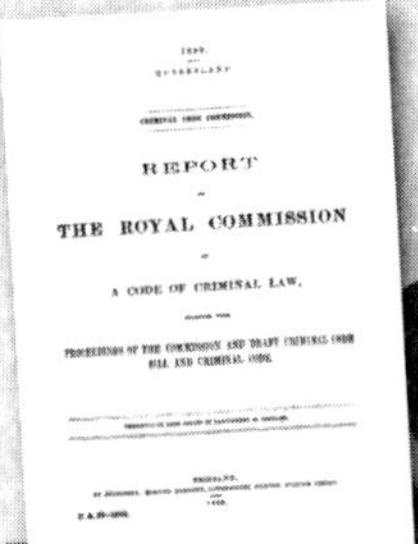

REPORT

THE ROYAL COMMISSION

A CODE OF CRIMINAL LAW,

SIR Samuel Griffith served Queensland with distinction as Premier (1883-1888), Chief Justice of the Supreme Court of Queensland (1893-1903), and first Chief Justice of the High Court of Australia (1903-19). His enduring legacy to criminal law in Queensland, however, is his drafting of the long-surviving *Queensland Criminal Code of 1899*.

An explanatory letter to the Attorney-General in 1897 was attached to his first draft. As Chief Justice, Griffith pointed out that the existing criminal law of Queensland, quite apart from Imperial Acts, was in something of a mess, being scattered throughout nearly 250 statutes, not to mention common law principles which also applied. His draft Code was a massive undertaking, containing 733 sections, comprehensively covering issues of procedure, criminal responsibility, offences and defences.

He invested an 'extraordinary amount of laborious care' into the task, to the extent that his 1899 Code still remains in force in Queensland, although with changes being made 100 years later, in 1997 and 2000, to reflect revolutionary societal and cultural changes since the 1960s.

Fragments from the FILES of FELONS

1898. IN the early morning hours of 9 January, the sergeant of police at Charleville was called to investigate a disturbance out of town. In the tent of Henry Hasted, he found the man hiding under a bed, choking, with his throat cut by his own hand. On the bed was his slaughtered wife. The court was later told that the couple had had a violent argument over the wife's extramartial mischief and Hasted, no longer able to tolerate her constant taunting, had taken a double-barrelled shotgun and blown off her head. Throughout his long gaol term on St Helena, Hasted required constant medical treatment for the damage he had done in slashing his own throat back in Charleville.

1899. NEDDY, an aboriginal stockman at Arabury Station via Roma, killed another aboriginal, Tony, during a 'trial of skill' contest. He admitted throwing six boomerangs – but a seventh smashed Tony's skull – and earned for Neddy three years for manslaughter.

1899. BILLY Broom was hanged in June for murdering 13-year-old Mary Le Blowitz near Childers. Mary had disappeared late on 24 December, after the blacktracker had afternoon tea with the family. Over several days, with police and neighbours in tow, the blacktracker led search parties in the opposite direction to where the decomposed body was later found. Broom's apparent deception, and hidden bloodstained clothing and knife, brought about his downfall – although on the gallows he strenuously denied the crime and named whom he believed was the true killer.

The fake suicide

Charles Beckman was a man on the run in January 1901. He knew that police were looking for him in relation to the disappearance of his prospecting mate, Alfred Anderson. In mid-January, police issued a warrant for his arrest; they knew, at least, that he had Anderson's horses. He was spotted from time to time in the Bowen area, but he had managed to elude his pursuers.

Beckman devised a scheme to throw the police off his trail. On the night of Friday 25 January, he left some of his belongings and a suicide note at the end of the Bowen pier. In the note, he confessed that he had accidentally killed Anderson and buried him near Gipsy Creek. His anguish was such, he claimed, that he had decided to end it all by drowning himself. The note was found early next morning by a wharf labourer.

Police dragged the jetty's surrounds, but they found no trace of Beckman's body. They suspected that the episode was probably 'a ruse', and their hunt for the suspect continued.

A week later Beckman was located by native trackers in his camp deep in scrub four miles north of Bowen.

Beckman later told his story to the arresting police:

"On 16 November 1900, Anderson and I left our camp in the morning. Anderson was carrying a double-barrelled gun. We travelled to the head of Gipsy Creek. When returning, the country was very, very rough and Anderson, not being accustomed to rough country, I took the gun from him. We travelled some distance down the creek, when Anderson tripped and fell.

BOWEN, January 28.

Last Saturday morning a wharfinger named Wilson found on the outer end of the jetty a swag, gun, and a letter, purporting to be from Beckman, the man connected with the disappearance of the missing man Anderson. The letter was written in pencil, and stated that Anderson was accidentally shot dead from behind, while both were proceeding up Gipsy Hill Creek, and that he buried him (indicating the position), and that, being weary of continual hiding, he determined to commit suicide. Dragging operations up to the present have had no result. The police have proceeded to the spot indicated for the purpose of exhuming Anderson's body. The general belief, however, is that the affair is a ruse on Beckman's part.

The Queenslander, 12 February 1901

I laughed at him... We only travelled a few yards when *I* then tripped and fell. The stock of the gun struck the rocks, which caused it to explode, striking Anderson in the back of the head and killing him instantly. He was only two or three feet from me at the time. I was nearly mad at what had occurred. I went to our camp and got a bag and covered the body with it. I remained with the body all night and buried it in the creek. I then got the horses and cleared out."

SEVERAL days later, Beckman led police to the site. Anderson's bones were discovered in the creek under a bag covered with stones. The next day, the remains were taken to Bowen where they were examined by doctors.

Suicide note admission aside, when Beckman was brought to trial in Townsville in early March for the murder of Anderson, the medical evidence was strong: the victim had *not* died from a gunshot wound – it would have been impossible for a gunshot to break the skull into so many pieces. More likely, said the doctors, the skull had been smashed by a large stone dropped from a height or, more probably, by a tomahawk or similar weapon.

Why did Beckman commit the crime? One view suggested that evidence presented might have led the jury to believe that the pair had been engaged in a homosexual relationship for about six years, and that 'a lovers' quarrel' probably led to the 26-year-old's untimely death.

Found guilty and sentenced to death by hanging, Beckman, aged 35 and still proclaiming his innocence, was transported by coastal steamer to Brisbane where his execution was carried out on 13 May 1901. ■

Fragments from the FILES of FELONS

1900. OLD Alfred Burnstead's murder was a callous and senseless affair. It happened on 25 December in Ayr.

Shortly after Christmas dinner, three kanaka plantation workers took a walk across the local creek, carrying tomahawks. As they approached the house of old Alfred, one of the kanakas, Wanti *(pictured)*, said to his companions: "You two fellows stop here. Me go killem old man."

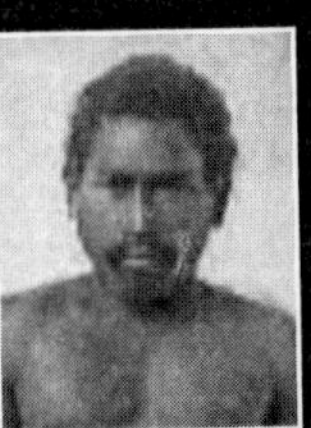

"Good day," said Wanti as he approached the old man sitting on a bed outside the door.

"Good day," replied Burnstead.

In conversation, the kanaka walked behind the old man and struck a blow to his neck with his tomahawk. When Burnstead fell to the floor, Wanti battered him further.

In turn the other two kanakas, Neagh and Bowlea, then wielded their weapons on the lifeless body.

When arrested two days later, Bowlea was asked why they took the old man's life: "We altogether kill him for nothing."

He continued: "Wanti killed him first time, Neagh kill him second time, me kill him last time. He dead finish."

A jury later found the South Sea Islanders guilty of murder and all three were sentenced to death.

Executive Council commuted the life sentences of Neagh and Bowlea to life in prison, after all, it was argued, a person cannot be murdered three times.

Wanti was hanged in Brisbane at Boggo Road on 27 May 1901. On the scaffold 'his initial nonchalance forsook him as the noose was being fixed, and he wailed dismally to the end'.

The jockey who sought revenge

ROCKHAMPTON RACES.

(By Telegraph from Our Correspondent.)
ROCKHAMPTON, August 6.

The Rockhampton Jockey Club races held on Saturday were fairly successful, the profits amounting to about £30.

The August Handicap resulted as follows:—Glendennon, 1; Barcoo, 2; Frilette, 3. Won easily. Time, 1min. 46½sec.

Glendegnon and the jockey Jack Smith were disqualified during the pleasure of the stewards, on account of the suspicious running of Glendennon in a previous race.

The Queenslander, 11 August 1900

The above newspaper clipping, revealing the disqualification of well-known Rockhampton trainer-jockey Jack Smith in August 1900, foreshadowed an incident that would deliver even more sensational news less than a month later.

Jack Smith was a respected licenced trainer and jockey, who from time to time was known to get up to a few 'tricks' with his mounts.

At an RJC race meeting in early August 1900, Smith rode the favourite, Glendennon – and it ran a poor third. At the next meeting, Glendennon came from behind to win a more lucrative purse by two lengths. Stewards were suspicious and an inquiry was held into the earlier race. The outcome: Smith was disqualified as a trainer and jockey. Although he twice appealed the decision, the suspension stood.

The RJC committee members met on 4 September to determine the length of the disqualification. Later, on the footpath outside the club secretary's office, Smith was told of the committee's decision – six months, a penalty which greatly angered him.

"Right," he responded. "I'll shoot the lot of you!" His remark was taken in jest.

Later that day, Smith turned up at the Union Hotel where he discussed his disqualification with a racing enthusiast, local dentist William Ross. Smith asked if Ross knew the address of one of the committee members. He didn't – and when Smith produced a revolver and repeated his threat to shoot the committee members, Ross wrestled the gun from him and told him to go away and rethink the consequences of such anger.

But when Smith left the hotel, he called a hansom cab and asked to be driven to the local gunsmith, where he purchased a second revolver and cartridges.

Back in the cab, he asked to be taken to the residence of RJC committeeman Arthur Headrick. No one was home.

He asked the cab driver to take him to the homes of committee members Symes or Bolton. Neither Smith nor the cab driver knew the addresses.

"Well, take me to John Henderson's home at Athelstane Range," said Smith.

When they arrived at Henderson's home, the driver was told to go to the front door and tell Henderson that there was someone in the cab who wished to talk to him.

At the cab, Smith identified himself to Henderson and asked him if he would lift the disqualification. When Henderson replied that there was nothing he could do, Smith produced his revolver and responded: "Then I will shoot you!" And he did.

As Henderson staggered back to the house, bleeding from the stomach, his assailant ran off. It took several weeks for Henderson to recover.

POLICE scoured the district for Smith. Wharves and roads were watched, as was the only railway line out of Rockhampton, to Longreach.

The assailant eluded capture for over a year until an alert constable at Urandangi, in far western Queensland, having recognised the fugitive from his description in the *Police Gazette,* arrested him on 2 February 1902.

Jack Smith was tried before Justice Power at Rockhampton Supreme Court on 20 August 1902, found guilty of attempting to kill John Henderson, and sentenced to 12 years hard labour. He was released after nine years. ■

ONE evening in 1911, Mrs Henderson answered a knock at her front door. She was stunned to find Jack Smith standing there. A few weeks earlier, Smith had been released from St Helena Island, where he had worked at the prison tending livestock. Smith had returned to Rockhampton, and he had come to apologise to John Henderson, he said.

Later, on 19 May 1911, at an executive meeting of the RJC, Jack Smith's training licence was reinstated. The motion had been seconded by John Henderson.

1900. DURING a spear fight between two Aborigines, Tommy and Redcap, one of the weapons, thrown by Tommy, glanced off a tree and killed an Aboriginal child named Minnie who was standing nearby. Both men were sentenced to death, commuted to seven years in prison.

1901. JOHN Reubens *(left)* had evicted his live-in lover Fanny Hardwick and daughter. In June he wanted her back, visiting her at the Rockhampton boarding house where she was living with her young daughter and her mother – and a new lover Charley Price. Refusing to return, Fanny was repeatedly stabbed by Reubens, a murder witnessed by the daughter and two others. Reubens was executed at Boggo Road on 30 September 1901.

1901

BROWN

DAVID BROWN

Crime: **MURDER**

Location: **CHARTERS TOWERS**

Penalty: **DEATH**

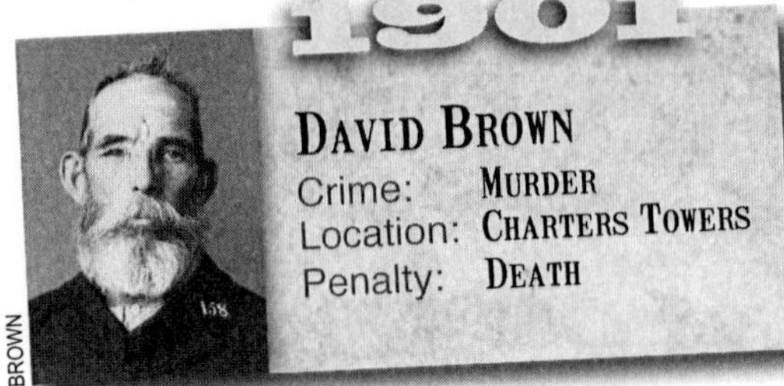

Bullets in the boardroom

In 1901, Charters Towers was Queensland's second largest city with a population of 30 000, many of whom were employed by the rich gold mining companies. Over 100 such companies were registered on the field and most of them were paying huge dividends on the Stock Exchange.

The Charters Towers Pyrites Company was an exception, however. The works had prospered until the advent of the cyanide process for gold extraction. Then there was a distinct slump in company profits.

Early in July 1901, in an attempt to pull the company out of its financial difficulties, the directors decided on a policy of retrenchment and cost-cutting, and an extraordinary meeting of shareholders was called for 10 July to announce such measures.

It was 8 o'clock on the evening of 10 July and about a dozen directors and shareholders had gathered in offices in the Australian Bank of Commerce in Mosman Street. The participants in the unfolding drama of that night were seated around a large conference table in the boardroom. At the head of the table, the chairman was Graham Haygarth, a popular town identity and well known in financial, racing and social circles.

The manager of the company's extraction works was also there. David Brown worked hard for the company, had sunk a considerable sum of his own earnings into the business and, as a result, was himself now in financial difficulties.

Brown was seething with anger that night. Earlier in the day, he had received a letter from the company advising him that his salary was to be reduced

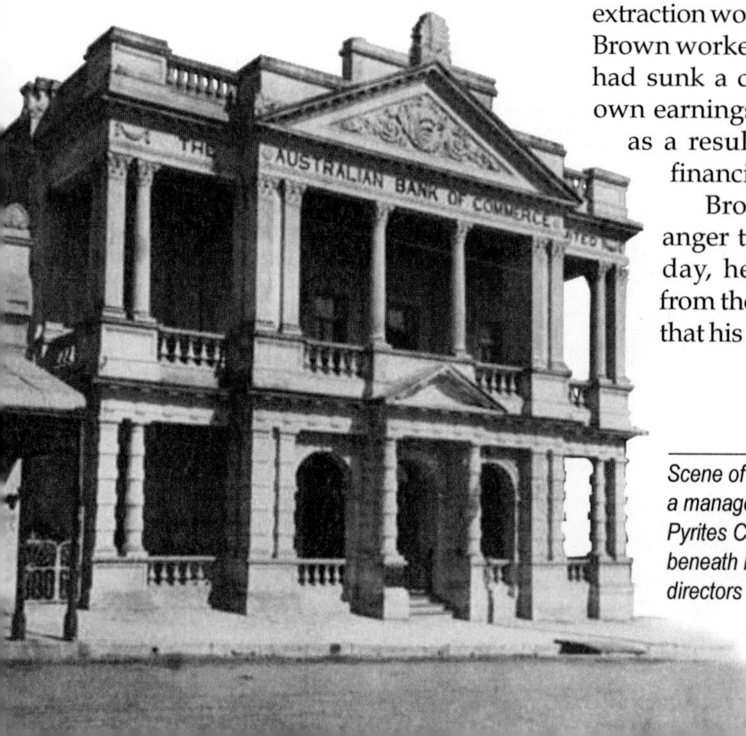

Scene of the boardroom meeting where a manager of the Charters Towers Pyrites Company pulled a gun from beneath his coat at the gathering of directors and shareholders in July 1901

from a weekly £8 to £6.

Brown took the letter from his pocket and threw it on the table.

"Before any other business is done at this meeting, I want to know what this letter means," he said. "I received it today from the Secretary, informing me that my wages have been reduced by £2 a week!"

"The company's retrenching," replied Jim Matchett from across the table, "and the retrenchments should have taken place years ago."

"I want to see the minutes of the Directors' Meeting," demanded Brown.

Chairman Haygarth responded. "This meeting is called for a special purpose and your letter cannot be discussed."

"You will give me the minutes!"

"I cannot produce them as your request is out of order," Haygarth repeated.

"By God, I'll show you!"

BROWN rose to his feet.

"I don't give a damn whether my request is of out of order or not. I came here as a shareholder to see those bloody minutes and I will see them in spite of you or anyone else."

"You are out of order. Please sit down and keep quiet," said the chairman.

Brown, getting noticeably angrier by the word, snarled at Haygarth: "You may be a bloody good handicapper at the races but you won't handicap me..."

He was wearing a long black coat at the time. He took one step back from the table, unbuttoning his coat as he did so, and pulled out a 16-inch Colt revolver.

"Brown, Brown, for God's sake!" yelled three or four men at once. "What are you doing?"

"I ask you for the last time to produce those minutes!" He waved the gun in the direction of the chairman.

Haygarth, always a plucky little man, seemed not the least intimidated by Brown's demonstration. He remained seated in his chair at the head of the table, shuffling the papers before him and taking no particular notice of the man menacingly waving the revolver.

"Look, Brown," said someone, "there is no man working against you."

"Haygarth, I ask you for the last time, to produce those minutes..."

In a fury at the little man's apparent lack of interest in his demands, Brown exploded: "By God, I'll show you..."

He raised the revolver, rested its long barrel on his left hand, pointing it at Haygarth – and shot him.

Haygarth half stood and then fell to the floor with blood pouring from his ear. He was dead.

Someone shouted: "Clear out!", and there ensued a wild stampede. Panic-stricken directors and stockholders alike made a dash for the doors – all except old Jimmy Matchett who was crippled with sciatica and just couldn't get moving fast enough. Matchett later recalled his ordeal:

> I remained sitting there by myself. There was some smoke coming from the revolver and Brown, pointing it at me, clicked the trigger once or twice. [In fact, the police later found the Colt had two empty chambers.] I said to him, 'Do you know what you're doing?' He didn't reply. He lowered the gun and walked down to a chair at the far end of the table.

He sat down and put the muzzle of the gun to his throat. Taking a deep breath, he fired, the bullet going in under his chin. He sat there, his left hand over his face, with blood gushing out and down his arm…

Brown had made an effort to blow his own brains out but the bullet had passed through the roof of his mouth and exited between his eyes, just above the nose.

The local ambulance was called and Brown was taken to hospital where, after lingering between life and death for some weeks, he finally recovered.

While there, Brown, a widower, was married to his mistress, by whom he already had several children. As a contemporary newspaper had earlier reported, his new wife, who was 'in a delicate and interesting condition, never recovered from the shock of the boardroom shooting, and almost immediately died'.

Brown was arrested in hospital and brought to trial some months later, protesting that he remembered nothing of the shooting since he had been drinking heavily at the time, a fact denied by those present on the night.

The jury returned a verdict of wilful murder. The judge read him a severe homily upon the enormity of his crime and, on 7 November 1901, sentenced Brown to death. ■

The Execution

AT 8 o'clock on the morning of 9 December 1901, the bell at Brisbane's Boggo Road Gaol began to toll as David Brown was led from his cell to the scaffold.

Weak, emaciated, and finding it difficult to speak because of the damage caused to his palate by his own hand that fateful night, his last words were: "…Now unto God I commend my soul, and truly hope that I will meet my maker in the next world. Oh, Lord, have mercy on my children and protect them in this world and in the world to come…"

And then came the sudden drop. A witness described the final moments.

'The authorities let the body hang for some twelve minutes, when all that remained of Brown was lowered into the rude wooden shell that the Government allows as the final shelter of the doomed.

When the hangman stooped to undo the noose from around the neck of the body in the coffin, he was compelled to raise, to some little degree, the front flap of the white cap which had been placed over Brown's face prior to the drop. It had been noticed previously by those down below that the flap was blood-stained. Most of us, naturally enough, imagined that the blood was from Brown's self-inflicted wound. But it was not. The blood came from the wound in his neck which the hangman's rope had caused. The glimpse that was given to the witnesses present was sufficient to show that Brown's throat had been severely lacerated by the cruel rope which had cut deep into his neck.

It was only a glimpse that we got of the gruesome sight, and when the attendant warders noticed that the wound had been observed, two of them came forward and diligently explained that the blood on the cap was from the self-inflicted wound.

We knew better.'

The railway rascals

As the train sped through the Victorian countryside on that day in 1896, Patrick Dwyer, a passenger, saw something that made him shout out in horror. The train was brought to a halt and a white-faced Dwyer reported that he had seen a man topple out of an open door as the carriage wobbled violently in taking a corner. The door had clearly been left open by a negligent porter or passenger, he said.

A frantic search was made back along the line and Dwyer's terrible story was proved to be all too true. Lying beside the line covered in dirt and with his clothes in ribbons was a James Harris.

The saddest fact of all was that the fall had paralysed Harris from the hips down. He had been 'ruined for life' and doctors had no trouble in testifying to that all-too-obvious fact.

When Harris sued the Victorian Railways for negligence, a sympathetic Court awarded the victim hefty damages for those days – £1000. Who could begrudge the poor fellow the money when the remaining years of his life had been so irreparably ruined?

Soon after the compensation had been paid, key witness Pat Dwyer and the tragic victim, James Harris, got together – to split the £1000, and to congratulate each other on the scam they had carried off so successfully.

Indeed, they pulled the same stunt in South Australia one year later for £400, in Western Australia in 1898 for £650, in New South Wales in 1899 for £1750. Then they moved to Queensland and, on a train out of Toowoomba on New Year's eve 1901, they tried again – and presented the Queensland Railways with a writ for £10 000!

But, this time, the pair's luck had finally deserted them. While the poor

For five years, from 1896 to 1901, Campbell and Henderson would 'fall out of trains' around Australia – and handsomely sue the colonial governments for negligence.

paralysed victim (now calling himself John Campbell) lay in Toowoomba Hospital, a newspaper in northern New South Wales carried the story of the accident and it was spotted by a visiting Perth doctor who had been involved in the Western Australian case. His letter to the Queensland authorities started a chain reaction – and railway authorities throughout Australia soon began comparing notes.

In the end, on a stretcher, Campbell found himself in Court where he continued to feign paralysis – until he was sentenced to 10 years on St Helena, a shock which apparently cured his ailment.

His partner James Henderson had taken flight, only to be picked up in Sydney and sent back to Brisbane where he, too, received ten years on St Helena Island for his wickedness. ■

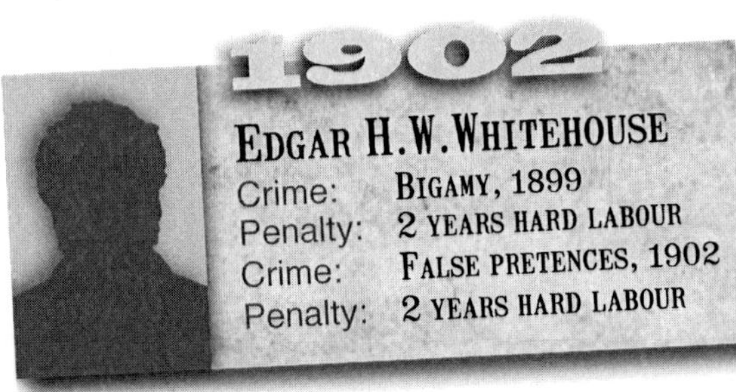

"The very man I wanted to meet"

Over thirty years, Canadian-born Edgar Whitehouse would gain a reputation as a conman-trickster *par excellence*.

In the 1890s he had spent time in a New South Wales gaol for false pretences and embezzlement and, on another occasion in an insurance company fraud, had evaded imprisonment by outlawyering the lawyers. Indeed, in Queensland he almost succeeded again in bluffing his way out of bigamy charges but ended up on St Helena Island in 1899 serving a two-year sentence.

Shortly after his release, the sweet-talking Whitehouse interviewed the Queensland Premier, representing himself as a journalist from the *Liverpool Mercury*, who had been sent to Queensland to write a story on the sugar industry.

At Whitehouse's request, the Premier presented him with a free railway pass to Bundaberg where he proceeded to 'take all Bundaberg by the nose, procuring a press camera in a local store under false pretences, and had all the swanks and swankesses of the district posing in the gardens of their homes, in the ballrooms by flashlight, and in the sugar works of the district, for pictures for the English journal' – and all the time, it was later revealed, the camera was entirely empty of plates or film!

One of those 'photographed' was the local magistrate who, after playing cards with the handsome and distinguished young visitor the night before, had to send him for trial the following morning, on a charge of being an imposter and a swindler.

The Bundaberg episode cost Whitehouse another two years of his life on St Helena Island. There he became the organist and choir master for the visiting chaplain and spent the rest of his spare time on the island writing a novel.

In one of his most impudent swindles, he once impersonated a Congregational parson in Gympie. The rascal had stolen the papers of a recently deceased minister acquaintance and presented himself to the people of Gympie...

As one contemporary account said: 'He was smart, small, bearded and an immensely pleasant man, and the congregation welcomed him with open arms – especially the feminine section of it. The girls lost their heads and hearts on every side to the charming new preacher and he reigned as a social, as well as an ecclesiastical success, admired, feted and trusted by the cream of Gympie society until the crash came.'

One of the little swindler's often-used sayings was: 'The very man I wanted to meet', on being introduced to a fresh victim. In the months after Whitehouse departed, if one wanted the cold shoulder or the glassy stare 'in swell Gympie circles' where he had left a trail of disappointed matrons, heartbroken daughters and angry fathers behind him, one needed but to greet someone with: 'The very man I wanted to meet...'

In 1909 Whitehouse served three years in Hobart Gaol on false pretences.

After World War 1, he reappeared in London as a bogus Australian baronet where in 1919 he organised a successful charity ball – but was subsequently arrested and charged with 'unlawfully wearing an officer's uniform', a charge which found him being detained at His Majesty's pleasure for yet another year of his life. ■

For master conman Edgar H.W. Whitehouse, Gympie in the early 1900s was a town ripe for picking.

1902

PATRICK KENNIFF
Crime: MURDER
Location: UPPER WARREGO
Penalty: DEATH

JAMES KENNIFF
Crime: MURDER
Location: UPPER WARREGO
Penalty: PENAL SERVITUDE FOR LIFE

The last of the bushrangers

A crime that fired public imagination

THE murder of police constable George Boyle and cattle station manager Albert Dahlke, whose incinerated remains were found in a gorge of the Carnarvon Range in 1902, caused a sensation such as few Queensland crimes ever created.

On trial for the murders – and convicted – were brothers James and Patrick Kenniff.

As one commentator summarised the affair:

'Public interest was aroused to an extraordinary pitch; sides were taken, and the whole community was divided into factions; judges of the Supreme Court wrangled publicly on the Bench; meetings of protest against the execution of the criminals were held, and largely attended; while petitions sent to Brisbane from all over the state for the reprieve of the condemned men were rejected....

And, quite apart from sympathy for the offenders, the wild setting of the crime; the struggle of a family of nomads against constituted authority; the vendetta between one of the brothers and one of the victims; and the escape of the suspected men, their complete disappearance for three months in the bush, and their capture only after a great body of police and nearly all the residents of the district were engaged in the chase – all these features of the crime appealed powerfully to the public imagination.' [1]

Patrick and James Kenniff were 'wild colonial' brothers, who already had convictions for stock stealing in northern New South Wales before the family moved to a leased property in the Upper Warrego ranges, north of Mitchell, in 1893.

There they worked at the usual bush occupations, as stockmen, kangaroo shooters, horse-breakers - and, as a sideline, began stealing cattle and horses from neighbouring properties.

The pair clashed constantly with police over their activities. Indeed, in 1895 both bothers spent time on St Helena Island for horse stealing - Patrick a four-year term, Jimmy three years.

When they returned to the ranges after their gaol terms, the reception they received from the graziers was a cool one - even more so when the brothers took to carrying Winchesters and Colt revolvers, which they kept in holsters inside their shirts; and more stock began to disappear.

The complaints of neighbours led the government to establish a police station on the Upper Warrego and to terminate the Kenniffs' lease in 1901.

Forced to live like nomads, the Kenniffs shifted their base across the Great Dividing Range to Lethbridge's Pocket, in the wild Carnarvon Ranges, a most convenient spot for hiding stolen stock. And the brothers became more openly belligerent, as they rode armed throughout the district.

By Easter 1902 the situation reached a dramatic climax.

The crime

ON Good Friday, 28 March 1902, Constable George Doyle of the Upper Warrego Police Station set out for Lethbridge's Pocket. He was armed with a warrant for the arrest of Patrick and James Kenniff, for the theft of a bay pony, the property of a resident in nearby Springsure.

Accompanying Constable Doyle were Christian Dahlke, manager of Carnarvon Station, who had previous unfavourable dealings with the Kenniffs, and aboriginal tracker, Sam Johnson.

Johnson would later play a vital role in the conviction of the Kenniffs in the Brisbane Supreme Court.

On Easter Sunday morning, 1902, the police party surprised the Kenniffs at Lethbridge's Pocket. Patrick Kenniff escaped but after a brief chase they took James into custody.

Sam Johnson was sent back to collect handcuffs from the pack horses tethered some 200 yards away and, while doing so, he heard a shot. Through the bush he saw Dahlke fall from his horse. Four more shots... and as he ran back to assist, suddenly the Kenniff brothers were galloping towards him. Johnson fled down a slope and into the scrub. He later rode 12 miles to an outstation to raise the alarm.

Returning to the site with a Carnarvon man, he found a hat and two packs, along with Dahlke's horse, grazing nearby, its neck and saddle stained with blood.

A subsequent search revealed evidence that a gun fight had occurred at the site. Constable Doyle's grazing horse was located with the saddle bags stuffed with charcoal, later

Murdered police constable **George Doyle** was the officer-in-charge of the three-man Upper Warrego Police Station. He and Albert Dahlke were shot, incinerated, and their ashes stuffed in saddle bags by the Kenniff brothers.

Murdered 27-year-old **Albert Christian Dahlke**, as newly appointed manager of Carnarvon station, was determined to put an end to cattle- and horse-stealing. He was 'a most trusted and efficient employee'.

Tracker **Sam Johnson** was the sole surviving witness to the events at Lethbridge's Pocket. His evidence helped convict the Kenniffs, despite the defence urging the jury not to convict on the 'evidence of one blackfellow'.

Seeds of hatred

BAD blood between the Kenniffs and the manager of the Carnarvon Station, Albert Dahlke, developed into an intense hostility at a country race meeting a few months before Dahlke's murder. Itching for a fight, James Kenniff tried to fell Dahlke with a 'king hit' but the agile manager soon reduced Kenniff to 'a battered wreck'. Kenniff skulked away, muttering foul threats as to what would happen in the future... an incident not forgotten at the outlaw's trial a year later.

identified as burnt human remains, and bits of metal and buttons from Doyle's and Dahlke's clothing.

Elsewhere in the Pocket, a few days later, searchers found a large flat rock which had recently been splintered by the heat of a very fierce fire. On the rock were blood stains, and 'several fragments of human bone, a human tooth, a shirt button' and other items. And nearby, two partly burnt skulls.

It became apparent that the Kenniffs had burnt the bodies of Doyle and Dahlke and intended to dispose of their ashes in an attempt to conceal the crime.

Capture and trial

A £1000 reward was offered for the capture of the Kenniffs. A party of 50 police and 15 aboriginal trackers searched for three months until they found the brothers at what has become known as Arrest Creek, just south of the town of Mitchell.

Far from the final scene being the show-down that many people expected, the Kenniffs surrendered to the police without a fight.

The brothers were transported to Rockhampton, where they were committed for trial at the Supreme Court in Brisbane, for the wilful murder of Constable George Doyle and Albert Dahlke.

In November 1902, both Patrick and James Kenniff were convicted of murder and sentenced to death by hanging. ■

Amid public outcry

EVEN before the murder trial of the Kenniff brothers, there was considerable public sympathy for them.

According to historian Grenfell Heap[2], 'this was partly a manifestation of public discontent' due to widespread unemployment, an ongoing drought, and a revival of the old antipathy between rich squatters and cockatoo farmers (such as the Kenniffs)'.

Chief Justice Sir Samuel Griffith presided over the Kenniffs' trial in Brisbane. Found guilty of wilful murder, both prisoners were sentenced to death but execution was deferred, pending an appeal.

The appeal, financed through funds contributed by supporters, was dismissed by a full bench of the Supreme Court; the only dissenter was Mr Justice Real who was not convinced of James's guilt.

Patrick was executed on 12 January 1903 and buried in South Brisbane cemetery with Catholic rites. James was spared and given life imprisonment.

Sympathy for the Kenniffs was greatly aroused by the spread of two popular ballads at the time, 'The Kenniffs' and 'The Hanging of Paddy Kenniff'.'

Heap concludes: 'Exacerbated by sectarianism, public controversy over this case gave a strong impetus to moves for the abolition of capital punishment in Queensland.'

SOW TOO LOW

One killing was not enough

Anti-kanaka sentiment

LATE in the 1800s, Mackay had become one of Queensland's major sugar growing centres. The industry was founded on cheap South Sea Island labour, recruited through a dubious practice known as 'blackbirding', where Islanders were often kidnapped to work on the plantations.

By the turn of the century, Mackay had earned an unenviable reputation for the number and variety of crimes committed in the district, and a series of murders remained unsolved. It was easy to blame the situation on the non-white population.

Advocates of a 'white Australia' policy were quick to note the unrest in places such as Mackay. The style of journalism featured in such newspapers as the *Truth* – high pitched, sensational, racist and melodramatic – helped keep the issue at fever pitch. 'The Mackay district has turned into a plague spot,' seethed *Truth* in 1902. 'Opium, grog, vice, crime, murder – these are the normal characteristics of the place. Hundreds of coloured aliens of indefinite breed, Chinese-cum-Cingalese-cum-Kanakas swarm everywhere. Vice of the most awful description prevails...'

It was in such a social climate that the crime of kanaka Sow Too Low in 1902 helped those in favour of a strict immigration policy to reinforce their case for the exclusion of those of non-European descent...

On 26 October 1902, the body of twelve-year-old Alice Gunning, the stepdaughter of a selector at Habana, some 15 miles north-west of Mackay, was discovered under bushes beside the road.

Within an hour of the discovery, local police had rounded up the district's 90 kanakas. One man was missing, an Islander named Sow Too Low. He was known to police: one week earlier they had received a report that the girl had been intercepted on The Leap Road and threatened by this same knife-waving kanaka.

With the help of native trackers, police at once set about locating Sow Too Low. The Islander's humpy was kept under surveillance and this was rewarded that night when the suspect appeared.

His clothes were blood-marked but this, he claimed, was the blood of a possum that he and two other Islanders had killed earlier. The two, when interviewed, denied that they had been on any possum hunt.

Sow Too Low was detained and next morning confessed to the murder.

He took a police party to the place where he had waylaid the girl as she was returning from mass that morning. He had stopped the girl's horse by grabbing hold of the reins. He explained that he 'intended to molest the girl in a certain way and to this end put a question to her'. She resented his conduct and called him 'a dirty blackfellow'. This so enraged him that he struck her on the head with a stone, stunning her, so that she slumped forward on the horse. Leading the horse to a spot further up the road, he lifted the unconscious girl down from the saddle and carried her to the site where the body was later found. There he ended her life with a large stone.

"Me been killum little girl," he later admitted. "I wantum die; suppose big fella want me die, I die. Suppose he want me live, I live and go alonga island."

As to why he had killed the girl, he replied: "Head belonga me no good."

But, as Fate would have it, Sow Too Low would *not* hang for the murder of Alice Gunning.

The slaughter continues

THE prisoner was taken to Mackay Gaol to await his trial.

While in the exercise yard with other prisoners on 29 March 1903, Sow Too Low savagely attacked a white prisoner named John Martin, killing him instantly with a blow from an axe he was using.

The alarm was raised and the lockup-keeper, David Johnson, entered the yard.

A prisoner warned the warder that the Islander was armed, but Johnson brushed him aside and walked hurriedly to the body of the prisoner on the ground.

While he was stooping over the body, the murderer, who had been hiding behind a wood heap, rushed out and brought the axe down on the warder's head, killing him also.

The kanaka then turned on the

Warder David Johnston, murdered by Sow Too Low at the Mackay Lock-up in 1903

other prisoners who ran from the yard and locked themselves in their cells.

By this time, other warders had come running. After a violent struggle, Sow Too Low was overpowered.

ON 12 May, Sow Too Low faced Mr Justice Power and a jury in the Mackay Circuit Court. The triple slayer was found guilty of murdering warder David Johnson and sentenced to death although, with the blood of *three* people on his hands, an appointment with the hangman at Brisbane's Boggo Road gaol was inevitable. ■

NO, we're not wasting too much space on the departed Sow Too Low. He was a savage, straight from the lap of barbarism. The native appeared to have no idea of the sacredness or value of human life...

The barbarian told the Rev. Mr Calger that he had committed half a dozen murders on the island from whence he came [Malayta in the Solomons]. He added another three to his bloody tally during his residence in Queensland. How many more may he have committed during the years he has worked in the various sugar districts of Queensland we have no idea...

– *Truth*, 28 June 1903

Following the execution, the body of Sow Too Low was lowered into the coffin prior to burial in an isolated corner of South Brisbane cemetery.

– Illustration drawn on location by *Truth's* artist, 22 June 1903

The Execution

ON 22 June 1903, very little time was lost in the judicial removal of Sow Too Low. At 8 o'clock he walked straight upon the scaffold at Boggo Road in bare feet and then looked curiously about him. The hangman wasted no ceremony in strapping the prisoner's legs together below the knees.

It was recorded that the kanaka 'looked down several times and then cast his eyes up at the snakey-looking rope dangling from the beam above his head.'

The report continued…

> 'The noose was quickly settled about his bare throat, and then the little white bag was pulled down over his head. It was too small for the condemned man's head, but the length of the shield enabled it to cover the face effectively. It was no sooner fastened than the Sheriff gave the signal, the hangman stretched forth his brawny arm, seized the level, and pushed it forward. All that was mortal of Sow Too Low tumbled through the trapdoor. He came up with a jerk, and then his knees drew up to his breast convulsively twice, after which they stiffened out, and the body swung gently two-and-fro in the slight breeze from the open doorway. He hung for 15 minutes and then was lowered into the coffin and carted away.
>
> The job was done neatly, quickly and cleanly.'

Fragments from the FILES of FELONS

1903. THOMAS Tierney boarded the *Otter* at St Helena Island on 23 December 1902, having that day been released from the island prison. On board, he struck up a conversation with a Mr Halas who was returning from a day trip to Dunwich. Convinced that Tierney was intending 'in future to lead an honest life', Halas invited the ex-prisoner to spend a couple of weeks at his Annerley house until things got back to normal for him.

One week later, Halas unexpectedly walked in on Tierney who had broken in through the back door of the house he had locked while out shopping. Tierney ran off, with Halas in pursuit. When overtaken and handed over to police, he had £160 of Halas' jewellery in his pockets.

So it was back to St Helena for Tierney, to serve another two years in prison.

1903

Florence and Angus Macdonald

Crime: Murder
Location: Longreach
Penalty: Death commuted to life imprisonment

The Longreach Cinderella

In December 1903, at every railway station from Longreach to Rockhampton, small groups of angry people gathered to hurl abuse at the passing mail train. At its destination, the Stanley Street station in Rockhampton, the largest and angriest crowd of all had assembled – one man even carried a noose. Fearing trouble, police arranged for the train to bypass the platform and to continue on to Archer Park station. Here two special passengers were quickly whisked away to the nearby gaol. To most Queenslanders, Florence and Angus Macdonald were monsters beneath contempt.

SINCE 1899, following the death of her mother, young Grace Macdonald had been living in Brisbane with her aunt. She was excited when her father, Angus, sent for her in March 1903 to join him and his new wife Florence on their pastoral station, Urandah, near Longreach. Like most teenagers, she was looking forward to station life, mustering and horse riding.

But her life soon turned into a nightmare: she found herself working from dawn to dusk, scrubbing floors, milking goats, looking after two toddlers, sleeping on the floor, eating with the dogs, having no warm clothes in winter, and being viciously beaten. She was dressed in hessian. On one occasion, when caught drinking milk from the dogs' bucket, she was flogged and locked up in a small room for days, fed only on dry bread and water – a frequent punishment.

Between March and October of that year, few people saw Grace; she was never seen in town or in the buggy with the rest of the family.

By the end of October, Grace was dead. The doctor could not believe what he saw. She appeared to have

Left: *In 1903, Grace Macdonald was a happy and healthy 13-year-old living in Brisbane. All that would change within eight months.*

Right: *After her death, Grace Macdonald's body was buried in Longreach cemetery. Chains from a wool wagon were originally draped around the grave, symbolic of the child being tied up like a dog towards the end of her young life. The chains have since been removed.*

been starved, she had broken ribs and wrist, bones were protruding from her right arm, and pieces of skin had been torn from parts of her body. Large sores showed that she had crawled around on her hands and knees, too weak to walk. Stones were embedded in the wounds. Her sunken eyes were black and pus-filled.

The Macdonalds admitted to exposing the girl to extreme starvation, harsh physical brutality, ill-treatment and wilful neglect. To the law, it was murder.

And the motive? It was learned that Grace had been left £2000 and land by her mother but, if she should die before reaching 21 years of age, Angus Macdonald would be the beneficiary. Motive enough for slow and deliberate murder?

The Macdonalds' trial, held in Rockhampton, aroused massive public interest. Both of the accused were found guilty and sentenced to death. Neither expressed any remorse for the death of Grace, who had become known to the public as "The Longreach Cinderella".

When their sentences were commuted to life imprisonment, here was a fierce public backlash; many believed that Angus Macdonald had used friends in high places to gain political sympathy.

Angus served his term on St Helena Island. Inside the women's prison at Boggo Road gaol, Florence's file recorded her as a model prisoner and devoted Christian.

But the Queensland public had a long memory: another storm of criticism erupted when the pair was released fifteen years later. ■

Fragments from the FILES of FELONS

1902. IN March at Georgetown on the Gilbert River in far north Queensland, an Aborigine named Barney was speared to death by Joe and Old Man, in a dispute over Barney's female companion. The pair would later lead police to Barney's body, with three spear-heads in it, buried under an ant bed. Both were sentenced to death, commuted to life in prison.

1903. DURING the night of 31 August, two valuable copper plates were unscrewed and stolen from the Monitor gold crushing mill in Georgetown on the northern diggings.

On the following morning, police and a tracker were able to follow footprints along the river and into the scrub where they found the stolen plates in an old mine shaft 100 yards off the well-beaten track. The culprit had planned his night theft well (he thought), having left tell-tale white paper markers on a tree to show him where to turn off the path and to the shaft in moonlight.

That night, all the following day, and into the next night, two policemen hid in wait near the shaft in the hope the thief would return for his booty.

Their patience was rewarded around 1 a.m. on the second night, when the local Chinese baker Tommy Chin Mow turned up, cautiously looked around, climbed down the shaft, and reappeared with one of the plates. He fled when the police emerged from hiding, but surrendered when a shot was fired in the air.

"Me welly bad luck," he wailed.

In court, the Magistrate commended the police 'for the clever way they brought the case to a successful culmination'.

The Boonah publican

It was a Tuesday night in May 1904. A travelling circus was visiting the quiet little farming settlement of Boonah about 80 km south-west of Brisbane and among those who had come into town for the event were the O'Brien brothers and some of their rowdy friends who were working as road contractors outside the town.

The circus performance had ended some hours earlier and the group had been drinking quite heavily. At midnight, the men found themselves outside the Royal Exchange Hotel, on the corner of Park and High Streets, and, after banging on the closed door and demanding that the bar be opened for them, were informed by the 16-year-old son of the publican that the establishment was closed and that his father had gone to bed. They trudged off into the darkness.

Shortly afterwards, the men returned, once more sought admission, but were again refused entry, this time by the publican, Robert Denner.

A little while later, the group returned a third time, accompanying their demands for a drink by shaking the hotel door, threatening to break the windows, and screaming abuse at Denner and his wife.

In the hotel bedroom, Denner's wife persuaded her husband to let her go out, arguing that she would be more likely to quieten the group than he. Moments later Denner heard his wife calling. 'Robert! Robert! Murder! Murder!' she cried.

Denner leapt out of bed, grabbed a gun which he kept in the bedroom and rushed out into the passage. Down in the public bar, John O'Brien had his hands around Mrs Denner's neck and was forcing her to the floor.

'Leave her alone, you brute, you're going to murder the woman! Leave

Scene of the crime, the old Royal Exchange Hotel, Boonah

her go!' shouted Denner and he fired a warning shot into the ceiling. O'Brien lunged at him, grabbing the barrel of the rifle. The gun went off a second time and O'Brien fell to the floor. He died soon after.

IN the days that followed, while in the solitude of his cell awaiting trial, Robert Denner was able to contemplate the seriousness of his situation. It had all happened so quickly. He had taken over the Royal Exchange as licensee only three months earlier after coming from Western Australia and had made a great number of friends in the short time that he and his family had lived in Boonah. He had been under considerable provocation that night and had committed an act which would find him on trial for murder.

Three months later, a jury found Denner guilty of manslaughter with a strong recommendation for mercy.

The judge agreed with the jury's verdict but regretted that he was not able to deal leniently with the prisoner – that was for those who had the power of mercy and he would not be sorry to hear the Executive exercise those powers. But he had a duty to the community and inflicted a heavy sentence: five years imprisonment with hard labour.

Denner was released after two years, on 7 August 1906. ■

1903. THERE had been a house fire in Kent Street, Maryborough on 25 November. The next day, Robert Butterworth commented to his neighbour Nellie Coffey that 'it's not a bad money-making game for insurance having these fires…'

In the days that followed, this became a topic of conversation for Butterworth's wife Agnes and Nellie Coffey.

On 8 December, Agnes Butterworth proposed to Mrs Coffey: "Robert could burn down your house. Just pack up your boxes and he'll send them wherever you want them sent." And he'd do the job for only £3.

Nellie Coffey agreed. She packed her belongings and took them to the Butterworths' house.

But on the night of the planned fire, 9 December, she put her three children to bed and went over to the Butterworths' house, telling Butterworth that she was 'feeling nervous' and that she wanted the burning 'postponed until some future time'.

"No, it will be all right," he replied, and he accompanied her home. He began breaking up a cardboard box and a few pine boards.

"You'll need to take off that dress and put on a nightgown – it would then look as if you'd been in bed," he said. Nellie Coffey returned to the Butterworths' and changed.

Robert Butterworth entered shortly afterwards.

"Everything is all right. I've set it going with kerosene."

"My God," screamed Coffey. "My children! My children!"

With Butterworth following, she ran back to her house, where they removed the youngsters and took them back to Butterworths'. It was close to midnight.

Meanwhile, three young men were passing the Lennox Street house and, seeing the glow of fire, ran inside and extinguished the flames. Police would later find traces of five different fires in the house and the strong smell of kerosene.

At their trial in March 1904, the three conspirators were found guilty of arson: Robert Butterford was gaoled for five years; and his wife and Nellie Coffey two years each, to be freed after three months.

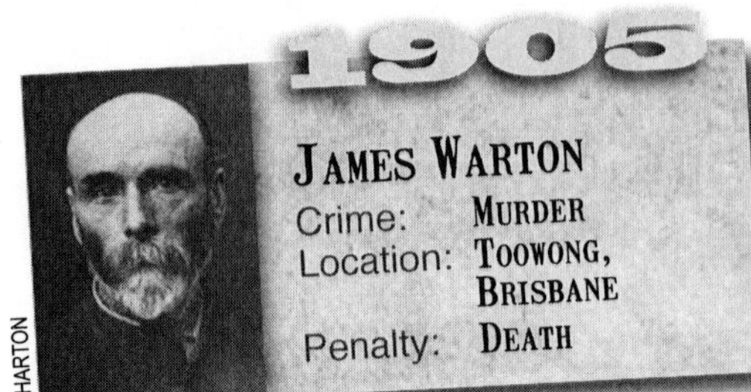

One crime too many

"That was a shot!" said Toowong storekeeper Edwin Richards. Shortly afterwards, he heard the cries of someone in distress. It was 7.45 on the night of 23 March 1905.

Richards ran outside, and across Moggill Road. There he saw a man stumbling along with blood running down his arm. He knew him; it was William Munday, a local family man. He helped the exhausted victim to the nearby surgery of Dr Samuel Hammond, who, by the light of his lamp, discovered a flesh wound to the arm but a more serious gunshot wound in the lower chest.

Police were summoned and a ambulance cab was soon rushing Munday to hospital, but not before the victim was able to tell them that he had been shot by a man in a white coat.

An arrest is made

THREE hours later, and already briefed on the details of the earlier shooting, Police Constable Hennessy was cycling along River Road [Coronation Drive] towards Toowong. When about 100 yards on the city side of the Regatta Hotel, he saw a man in a white coat walking along the footpath in the direction of the city. Hennessy turned his cycle around, and doubled back towards him.

Dismounting, he said: "I say, can you give me a match?"

The man handed him a box of matches and began walking away.

Scene of the Toowong Tragedy.

"Don't go. I want to speak to you."

Hennessy then noticed something under the man's coat: "What have you got there?"

"I will soon show you," he replied as he reached into his trousers pocket and pulled out a revolver.

The constable grabbed him by the hand and threw him to the ground, taking the revolver from him.

"You answer the description of a man we're looking for," said Hennessy as he handcuffed the suspect. He found a parcel under the man's coat. It contained a five-chambered revolver, with one empty chamber, recently discharged.

Crime and punishment

TWO days later, William Munday died from his wounds and a long line of horse-drawn carriages accompanied the hearse along spectator-lined streets to Toowong cemetery. The well-respected 41-year-old left a wife and five children, for whom a benevolent fund was later established.

From his hospital bed, Munday had described the events of the 23rd and identified James Warton whom police had taken to the bedside:

> Munday was walking from his Taringa residence to nearby Toowong that night to attend a masonic meeting. Near the High Street bridge, he saw a middle-aged man, bearded and wearing a white overcoat, step out into the moonlight from under the shadow of a tree.
>
> "Fork out what you have got, and be sharp about it," he said.
>
> Instead of complying, Munday attempted to brush him aside. The man drew back quickly, whipped out a revolver, fired, and made off as fast as he could.

At the trial in April, witnesses placed Warton in the area. John Harding, for example, heard the gun-shot, saw the flash some 130 yards distant, and hid behind a tree as a man in a white coat came running by in the darkness.

JAMES Warton was executed at Boggo Road Gaol. He was allowed to play hymns on the organ at the gaol in the days leading up to his hanging on 17 July 1905. On the scaffold his last words were: "I am truly sorry for the wrong and evil I have done, and now I hope I shall be forgiven"... and as the white cap was adjusted, he uttered: "Oh, my God! Oh, my God!" The force of the drop almost severed the head from the body, and death was instantaneous. ■ ▶

Fragments from the FILES of FELONS

1905. IN Brisbane Gaol at Boggo Road, the Solomon Island kanaka Charlie Gos Ano was finally made to realise his fate: he was to be put to death for the murder of a Portuguese man named Jack Parsons.

"How long it take – three hours?" he asked. It was his belief that death as atonement for his crime meant slow torture. But, assured that his hanging death would be immediate, he became resigned to his fate – and the barefooted kanaka plunged through the trapdoor at the Boggo Road scaffold at 8.02 a.m. on 17 April 1905.

Several months earlier, about 2.00 a.m. on 28 November, Charlie and his kanaka mate Harry had approached John Parsons' humpy at a camp in sugarcane country about a mile out of Ingham. They had given Parsons £1 three weeks earlier so that he could buy grog for them. Their persistent requests for the grog, or the return of their money, fell upon deaf ears.

On the morning of the murder, a fellow camper was woken at that early hour by a 'rustling' noise; he saw the three near Parsons' humpy, but fell back to sleep.

Parsons was found the next morning, his head in a pool of blood. He was quite dead, and close to the body was a tomahawk and a broken handle.

When Charlie was arrested, he confessed: "He cheat me and called me blackfellow. That why me cross and kill him. Me kill him with tomahawk. Me hit first time behind ear. Handle broke. Me then hit him cane-knife above ear. Me finish him alonga cane-knife."

At the trial in Townsville on 28 February 1905, Charlie was found guilty of wilful murder and sentenced to death; Harry was found not guilty and discharged.

1905. William Ohley was sentenced to three months hard labour for attempting suicide. He was caught swallowing the heads of 300 matches, at Warra near Miles.

James Wharton's long life of crime

A PULL of the lever at Boggo Road gallows in July 1905 ended the life of an habitual criminal.

James Wharton had arrived as a lad in Victoria from Ireland in 1855. By 1876, when he left for New Zealand, he had spent 18 of his 21 years in Victoria in prison – for such crimes as vagrancy, being illegally on premises, larceny, robbery under arms, receiving stolen property, and burglary. In gaol, he read and studied, becoming an authority on music and history.

"ill-tempered, malicious, destructive, cowardly and treacherous"

– Fellow prisoner's description of James Wharton, Lyttleton Gaol, NZ

Less than a fortnight after arriving in New Zealand, he was gaoled once more, serving four years for committing a string of burglaries.

Shortly after his release in February 1880, two houses in Dunedin were burnt to the ground.

From the first house, a number of items had been stolen (and later traced to Wharton); in the second, a young couple named Dewer and their baby were murdered and the house set alight.

Wharton (then known as Butler) was arrested for murder – only days earlier he had boasted to a detective that he 'could commit murder in such a way that nobody would be able to bring it home to him'.

The prisoner admirably conducted his own defence and showed great shrewdness in cross-examination. His speech in his defence lasted six hours. After three hours deliberation, the jury found him not guilty of murder – not because they thought him innocent, but because he had shown there was insufficient evidence to convict him. In the process, however, he had to admit to burglary and arson, and was gaoled for 18 years.

Back in Victoria in 1896 he was in prison once more – 10 years hard labour for house-breaking.

Wharton was later to write that, on his arrival in Brisbane in early 1905, aged sixty, 'half-starved, bewildered, despairing, my actions became those of a fool; my mind and will had become a remnant guided or misguided by unreasoning impulse'.

And it was under the influence of such an impulse that on 23 March 1905 Wharton had met and shot William Munday at Toowong.

"During his long career of crime, Warton proved himself to be a most unscrupulous scoundrel. He robbed everybody he could. One of his methods, according to a prominent Melbourne police officer, was to bail people up in the city late at night, poke a revolver in their faces, and make them shell out everything they had.

This clearly was his intention when he stuck up poor William Munday. Had the unfortunate victim 'disgorged on demand', Munday might have been alive today."

– *Truth*, 23 July 1905

Odd spot

JAMES Warton was allowed to play hymns on the organ at Boggo Road Gaol in the days leading up to his execution on 17 July 1905.

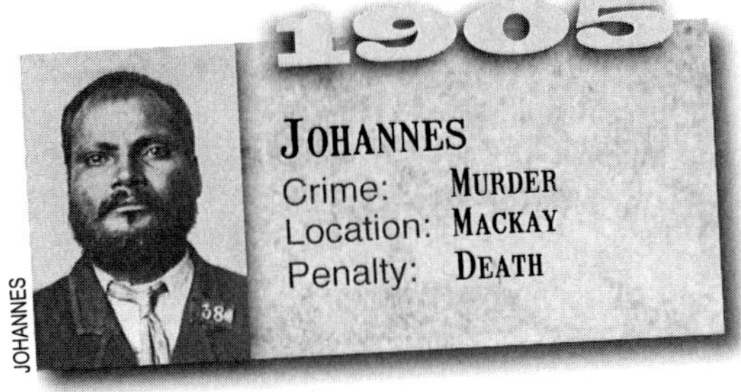

Death of a policeman

Mary Price was the wife of Mackay police constable Albert Price. They had four young boys, aged 3 to 7 years, with another on the way.

Mrs Price loved singing. On the night of 23 December 1905, she was performing at a Christmas concert. Whenever his wife sang in public, husband Albert always tried to attend. He promised to be there that night; she looked out for him but apparently on this occasion his policing duties had kept him otherwise occupied.

At a little after 8.30, she went outside the hall to look for him. She saw crowds hurrying along the street and, wondering what was happening, she asked an approaching woman.

"Don't you know?" the stranger replied. "Poor Constable Price has been murdered by a blackfellow."

Mary Price collapsed to the footpath, sobbing hysterically. It was reported she 'became semi-demented and was taken to her home in a cab'.

The funeral of Constable Price was held on Christmas Eve and, as one newspaper reported, 'was attended by a large number of citizens, and the pitiful sight of the widow screaming and raving will be long remembered by many'.

The crime

AROUND sunset on 23 December 1905, a mob of drunken kanakas was fighting with some Aborigines in Chinatown, Mackay. After three of the combatants had been arrested, and the others quietened, Constables Cameron and Price, along with Sargeant Mulvey, were sent to arrest a Cingalese man who was said to have supplied alcohol to the men.

The Cingalese, Johannes, kept a small fruit shop – although to the police, it had a reputation as a 'den', a place where liquor was supplied to kanakas and Aborigines, and native women were harboured for immoral purposes. In consequence, the shop had been kept under close surveillance in the past, particularly by Constable Cameron.

At 8.15 that night, Cameron and Price entered the shop but found it empty, except for an aboriginal woman in a chemise lying on a stretcher in the back room.

Walking outside, they found Johannes in the street and arrested him. Each constable seized an arm and started for the lock-up.

"All right, I go quiet," the man told them.

"I can manage him," Price said to Cameron. "You see to the woman inside."

As soon as Cameron let go, the Cingalese pulled out a knife from his belt and made a lunge to stab him.

Price yelled, "Look out, he's got a knife!" Cameron took evasive action and the blade cut his tunic.

Desperate to get loose so that he

could better stab Cameron, Johannes swung around on Price, plunging the 9-inch knife into his chest, through his heart. He died instantly.

Sargeant Mulvey ran to intervene, and he too was slashed.

Johannes ran off, into the Victoria Hotel. There, the publican asked for the weapon – and the murderer threw it to him. Cameron rearrested the Cingalese and locked him up.

The aftermath

THE town was crowded that night with the usual Christmas visitors. The startling news of the murder of Constable Price rapidly spread around Mackay and large crowds of people hurried to the scene. The press reported as follows:

> '...The whites became greatly enraged at the coloured man's awful act of assassination. Kemp, the well-known horse-breaker, led on to the gaol a mob of people who in raucous voices howled "Lynch him! Lynch him!" Needless to say the prisoner was kept safely ironed and secure...'

The 'galant, 6ft 2in Constable Albert Price', stabbed to death in the line of duty, by Johannes at Chinatown, Mackay in 1905

JOHANNES' trial was held in Mackay in January 1906.

"The trouble was Mr Cameron," he told the court. "I came from Plane Creek and open that shop for my living. He watch me all time in Chinatown. He tell kanakas he want to catch me selling grog. They told me. I no give grog to them. He watch me all time. If Cameron not let go my hand, I not kill Mr Price."

Two weeks before the murder Johannes told his mate he thought he would kill Cameron one day, and even in his final moments, he would continue to curse the constable who persecuted him.

On the gallows in Brisbane on 14 May, with his legs strapped together and the noose around his neck, his parting words were: "Mr Cameron is a bloody bastard! Mr Cameron is a bloody cow! That's all." ■

IT seems that Mrs Price showed a great deal of compassion for her husband's killer, Johannes.

In an interview after the trial, the widow said she firmly believed he had no intention of killing her husband. "As a matter of fact, Johannes was a very kind man, and was always kind to Bert. On the day of the murder, he gave my children a great deal of fruit – so much, indeed, that they had to take a cab to bring it home. He was always kind to the children, and I am sure he did not intend to hurt Bert. He certainly had a grievance against Cameron, but he was always very respectful to my husband... Poor wretch. I'm sure he didn't mean it."

FOLLOWING the shock of her husband's murder, the pregnant Mrs Price's troubles went from bad to worse. She became ill and, with her four young children, one being 'deaf and dumb', was forced to move to Brisbane for treatment. Her child was still-born. Released after several weeks in hospital, the children boarding in the meantime with the Salvation Army, she found her clothes and house linen had been stolen. She moved into a small cottage on Petrie Terrace with the children, opposite the Police Barracks, where she took in washing to make ends meet. Her husband's insurance payout of £100 was soon gone.

Four years later, a newspaper took up the cause for the widow of a policeman killed in the line of duty, and neglected by the State... 'Mrs Price is still working as a laundress, by hard and laborious work supporting herself and her children. As a worker, she has proved herself a veritable Trojan. Right throughout the time from her husband's death, her conduct has been extremely meritorious, and proving her in every way worthy of the State's considerate treatment.'

A final note

JOHANNES

DESPITE the tragedy of it all, Mary Price penned the following letter, the essence of which was communicated to Johannes ten minutes before his execution:

To the Sheriff, Brisbane

Sir – If it be in order, will you please tell the poor man Johannes, who is to hang for the murder of my late husband, Constable Albert George Price, that I, his heart-broken widow, do now fully and freely forgive him for the cruel wrong he has done me and my children by taking my dear husband from me, and that my prayer is that God will have mercy on his soul. These are the true sentiments of my heart, as I hope to meet my dear husband in a better world. God help Johannes in his last hours of misery; cruel though his crime was, his end is worse. Therefore, and for God's sake, I forgive him from the bottom of my bleeding heart.

Yours sincerely

MARY A. PRICE

Widow of the Murdered Constable

The condemned man simply replied, "Thank you", and a few moments later he was taken charge of by the hangman.

Dobbed in by his wife and son

On the Booie Road out of Nanango, in 1906 a Russian Pole named August Millewski owned a bush homestead on a small selection. He had a wife and three teenage children.

The adjoining selection was owned by Wallum Nabby, an unmarried Indian who lived in a humpy some 300 metres from the Millewski dwelling.

Since October 1905, there had been trouble between Millewski and Nabby after the Russian's barn had burned down. Nabby was tried on a charge of arson but was found not guilty.

The key witness at the arson trial was a Johnny Doo, who testified against his fellow countryman, Nabby. Within a month of the trial, Doo was murdered. The prime suspect of course was Wallum Nabby, but a Brisbane jury found him not guilty of the killing and he returned to his Booie Road property – much to Millewski's displeasure.

WALLUM NABBY.

So who murdered Johnny Doo?

The crime for which Wallum Nabby was tried in 1905 – the murder of Johnny Doo, and found not guilty, was never officially solved. However, Millewski's wife later admitted that *Millewski* had killed Doo with a shot to the head. An exhumation of the body found no evidence of this, owing to the battered state of the skull. Perhaps Millewski *did* murder Doo, believing that his Indian neighbour Nabby would be forced to wear the full penalty for avenging Doo's testimony against him.

IN August 1906, Wallum Nabby had disappeared and, as part of their inquiries, police visited the Millewski homestead on 12 August. Millewski had just left by train to visit the Brisbane Exhibition.

Sargeant Dower from Nanango asked Mrs Millewski: "Wallum Nabby has been missing since Wednesday. Do you know anything?"

Her reply surprised him.

"I do not want to be drawn into the case – but I am afraid of my husband, so I will tell everything…"

And she did.

A family affair

TWO days before the murder of his neighbour, Millewski asked his son to help him 'do away with Nabby some night' and he spoke to him again the next day. Each time his son refused.

Similarly, Milleweski outlined his plans to his wife. As she confided in daughter Alice: "Tomorrow father wants me to hold the lantern while he is murdering Nabby."

"Don't go, mother," she said.

"But I will have to if he makes me."

AT 1 a.m. on the morning of the murder, 8 August, Millewski woke his wife and son: "We must kill Nabby *now* or else he will murder all of us!"

He ordered his son to get the revolver and to make sure it was loaded; his wife was to carry the lantern.

"Walk quietly," he said, as they made their way through the garden into Nabby's place.

Inside, the trio found the Indian asleep under a blanket on a bunk. Millewski fired through the blanket at the sleeping man's head. Nabby, though wounded, was able to spring up, crying out 'Millewski! Millewski!' at the top of his voice.

The pair struggled violently until Nabby became exhausted through loss of blood. Millewski fired two more shots and Nabby fell to the floor.

Father and son carried the body outside but found that the Indian was still not dead. Millewski used a hardwood rail to batter his victim's head.

Nabby's limp body was then placed in a large corn sack and carried into a nearby paddock. With his son, Millewski then tried to hide any blood marks and other traces of the crime in the house with dust and ashes. They bundled up the dead man's clothes and took them, and the body, to another nearby location, before returning home.

Later in the day, the body and clothes were shifted once more, into a hollow log. That night they set fire to the fallen tree so that all that remained was a heap of ashes.

After warning his family to say nothing about the entire episode, Millewski set out by train to visit the Brisbane Exhibition.

Arrest and trial

BEFORE Millewski reached Brisbane, however, the police were on his trail. Two detectives intercepted the southbound train at North Pine railway station around 7 p.m. They located the Russian and casually accompanied him on the rest of the journey to Brisbane. When they arrived at Central Station, they identified themselves and arrested him for the murder of Wallum Nabby.

Back in Nanango, mother and son were also arrested.

The husband and wife were arraigned on the capital charge; the charge against the son was later dropped when he agreed to give testimony against his father.

The Crown had a strong case.

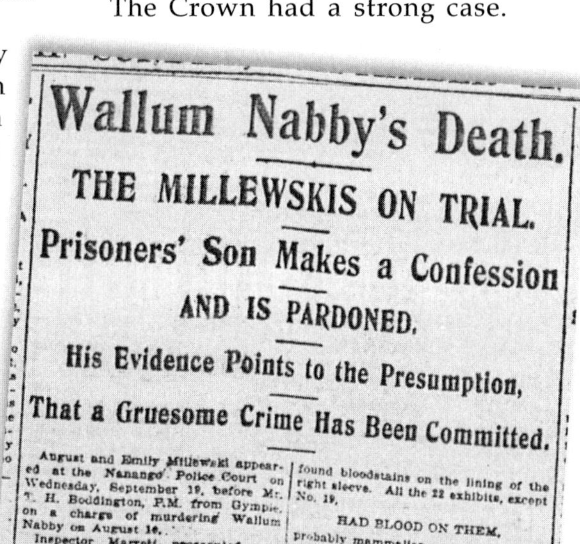

Wallum Nabby's Death.

THE MILLEWSKIS ON TRIAL.

Prisoners' Son Makes a Confession

AND IS PARDONED.

His Evidence Points to the Presumption,

That a Gruesome Crime Has Been Committed.

August and Emily Millewski appeared at the Nanango Police Court on Wednesday, September 19, before Mr. T. H. Boddington, P.M. from Gympie, on a charge of murdering Wallum Nabby on August 16.

Inspector Marrett prosecuted, and Mr. W. J. McGrath, of Brisbane, defended the male prisoner, the female being undefended.

Martin Hayes, first-class constable, South Brisbane, deposed that the male defendant was handed over to him on September 16 to take to Nanango. The [illegible]

found bloodstains on the lining of the right sleeve. All the 22 exhibits, except No. 19,

HAD BLOOD ON THEM.

probably mammalian.

On Friday, Alex Millewski, son of the prisoners, who had been granted a pardon in connection with the murder, was called, but Mr. McGrath objected to his evidence being taken on these grounds: (1) On their evidence the police did not caution the witness or his mother previous to arrest; (2) at no [illegible] informed

Sieving of the still-warm ashes of the burnt-out tree revealed buttons, boot sprigs, a trousers buckle, and human bone fragments. A hardwood rail at Wallum's hut was blood-stained, as were Millewski's clothes and boots. A witness was found who testified that, in 1905, Millewski had offered him £1 to kill the Indian. And there was the damning testimony provided by son, daughter – and mother.

In September 1907, the husband and wife appeared in the Maryborough District Court before Chief Justice Pope Cooper and a jury.

After a hearing lasting three days, Mrs Millewski was found not guilty, having pleaded that she had acted under her husband's 'evil compulsion'. August Millewski was found guilty and sentenced to death.

Message from the scaffold

AUGUST Millewski was scheduled to hang at Boggo Road Gaol at 8.00 a.m. on 16 December 1907.

In his final weeks, gaol officials reported that the death sentence seemed to make no noticeable change in his demeanour. At first he was anxious about obtaining a reprieve but, that being unobtainable, he turned his attention to managing matters relating to his farm at Nanango, and the welfare of his two young daughters.

On the day of the execution, the condemned man showed no fear and walked firmly to the scaffold. To the last, even with the rope around his neck, his thoughts, as expressed in the short speech he made, were revengeful and sordid for, with his next-to-last last breath, he cursed his wife. There was not a vestige of tremor in his voice when, 'in his pronounced foreign guttural sort of accent', he said:

> "I wish to say it is because of my wife that I have to stand here. I know nothing about this affair. I wish that my wife will be put into a furnace and burned to ashes for swearing such lies about me to the court." ■

> THE execution of Millewski removes one who, there is every reason to believe, has been a moving spirit in a series of outrages which have for some considerable time past kept the district in which he resided in a state of unrest… In no fewer than three murders was Millewski said to be implicated if, indeed, he was not the actual perpetrator. In one case, in particular, in which a local man was murdered under circumstances of exceptional brutality, the body of the victim is said to have been boiled down and fed to the pigs. It is to be hoped that the unenviable reputation which has hitherto attached to the Nanango district will now cease, and that a reputation for active virtue will take its place.

– *Truth*, 22 December 1907

Fragments from the FILES of FELONS

1904. THE discovery of the body of an Aborigine in a grave near Cardwell led to the arrest of two Aborigines named Davey and Fred. The pair were found guilty of a revenge killing in which the victim had been speared, despatched with a nulla-nulla, his flesh cut out, and the blood drunk. The jury recommended mercy on the grounds that the men were 'acting in accordance with tribal custom'. Their death sentence was commuted to life in prison.

The threepenny murder

About the time when many Queenslanders were having breakfast on Monday, 31 December – the last day of 1906, a Chinese cook by the name of Look Kow dropped to his death at the end of a rope, on the gallows at Brisbane Gaol at Boggo Road.

The 62-year-old had paid the penalty for killing a countryman over a threepenny gambling debt in Townsville.

THE Chinese gambling dens of Townsville in the early 1900s operated day and night. They were to be found in the hotch-potch of jerry-built shanties covering an area of less than an acre in Flinders Lane, 'an abominable imitation of architectural designs that would confound Confucius'.

It was at the gambling dens that Look Kow arrived in the early hours of 26 August 1906. He and Tommy Ah Sing entered Lee Hoy's shop around 1.00 a.m. and bought cake and tea for sixpence.

Here they met up with a 27-year-old Chinaman Lee Chay Yuen, with whom Look Kow had earlier been playing 'dow now', a game in which dice play a central role, and during which the pair had a difference of opinion over a threepenny wager.

At tea, the dispute was apparently again raised, because, as the trio was leaving the premises soon after, as Lee Chay Yuen stepped from the veranda into the lane, Look Kow struck him from behind with a tomahawk. He died within twenty minutes.

Police later found the tomahawk and Look Kow under a nearby bridge. On 20 November, he was found guilty of murder and later died on the Boggo Road gallows. ■

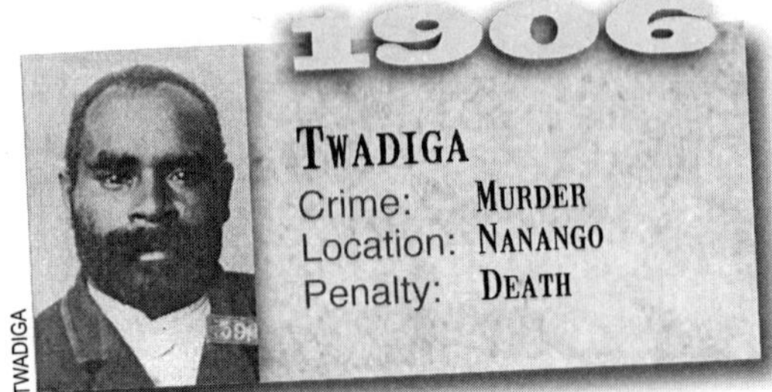

A killing in the kitchen

One of the first pieces of legislation passed by Australia's new Federal Parliament was the *Immigration Restriction Act* 1901. The so-called 'White Australia' policy was enacted to "place certain restrictions on immigration and... for the removal... of prohibited immigrants". As a result, South Sea Islanders (kanakas), many of whom had been working for decades on Queensland's northern plantations, were under threat of deportation to their islands of origin. Many, however, did not want to leave the new state.

One such labourer, working for Mackay cane farmer Charles Baulch in 1906, was Twadiga.

On 21 January of that year, Twadiga was told in conversation with four white workers that Baulch was intending 'to get rid of him' - which to the kanaka meant that his employer was going to kill him.

Confused and upset, Twadiga entered the kitchen of the Baulch homestead armed with an axe, where he confronted the farmer's wife and grandson Billy.

"You intend killing me, missus?" he blurted out angrily.

The woman ran, terrified, from the room to find her husband.

When they returned to the kitchen shortly afterwards, they found the kanaka behind the door with the axe still in his hand. On the floor, covered with a rug, was the body of the young grandson, Billy Baulch.

The distressed Twadiga would later say that, when Mrs Baulch screamed and ran out, he had become frightened, that 'his head was wrong through fear', and that in panic he had struck the boy a blow to the head with his axe, killing the lad instantly.

A Mackay jury took eight minutes to find Twadiga guilty of murder and he was executed in Boggo Road Gaol in Brisbane on 21 May 1906. ■

1905. AMELIA Linke was a young unmarried mother, who had left the train at isolated Vernon Siding, west of Fernvale on 12 September with her 12-month-old son, returning to the station later without the infant. It turned out that she had smothered the baby in a nearby paddock, where the child's remains were found a month later. She was sentenced to death in April 1906 for wilful murder but was granted clemency on account of her 'unsound mind', and was finally released in August 1908 after spending time at Goodna Mental Asylum.

1906. "IT is a pity flogging has been abolished. Corporal punishment would do these lads more good than anything else," said Judge Miller in sentencing Reg James and Bill Munro to 18 months hard labour for having stolen with violence a military medal and ten sovereigns from Badam Singh.

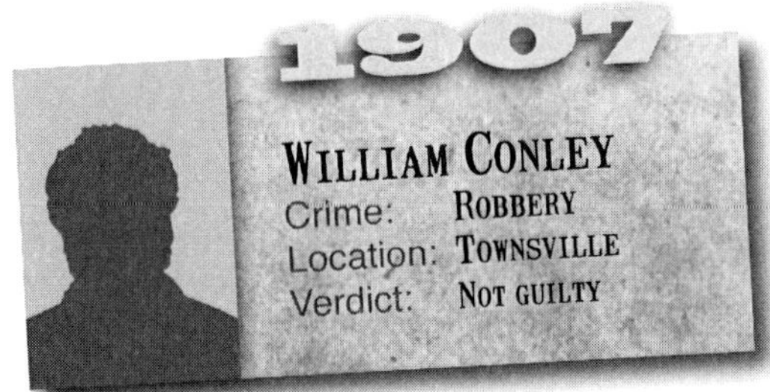

The Townsville railway station robbery

Early on Christmas morning, a messenger arrived at the residence of William Conley, assistant station master at Townsville Railway Station. He was there to pick up the key to the safe. He returned a short while later – the open safe was empty. The station had been robbed!

"By heavens, if this is a joke, someone will pay for it when I get to the office!" said Conley.

A MONTH later, in February 2007, station employee Albert Griffith, already known to police as 'a thief and liar', was charged with having stolen £1567 from the station safe.

Within a few weeks, William Conley would join him.

In time the police withdrew the charge against Albert Griffith and would call him as a witness at the trial, having turned state's evidence against Conley. In court in March 1907, Griffith testified along these lines…

'On Christmas morning, I went to work about 4.15 or a little earlier. When I went to put the key into the lock of the front door, it just shoved open. I went inside and the first thing I saw was the door of the safe open, and a man in front of the safe on his knees with a lamp. It was William Conley. He had a railway towel on the floor with something in it, and he was just about to tie it up.

"Well, Griff, what's it to be – a quarter of the spoils or nothing?"

"Do what you like," I replied. "I've seen nothing."

I turned and walked out of the office, and went home and had breakfast, returning after 8 o'clock when I heard about the robbery. I said nothing.

On 4 January, I was on the platform when Conley gave me a small parcel. I took it home, opened it, and found it contained £74 in bank notes. An accompanying letter said that there

We'll never know for sure who took £1567 from the safe at the Townsville Railway Station on Christmas Eve 1906.

was £274 in the safe and that this was my share – a quarter. I have none of the money left; I spent it all."

Griffith claimed he had later tried to meet with Conley, but was constantly avoided. He said he had then received on 28 February a letter, signed 'W.C.' which, when he was arrested, Griffith handed to the police. The letter read, in part:

> 'Dear A., ... I find I am 2 closely watched to meet. It would B hard 4 U to prove what U saw on Xmas morning B cause I can get proof that I was home the time U would say U saw me...... W.C.'

SEEMINGLY desperate to convict Conley, the police undertook what the prisoner's defence later claimed were underhanded tactics, of a type 'that had never been heard of'.

The defence deplored the police use of threats to force the prisoner's sister in Helidon to surrender recent letters she had received from Conley. As well, police had deceptively told the prisoner's father and brothers that Conley had in fact confessed to the robbery, in an attempt to extract information.

And worse, while in remand, 'the prisoner had eight interviews with his wife, which were supposed to be private and, each time, under a counter, on a small shelf, a constable was concealed. They had him so cramped up that they had to cut a hole in the floor for him to breathe through. They had this man spying on the most sacred conversations between husband and wife...'.

"Your worship," defence counsel Macnaughton concluded, "I say unhesitatingly that while the unfortunate prisoner has been in custody we have witnessed the grossest parody on justice..." (Applause in court)

The judge, Justice Charles Chubb, expressed similar concerns and doubts. For example, he asked if the initials and writing on the letter of 28 February were indeed Conley's, to which the Crown Prosecutor replied 'not absolutely'. The judge responded: "If that's the case, you had better not open that up to the jury."

Justice Chubb finally addressed the jury: "Griffith on his own admission was a thief, and his evidence – the evidence-in-chief – must not be believed *unless* it is corroborated. He is an acknowledged thief and liar, who admits that he had in his possession a fourth of the stolen money. The only evidence before the jury is that of an accomplice, and a jury cannot convict on that alone."

The jury retired, only to return in three minutes, finding William Conley 'not guilty'.

Judge Chubb: "I agree with the verdict. Conley, you are discharged." And those in the gallery applauded.

Two months later, Albert Griffith was convicted of stealing a buggy harness, basket and macintosh.

But the question remains: just who did steal £1567 from the Townsville Railway Station safe on Christmas Eve 1906? ■

Justice Charles Chubb advised the jury that, when evidence-in-chief was given by an accomplice to a crime, as Albert Griffith was, there must be corroborative evidence on all material matters. The jury took three minutes to find the accused thief 'not guilty'.

The bungling bank robber

The manager of the Commercial Bank in Gayndah, west of Maryborough, was out of town that Sunday night in October 1908. Normally he would sleep in a back room of the building, but in his absence he asked his young bank clerk Edmund Muir to do so.

At a little after 9.00 p.m., Muir entered the building to spend the night there.

SEVERAL minutes later, a railway clerk was passing the bank when he heard the clatter of breaking glass, the sounds of a struggle and shouting, followed by two or three shots.

In the house next door, a woman was aroused by the same disturbance. Rushing to a window overlooking the allotment behind the bank, she saw a man leave the premises by the back door, hurry across the yard, jump the fence, and head towards the Burnett River.

Within minutes the police had been summoned and, accompanied by a few men from the town, they entered the building by the back door.

Inside, in the bedroom, they found the body of the young clerk, bashed

The Commercial Bank situated on the corner of Pineapple and Capper Streets, Gayndah, scene of the murder of young bank clerk Edmund Muir in October 1908

and shot. Muir's straw hat was battered on the side, suggesting that an intruder had struck him down when he entered unexpectedly.

On the floor, they saw fragments of glass from a broken lamp, a pair of boots which, it was later discovered, belonged to neither the clerk nor the bank manager, and a 'brownish-green' felt hat.

A policemen recognised the hat as belonging to a recent arrival in the town, Arthur Ross. They crossed the street to a boarding house where Ross had been staying. Breaking in, they found the room empty and the bed undisturbed. A quick search located an opened box of bullets.

Strips of cloth

AT daybreak a party of police and townsmen began the search for Arthur Ross. Helped by an aboriginal tracker, police followed footprints of someone wearing sox or bandages on his feet instead of boots, from the back of the bank building, to the river, and along the bank towards the camp of a man named Doherty. On the way they found a dagger and a kitchen knife, and a heavy blood-stained baton, cut from a tree, with a loop of fishing cord fixed to one end. Arriving at Doherty's tent, they found it ransacked, and a pair of boots stolen.

On the ground near the tent they discovered strips of serge cloth and cord. Parts of the cloth were covered with mud, other parts were relatively clean. It was obvious that the cloth had been muddied in a manner consistent with a person having earlier worn these strips wrapped around his feet. And the cloth had been tied to the feet with the same fishing cord attached to the home-made baton.

One of the policemen identified the rag strips. They had been torn from a pair of trousers he once owned and accidentally left in a room he had previously rented in the boarding house opposite the bank – the same room now rented by Ross!

It was later argued that, to avoid leaving identifiable tracks, Ross had bandaged his feet with the strips he had cut from the trousers he found in his room in the boarding house. He had carried his boots in his hand when entering the bank to rob it but, in his haste to leave, he had left them at the murder scene.

TWO days into their search the posse caught up with the fugitive, on the river bank not far from Gayndah.

One of his pursuers later related the capture:

> "We saw Ross about 20 yards away. He did not see us, as his back was towards us.
>
> 'Hands up or I'll fire," I said.
>
> 'What's the matter?' replied Ross, turning.
>
> 'Throw down the weapons!'
>
> He did, a loaded revolver and a handful of cartridges."

Ross was taken back to town. Tellingly, the boots he was wearing, stolen earlier from Doherty's camp, appeared much too large for him. ▶

Ross was tried for murder – twice – before Justice Pope Cooper (right). *Because of his age, mass protests would follow the sentencing.*

Gaydah Murder.

Young Ross Executed.

Efforts to Reprieve Prove Futile.

The Cabinet Obdurate.

Final Scene at Brisbane Gaol.

Indignation Amongst Queensland Citizens.

Trial and punishment

Crowds gathered throughout Queensland to plead leniency for the youthful Ross.

THE trial of Arthur Ross for the murder of the Gayndah bank clerk was held in Maryborough before Judge Pope Cooper. It resulted in a hung jury.

It later came to light that the sympathies of a couple of the jury members lay with the growing Abolitionist Movement, which was advocating an end to capital punishment. Unable to reach a verdict, a second trial was ordered.

Both prosecutor and judge at the new trial made their thoughts clear about the task at hand. Prosecutor Kingsbury told the jury not to be influenced by 'any academic fads or false humanitarianism'. Judge Cooper was even blunter: 'If a jury took the oath to decide according to the evidence and, at the same time, made up their minds to decide according to their prejudices, then they were unfit to be members of the community, and were, in fact, perjurers.'

In the end, the jury found Ross guilty of murder, not wilful murder (on the assumption that the death penalty could be avoided). But Judge Cooper sentenced Ross to death.

Huge protest meetings followed in Rockhampton, Maryborough (producing a petition of 3000 signatures), and at Charleville and other western centres. A huge rally in Brisbane on the night before the scheduled hanging ended with an unsuccessful deputation to the Lieutenant Governor.

On the gallows at Boggo Road on 7 June 1909, Ross's last statement, in firm voice, was: 'I desire to thank the people of Queensland for the interest they have taken in my life. I am very sorry for the deed I committed and I hope to be forgiven for my sins.'

In the days before his execution Arthur Ross prepared a long letter for his victim's mother in which he admitted that he had planned the crime while in Brisbane Gaol on an earlier charge. He wrote that he had made the heavy baton that dealt the clerk the first blow but, as its use was not sufficient to prevent the clerk from strongly gripping Ross by the throat, he shot Muir twice while still held.

Odd spot

In their pre-execution examination, doctors found that Ross had some striking physical peculiarities. He could move the little fingers on either hand round until they lay on the backs of the other three knuckles of the corresponding hand. As well, he had long prehensile feet, 'the soles of which he could bend inward as an ordinary person turns in the palm of the hand'. And he had a horselike habit of turning his eyes on objects almost behind him, without turning his head.

The Carron River killings

When Captain Setterfield of the Salvation Army responded to a knock on the door of his barracks in Croydon, he was greeted by Alexander Bradshaw. It was 7.30 a.m. on Monday, 20 September 1909.

"I've been sent by the Sunderlands of Carron River to fetch you," he said. "Mrs Sunderland and her daughter met with a cart accident while returning from Croydon yesterday. Nothing serious. I've come into town for a buggy so I can bring them to the doctor."

The captain got some breakfast for Bradshaw who ate a hearty meal. Despite frequent pleas by the captain for him to go and get a vehicle and return to the Carron, some 22 miles distant, Bradshaw remained seated, reading the paper and conversing until after 9 o'clock.

Captain Setterfield assumed the accident was indeed 'nothing serious'.

At 10 o'clock, Bradshaw walked into the Croydon police station.

"I want to give myself up for shooting Eliza Roberts," he said. "I shot her in the leg with a pea rifle out at Sunderland's place. She's limping a bit but she's not seriously injured."

The bodies in the cart

WHILE Bradshaw was detained, Constable Burke was instructed to proceed to Carron River to make inquiries.

When Burke arrived within a mile of the property, he met two lads driving a horse and cart towards Croydon. In the back was an injured

Thanks to the discovery of gold in 1885, Croydon in the Gulf country of north Queensland became the fourth largest town in the colony, with a population in its heyday of 7000. By the early 1900s (below), its population, including more than 30 surrounding townships, still exceeded 3000. One such satellite settlement was Carron River, site of the Carron River murders of 1909.

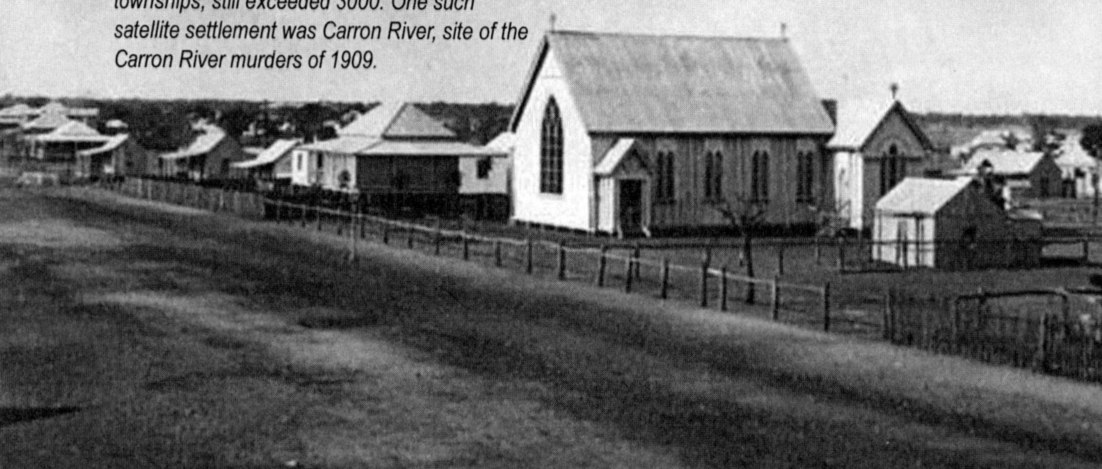

Eliza Roberts and her parents – Alice Sutherland was dead and her husband, George, was dying. Both had been shot.

The constable wrote a quick note and sent one of the lads off on horseback to deliver it to his sargeant in Croydon. The sargeant immediately headed off for the Carron in a horse cab with a doctor, arriving there at 8.30 that night.

Shortly after they arrived, George Sutherland died. Eliza Roberts, screaming with pain, was transferred from the cart to the cab and taken into the hospital at Croydon. The constable followed in the cart with the two dead bodies.

Next morning, in the lockup, Alexander Bradshaw was charged with murder.

"Are they dead? I shot them all on Sunday."

"Why?"

"Temper."

ON 9 April 1910, the trial of Alexander Bradshaw was held in Normanton before Justice Macnaughton.

There was an eyewitness to the killings that Sunday six months earlier – Eliza Roberts' 11-year-old son from her previous marriage. With his evidence, along with additional testimony from his mother and others, the jury would have little trouble convicting Bradshaw....

THE jury was told that Eliza Roberts had broken off her relationship with Bradshaw in Croydon and on Saturday, 18 September, returned by cart to Carron River with her mother. They arrived home at midday on the Sunday.

Later that day, Bradshaw arrived at the homestead.

"Can I speak with Liz?"

"It depends what you want to say to her," replied George Sutherland.

"Is it right, Liz, that you are not going to live with me any more?"

"Yes, I am going to live a better life," she replied. As one report stated, she said she had 'turned religious'.

Bradshaw began to weep.

He then asked Roberts to kiss him. She declined and he left.

A lover scorned

LATER he returned. Eliza was sitting on a squatter's chair on the verandah. Her son saw Bradshaw climbing through the sliprails with a rifle, but before he could warn her, she was knocked from the chair by a bullet which struck her in the thigh.

"For God's sake, Joe, spare me for the child's sake!"

1904. THE Burns brothers, James and Leslie, were sent to St Helena having been found guilty of stealing a brown mare at Roma and unlawfully killing it by cutting its throat.

The Magistrate said: 'In all my experience on the bench I never saw such ability displayed by the police as in this case. A small trail was followed faithfully and with keenness and intelligence by the police sargeant... The methods used were new in police practice and were worthy of the highest commendation.'

The methods referred to were the taking of plaster of Paris casts of all the tracks of the accused and their horses.

In the years that followed, the innovative Sgt Michael O'Sullivan was to rise through the ranks to become in 1921 Queensland's Deputy Police Commissioner.

The boy ran into the garden and hid amongst the mango trees, from where he would see all that happened.

When Mrs Sutherland heard her daughter's screams, she rushed out of the house. Bradshaw fired at her.

"Oh, my God. I'm shot!" She staggered back inside.

Bradshaw walked up to Roberts and said: "Where is that bastard of a father of yours? I have shot your mother and I will do for him too."

For 30 minutes he paced up and down in the yard until Sutherland returned from collecting horses.

As Sutherland dismounted the gunman shouted: "I've shot your wife and daughter, and I'll kill you too."

He fired and missed. Sutherland ran towards the house and Bradshaw followed and shot him.

Before leaving, the gunman lifted the wounded Eliza Roberts back into the squatter's chair. She begged him to get help from town and to send out Captain Setterfield of the Salvation Army.

Then, leaving all three of his victims helpless and suffering, if not dying, he rode into Croydon.

Above: *Salvation Army Hall, Croydon 1913. Eliza Roberts appeared quite happy living with Alexander Bradshaw until she joined a local Church and was badgered by members about 'living in sin'. Torn between a love for Bradshaw and commitment to her Church, Eliza moved from Croydon back into the home of her parents, the Sutherlands at Carron River, thereby breaking off her relationship with the man who would subsequently wreak vengeful havoc upon her family.*

AT this trial, Bradshaw pleaded not guilty. His defence called no witnesses but rather attempted to reveal the state of the accused's disoriented mind at the time of the killings.

The jury, however, took only 20 minutes to conclude that Bradshaw was guilty of murder; Judge Macnaughton sentenced him to hang.

On 13 June 1910, Bradshaw's final words were: "O Gracious God... take me to thy brilliant islands. I ask this in the hour of death. May my Lord comfort me and ensure my righteousness and peace forever. Amen. Amen."

Whereupon the hangman adjusted the white cap, checked the noose, and pulled the lever. ■

Sidelight

ACCORDING to historian Hugh MacMaster, 'a male member of Eliza's Church congregation, regarded by some locals as having a personal motive in encouraging Eliza Roberts to leave Bradshaw, was also afforded an early opportunity to meet his maker, courtesy of "unknown" locals who didn't fancy his hypocrisy.'

MacMaster tallied the final cost of this unfortunate saga at Carron River thus: One life forfeited to the Crown; two in the cause of the Church; and one to Gulf justice." [1]

Bismark, the murdering blacktracker

Thirty-year-old Janet Evitts, widowed mother of four children, lived with her brother Herbert Tomkins at Prairie Farm, a few miles out of Jundah in Central Queensland.

She helped to work the farm, was a good horsewoman and was familiar with the rough life of the bush.

On 14 January 1909, as was her custom, she set out in the afternoon to round up the cows for milking. Usually she returned from the paddocks around 5 p.m., but by nightfall that day, her brother had become uneasy and anxious.

With a small search party he set out to where he assumed his sister would have gone. The search continued for several hours. Then, around midnight, they made a discovery that at once suggested Mrs Evitts had met with foul play. They found the torn sleeve of her dress and also her blood-smeared hat.

Fearing her fate, Tomkins rode hastily to the police station where he informed Acting Sargeant Proctor of his concern.

NEXT morning Proctor, with a constable and the blacktracker Bismark, set out to where the sleeve and hat were found, in the hope that they could pick up the trail from that point.

It was here that the sargeant became suspicious: Bismark was acting oddly. The tracker said he could find no tracks – although he was seen obliterating some of them with his foot. Indeed the constable and others had no trouble following a trail for nearly two miles, to the riverbank and back. The tracks ended in the horse paddock near the police station.

The party returned to the river bank where Bismark was told to wade in to see what he could find. He hesitated.

The constable was sent in – and there he located the body of Janet Evitts.

Bismark was arrested that night for the murder of Mrs Evitts. In his hut they had found blood-stained clothes. Next morning, the blacktracker confessed, and outlined the events of the previous day…

BISMARK was out in the paddocks that afternoon, driving sheep, when he came across Mrs Evitts with some of her cows.

He claimed that the woman resented his presence in language that aroused and inflamed his anger.

He said that Mrs Evitts shouted something that caused him to retort: "If you call me that, I'll kill you. I'll murder you…"– at which point he caught hold of her bridle, but she galloped away.

He galloped after her and pulled her from the horse. With a stick he hit her across the head and she fell, only

Fragments from the FILES of FELONS

1909. IT would have been one of the shortest sentences in Queensland's criminal history. Edward Ikin appeared in court in December on a charge of having, on 6 November, attempted to kill himself. The *Brisbane Courier* reported the case as follows:

> 'Accused pleaded guilty, and said that at the time he had been in a low state, accentuated by financial trouble. Accused was sentenced to imprisonment for one minute, and discharged.'

1910. ARTHUR Starkey, a Nundah baker, one night in April noticed a man acting suspiciously outside an adjacent grocer's shop, before moving across the road to Dyer's lock-up store. Shortly afterwards, hearing strange noises, Starkey summoned the local constable.

At Dyer's, the constable arrested Alfred Seymour, having found him trying to force open the back door with a chisel. Wedges had been inserted in the door frame.

In court, Seymour claimed he was on his way to Sandgate and was looking for some place to sleep for the night. The chisel did not belong to him – and the skeleton keys found on him at the scene were 'used for locking his rooms'. And the jemmy? – well, he just carried that with him. In summing up, Judge Power said that Seymour had 'one of the worst records he had ever seen'. "You have been a criminal all your life, having received sentences aggregating something like 48 years... Well, now you can add yet another seven years' imprisonment with hard labour!"

to get up again, scream for help, and run for her life.

Bismark followed. He caught up with her a second time and, using a tree branch which he had picked up on the run, struck her across the neck. She fell, stunned and bleeding.

A contemporary newspaper report continued the tragic tale:

> 'The infuriated black had the lone and defenceless woman at his mercy and, showing all the worst instincts of savage and coward, beat his victim cruelly to death. And then, to make sure that no trace of life was left, he picked up two large stones and with these battered the woman's face.'

Bismark then made his way back to his quarters at the police station, arriving around 7 p.m., and got supper in the usual way from the police stores.

The same night, he returned to where his victim's corpse lay and, lifting it in his arms, carried it four hundred yards to the river. There he dropped it into a deep waterhole.

TWO months later Bismark faced judge and jury in Rockhampton. He was found guilty and sentenced to death.

On the scaffold, 'ghastly-looking and trembling', the 23-year-old Bismark met his fate.

"Bismark, you are going to die now. You want to say anything, you say it now," said the Chief Warder.

Almost inaudibly, he responded: "I sorry I kill the woman", and, after a short silence, "God have mercy on me, and forgive me, for Jesus' sake."

And then, a clattering thud as the trap door opened. ■

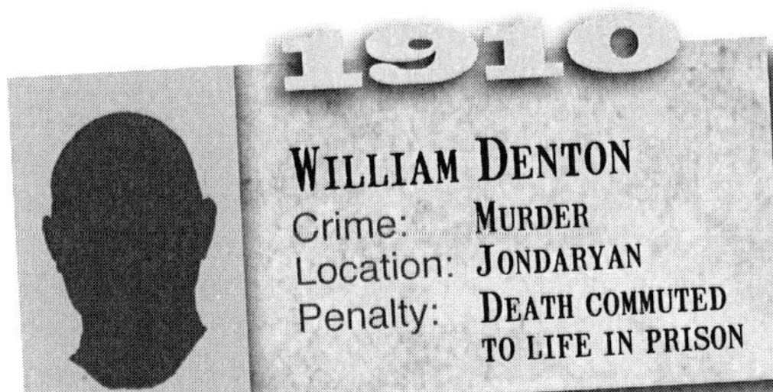

Tragedy in a tent

In 1910, the town of Jondaryan, north-west of Toowoomba, had a population of over 600, and boasted four hotels, several stores, a school, and two blacksmiths. It was the closest centre to the famed Jondaryan pastoral station with its 100m long woolshed capable of handling 3000 sheep at a time at 52 shearing stands. Jondaryan, however, was essentially a railway town.

The railway quarry at Jones's Camp was located just over two miles out of town. It accommodated in tents a team of men responsible for maintaining a large section of the western line out of Toowoomba to Charleville further west.

TWO of the railway workers from Jones's Camp spent the night of 15 October 1910 – pay day, drinking heavily at a hotel in Jondaryan. William Denton and George Kelly occupied the same tent back at the camp, along with another worker Arthur Blake. Usually the pair were the best of mates. However, on this night both were far from sober and very argumentative. On more than one occasion, in the hotel and in the yard, they quarrelled loudly and had to be separated.

Back at the camp, Blake was already in bed when, near midnight, Kelly returned to camp and also retired. Blake later recalled:

> Around 2.30 a.m. Denton entered the tent and lit a candle. In bed I turned my back to the light so as to escape the glare, and soon heard some chopping sounds from where Kelly's bunk was. I became alert when suddenly the light went out. Then I heard the defendant say, "My God, what have I done," and after that, I heard the sound of kissing…

1910. IT was a family flare-up that ended in tragedy that Sunday afternoon on 27 November at Dumbleton near Mackay. Peter Tynan with John Farrington was drinking beer at his brother William's house, when Peter accused William's wife of stealing his beer. An alcohol-fuelled argument ensued with Peter swearing at Mrs Tynan. William, described as 'a powerful man and a great athlete', thereupon knocked his brother down. Peter and Farrington then armed themselves with a cane knife and the metal part of a horse harness and, in the wild fight that followed, William Tynan was dreadfully chopped about and killed. Peter Tynan and Farrington were found guilty of murder and sentenced to death, later commuted to life imprisonment.

1911. HE introduced himself to the proprietor of the Marble Bar Hotel in Brisbane as William Thiele, a government health inspector, and asked to be shown over the premises. When this was done, he said that there were several things wrong – but if the proprietor would 'grease his palm with half-a-crown', he would say nothing. He tried the same scam at the Exchange Hotel in Edward Street… but Edward Gray found himself in court a few weeks later and sentenced to two years in prison for making false representations.

1911. PHILIP Palmer, 14, employed as a 'cow boy' on an Allora property, was found guilty of killing a mare and foal on 1 June. He had taken a pitch fork to the animals because the mare had kicked another lame mare he was attending. Judge Macnaughton sentenced Palmer to four years in the Westbrook Reformatory.

Immediately distressed, Blake began shouting for assistance from sleeping workers in tents close by. A couple came running in the darkness.

They found Denton kneeling beside Kelly's bunk, his face smeared with blood.

"Let me kiss you, Kelly. I have done for you," he wailed. "My God, what have I done."

Kelly lay on the bed, his head shattered and bloody. A blood-stained tomahawk lay nearby.

A distraught Denton slumped back on the edge of his bunk. "Give me a gun so that I might shoot myself," he pleaded. "Or a plug of dynamite or a razor…"

AT his trial in Toowoomba in March 1911, William Denton's defence claimed that he had no memory of the fatal night.

It was also revealed that Denton, a former sailor, had served in the Boer War and 'had spent much of his life in more than one madhouse' - in Islington, Canehill and Willowburn asylums in England, in Gibraltar, and Barcaldine. In recent years he had worked his way through New Zealand and Western Australia before finding himself working for the railway in Jondaryan.

The jury took twenty minutes to find Denton guilty of murder, 'with a recommendation for mercy', on the grounds that the accused did not know what he was doing and was incapable of controlling his actions.

But Justice Real had no choice other than to sentence Denton to death, although he passed on the jury's recommendation for leniency, and the sentence was later reduced to life imprisonment. ■

Butchery on a Sarina cane farm

It wasn't murder. It was butchery. With the exception of the father, an entire family – the mother and her five children whose ages ranged from 20 months to 17 years – was slaughtered on a north Queensland cane farm on an afternoon in November 1911. The episode shocked the nation.

FOR some months, George Silva, a native of Ceylon, had been employed by a Chinese cane farmer named Charles Ching on a property at Alligator Creek, a few miles north of Sarina. Ching had married a white woman and they had five children.

It was known that the eldest daughter, 17-year-old Maud, had more than once resisted the advances of Silva, thereby perhaps unwittingly precipitating the butchery that was to follow.

On 17 November 1911, Ching set out on a day trip to Plane Creek mill at nearby Sarina township, his family assembling to bid him farewell. Immediately afterwards, two of the children departed for the one-teacher school a couple of miles away.

From the 1870s, cane farms around Sarina pioneered Queensland's sugar industry. In 1911, one such farm became the site of one of Australia's most notorious mass killings.

Ching returned at 5.30 and was met by Silva who, he later recalled, had changed his clothes from those he was wearing earlier that day.

He found the house locked up and his family apparently away somewhere. Silva did not know where they were; he said he had been at a neighbour's farm for most of the day.

Ching, accompanied by Silva, unsuccessfully inquired at several nearby farms. Had anyone had seen his family that day? No.

The horror uncovered

RETURNING to his house and finding the doors locked, Ching climbed in through a window - and by the light of his hurricane lamp, inside he encountered the terrible scene.

Side by side upon the floor he found the bodies of his wife Agnes, daughter Maud (17), son Hugh (4), and baby Winnie (20 months). The bodies were covered with a blanket and, on top of it all, by some grotesque impulse, the family Bible had been placed.

Agnes and Maud had each been shot in the neck; the mother was horribly mutilated. And the two children, their brains had been dashed out with some kind of heavy weapon, wielded by a powerful hand. The interior of the three-roomed dwelling was in shambles and blood splattered the walls.

A distraught Ching sent Silva to a neighbouring farm to raise the alarm and police arrived the next morning by car from Mackay. They brought with them an aboriginal tracker who later located the bodies of the two remaining children, last seen on their way home from school at 4 o'clock the day before. Dolly (8) and Teddy (10) were found about a mile away, shot in the head and their skulls smashed in.

The slaughter of a mother and her five children – an episode that shocked a nation

It was not long before suspicion fell upon Silva. He had been unable to account satisfactorily for his movements and he told conflicting stories as to how and why he disposed of the clothes he was wearing on the morning of 17 November.

Silva was kept under surveillance for some days, during which time he became increasingly agitated and asked to be locked up because he was afraid a wild mob would lynch him - which was exactly what a few incensed locals were wanting to do. Police agreed to Silva's request.

In time, police discovered the remains of a fire in which Silva's blood-soaked missing clothes had been burned, along with a charred gold watch and other articles belonging to the Ching family. Eventually, Silva confessed his guilt, was arrested and taken to Mackay.

There the prisoner was tried before Mr Justice Lukin, found guilty of the murder of the Ching's oldest daughter Maud, and sentenced to death.

The community had been outraged by Silva's crime and a group of Mackay's citizens met informally and decided to take the law into their own hands - they were keen to string up the mass murderer themselves. But Silva was quietly and quickly escorted away from such hostility, to the security of Boggo Road Gaol in Brisbane. ▶

To the gallows

THE morning of George Silva's execution dawned bleak and wet. In the prison yard at Boggo Road in Brisbane, the flowers and shrubs drooped in the rain and the only bright spot around the quadrangle just before 8 o'clock was the lamp in the porch leading to the cell where the condemned man awaited his fate.

At 8 o'clock the procession began, with Silva the centre-piece, arms pinioned to his side. Chanting the 23rd Psalm, Major Wilson of the Salvation Army led the way up the stairs to the scaffold and Silva was placed on the drop.

Then began a strange and pathetic dissertation from the scaffold. As one eyewitness reported:

'The chief warder asked if the condemned man had anything to say, and George David Silva at once proceeded to let her go. He knew it was his last hour on earth and he made the most of it. For the next twenty-seven minutes by the clock he harangued and testified in a way that not one street-corner preacher could approach within miles.

His language was well-chosen and his diction good, and he rattled along like a human gramophone. He talked without cessation and, had he not been stopped, he would have been talking still. But the harangue was horribly blasphemous. Those whose duty compelled them to be present went to see a tragedy and they were treated to a farce.

He started by thanking the Governor of the gaol, the warders, the Salvation Army. Whenever the flow of his discourse was threatened with a stoppage, he fell back on his thanks dodge. No less than six times he repeated his lesson in his frantic effort to spin out his last moment as long as possible. Then he dived into the Scriptures and gave chapter and verse with a fluency that would have earned the envy of a top-notch preacher. An 'Our Father' gave him an extra ten minutes of life, for we counted no less than 12 times he recited that sublime prayer.

At first, practically everyone present thought they were dealing with a religious maniac, but as the minutes dragged by, they realised they were dealing with a cunning man who was simply talking against time, and the pity that was in their hearts turned to loathing and scorn. Had he confessed and asked pardon for his fearful crime, his harangue would have been all right; but he didn't, and he went down to death a blasphemous, unrepentant sinner...'

At 8.30 the officials began to get uneasy. Would the man never stop?

The chief warder came down the stairs and whispered to the Under Sheriff. Then he went back, but the harangue continued until, eventually, the Under Sheriff had to mount the stairs himself.

Silva seemed to recognise that the end was near, for he said: "I'm going to heaven now; going now; going now..." But he broke off to say: "God bless you all, dear friends. Take warning from me, and get out of the broad road, and take in the narrow way... " Off he went again.

Then, once more, he fell back into the Lord's Prayer, but this time Major Wilson joined in, the signal that the final scene was at hand.

Quickly the hangman stepped up and pulled the white cap over Silva's face, forever blotting out his vision of earth. The noose was adjusted within seconds, the signal was given, and the trapdoor opened. There were a few convulsive tremors, and then the limbs straightened out, and all was over for the butcher from Sarina. ■

The Turkey Station mystery

In 1912 Turkey Station was a well established grazing property south of Gladstone. Edie Anderson, the 17-year-old daughter of the assistant-lighthouse keeper at nearby Bustard Head, was employed in the homestead as a domestic.

Edie's father had sent Arthur Cogzell to bring his daughter home to Bustard Head, having been told that an 'intimate' relationship had been developing between her and a station stockman George Daniels, a young man of Kanaka-Chinese extraction. They set out for the lighthouse on horseback at 8.30 a.m. on Sunday, 11 February.

Less than two hours later, Fred Bowton came upon a severely bleeding Cogzell, with two bullet wounds in his back, lying on the bank of Danube Creek fewer than six kilometres from the station homestead. Cogzell was able to tell Bowton that he had been ambushed by Daniels, whose hat was later found nearby. And he had taken Edie with him. By the time help arrived from the homestead, Cogzell was dead.

For weeks, searching police and trackers could find no trace of the pair. Even a £500 reward, with posters at railway stations in the district, proved fruitless.

'Police needed. Shooting and abduction. Turkey Station.' *A heliograph message (flashing sunlight via a mirror) was despatched to the Bustard Head lighthouse* (above) *from Turkey Station* (below). The lighthouse telephoned Gladstone police.

Hopes were raised when a pensioner, a Mrs Leslie, reported being visited by Daniels, seeking food and clothing for Edie who was seen half-hidden behind a nearby tree, holding a gun. Mrs Leslie gave Daniels 'a good talking to', and the pair left. Police believed the old lady was senile and gave little credence to her story. (Suspiciously, some weeks later, her burned body was found inside her fireplace. Accidental death, said the police.)

Daniels and Edie were never located. The Turkey Station mystery of 1912 remains so to this day. ■

The last man to hang in Queensland

Samford in the early years of the twentieth century was a small valley community located some 20 kilometres north-west of Brisbane.

On the morning of Sunday, 8 June 1913, local farmer James Mitchell and his wife set out in their sulky to visit a neighbour several kilometres distant. With them was 11-year-old daughter Ivy.

On the way, they dropped Ivy off at the Frish family home where she would spend the day with the Frish children.

That was to be the last time the Mitchells would see their daughter alive.

IVY departed the Frish house at 4.20 that afternoon to walk the couple of kilometres home. She carried a bag of lollies and some flower cuttings, and was accompanied by her playmate May Frisch who walked part of the distance with her…

A gruesome discovery

THE Mitchells arrived home at around 5.30. At sunset, James Mitchell became anxious: Ivy had not returned. He and his son set out to find her. They called at the houses of farmers in the neighbourhood and learned that Ivy had been last seen about 5.30, walking along the road towards the Parker State School. A small party of concerned neighbours, carrying lanterns, joined the search.

In the dust of Cedar Creek Road, they found the tracks of small bare feet. These they followed as far as the school and there noticed ominously that, to the side of them, were also the marks of large hob-nailed boots.

Then, outside the school, the child's tracks stopped; the boot tracks continued, the wearer turning off into the scrub. By lantern light, the searchers followed.

It was James Mitchell who first came across the body of his daughter lying on the ground beside a log. Her throat had been slashed. Beside her were strewn her lollies and flowers. Nearby too was the handle of a home-made whip.

A newspaper report continued:

'The fact that Ivy had been deprived

Samford Hotel. In the early hours of Monday, 9 June 1913, a party of police arrived from Brisbane after riding during the night. At daybreak, they set about their task of seeking out the murderer of 11-year-old Ivy Mitchell.

of a certain garment, which was found on top of her body, as well as the position in which she was found, indicated with sickening clearness that another horrible crime, other than that of murder, had been contemplated, and attempted unsuccessfully, owing to the child's desperate resistance.'

Someone rode the five kilometres into Samford to telephone the police.

A little after midnight, a police squad arrived from Brisbane. The body was covered and plaster casts taken of the tell-tale tracks of the hob-nailed boots. A search revealed that the murderer had washed his hands of the victim's blood at a tap on the nearby school's tank stand.

Police questioning of locals quickly had them suspicious of a local farmhand named Ernest Austin...

A murderer revealed

ERNEST Austin had spent most of that Sunday unaware that his actions later that day would eventually cost him his life.

In the afternoon he called in on his former employer, farmer Christian Hansen, for a cup of tea and a yarn and to arrange for some of his belongings to be sent to his new place of employment.

Hansen's daughter recalled later that, when he was about to leave at 4.45 p.m., Austin had leaned against his horse and lifted his foot to examine a broken heel plate on his hob-nailed boot. She also noticed that he had a distinctive home-made whip in his hand – just like the one found later at the murder scene.

At 5.50 p.m. a farmhand named William Webster saw Austin galloping along Cedar Creek Road. He waved to Austin who pulled his mount to a halt and said: "I've done it this time."

Following a brief and obscure conversation, Austin spurred his horse and rode off, leaving a puzzled Webster staring.

Austin reached the farm of his new employer James Fogg. "I'm a little later than I thought I was going to be," he said as he hurried off to feed some animals.

After dinner, Fogg remarked that he was going to Brisbane the next morning and Austin asked him if he could take his boots to town to be resoled. Fogg agreed. Austin went to his room and began removing hobnails.

On the road next morning Fogg's sulky was stopped by police and the farmer was questioned. "And what's in the sugar bag?" he was asked. Austin's hob-nailed boots.

Austin was in the yard when the police rode up. His clothes and the cap he had worn the day before were examined, as were the boots. Blood stains were obvious. There were also blood stains on the inside of his large pocket knife. And he had three fresh scratches on his face. As well, plaster casts of the tracks on the road revealed a broken heel plate on the left boot – just like on Austin's. The police took him to Brisbane under arrest.

One night in his cell, while awaiting trial, he tore a prison blanket into strips, plaited them into a rope and tried to hang himself. A warder caught him in the act. Austin remonstrated: "I'll be hanged anyway. I admit I murdered the girl."

Despite the confession, he pleaded not guilty at the trial in August 1913. But his case was hopeless and he knew it.

Austin grinned as he swaggered in and out of the courtroom, making the most of the limelight that was briefly his. It took the jury only 49 minutes to find him guilty and Chief Justice Cooper sentenced him to hang. ■

The last man hanged in Queensland

NOT that he was aware of it at the time, but the Samford murderer would be the last person to hang in Queensland.

On 22 September 1913 Ernest Austin went to the gallows at Boggo Road calmly and with resignation. When asked if he had anything to say, he said, *inter alia*:

"I say straight out that I highly deserve this punishment. I did not know what I was doing at the time. I have asked the Lord to forgive me for all my faults and he has done so. I have made sorrow for my brother and sister, and not only for my own people, but for the father of the child. I ask you all to forgive me. I ask my mother to forgive me. May you all live long and die happy. God save the King."

Then the hangman pulled the white cap over the doomed man's face, but he continued speaking:

"God save the King. God be with you all. Send a wire to my mother and tell her I died happy. Yes, tell her I died happy – and with no fear at all. Good-bye all. Good-bye all."

And with that, the trapdoor was released and Austin, who only a few months earlier was singing in the church choir at Samford, was no more.

IN 1915, the Labor Party, which had long advocated the abolition of capital punishment, won office in Queensland. Because World War 2 and other political matters took precedence, it wasn't until the passage of a further seven years, marked by acrimonious debate, that legislation was finally passed in State Parliament abolishing the death penalty. In 1922, Queensland became the first Australian state to do so, followed by Tasmania – 46 years later.

EXIT—THE HANGMAN.

FROM childhood, Victorian-born **Ernest Austin** was in trouble with police. He repeatedly absconded from reformatories, only to add further petty crimes to his growing dossier. At age 19 he was sentenced to three years imprisonment for an attempted offence against a young girl. On release, he drifted to Queensland where, in 1913, he found honest work as a farmhand at Samford… until that fateful day in June 1913.

The Mayne timber yard tragedy

It was 3 o'clock in the morning when Sergeant Burgess looked up from his desk as Constable Nugent entered his office at the Valley Police Station.

"Sergeant, I've got a man here who says he has just killed his wife."

Burgess later recalled how the man, as he stepped into the room, was 'cool and quite collected, and exhibited no evidence of excitement'.

It was early Sunday morning on 18 January 1914.

"Yes, I killed Bridget in a timber yard down near the Booroobadin bowling green in Abbotsford Road, Mayne. She's been trying to poison me for the last two weeks by putting poison in my food."

"How did you kill her?"

"I hit her on the head with a piece of 6 by 6 hardwood."

LATER, at the Town and Country Timber Yard, police found near a timber rack the body of a young woman, lying on its back in a large pool of blood, with massive wounds to the head. Entangled in the hair was a pair of smashed, blood-soaked spectacles. Nearby they found a blood-stained piece of hardwood nearly four feet in length, along with a lady's hat and handbag.

"She was standing there, I was standing here. I hit her, and she fell in there. I hit her again, and then I got sorry…"

A question of sanity

HENRY Hopgood, 34, had married Bridget O'Callaghan, the 20-year-old daughter of an Allora farmer, only two months earlier. The couple had moved to Brisbane where Hopgood had found work as a horsebreaker and member of a touring buckjumping show.

But the shift to the city found Hopgood behaving strangely. In fact, during that time he soon sought medical advice.

Drs L'Estrange and Sutton would recall Hopgood claiming he 'was suffering from poison, which had been administered to him by his wife' – but neither could find any evidence of poisoning. Individually, the doctors concluded that their patient was 'under a delusion', 'suffering from illusions', and 'extremely depressed in mind'. They advised his wife that he was 'suffering from a disease of the mind' that 'could develop into suicidal mania'. In summary his mental condition 'needed to be watched'.

The doctors provided Hopgood with medicine to soothe his indigestion, and bromide to quieten him. In fact, after he was arrested, police found five medical prescriptions in his possession.

AT his trial in February, Hopgood told how the couple had walked from the city around 11 p.m. to a friend's house in Bowen Hills to stay the night. Finding the place in darkness, they walked over the hill past the bowling green, through the timber yard where he asked his wife: 'Will you admit giving me poison – and I'll forgive you?'

"She would not admit it, so I took up the piece of wood and killed her."

Others would testify to his odd behaviour. A jockey friend recalled him 'rubbing his stomach, rolling about, and groaning: "My wife is trying to poison me"'. A neighbour said Hopgood had told her that a doctor had informed him that he was being poisoned.

His mother recalled that as a boy Hopgood had a fall which injured his head, and he had had bad falls from horses since then.

Crown expert Dr A.H.Marks, President of the British Medical Association (Qld), said he had observed Hopgood regularly since his arrest. His conclusion: "The man was subject to fits of insanity. He suffered from delusions while in gaol. He said that people were breaking in horses in his cell, that people were trying to poison him… A belief that some one is trying to poison one is common in cases of insanity."

In summing up, Justice Chubb said the jury would be justified in finding a verdict of not guilty on the ground of insanity. It did. His Honour ordered the accused to be detained in an asylum 'during His Majesty's pleasure'. ■

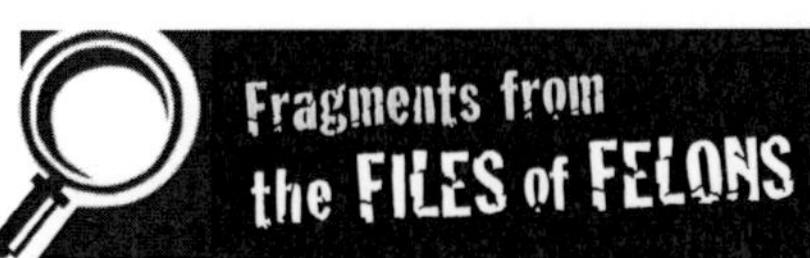

Scene of the shooting, Royal Exchange Hotel in Elizabeth Street, in the shadow of Brisbane's first skyscraper, Perry House, completed a year earlier in 1913

1914. THEY had arrived in Brisbane from Sydney only two days earlier and had spent the day at the races. That Saturday night, 18 July, Sidney Johns and his mate visited the British Empire Hotel in Queen Street, were refused a drink because they were too drunk, and started an altercation which had Johns drawing a revolver and threatening the barman before leaving.

At 10.15 p.m. the pair were walking down Elizabeth Street and, when outside the Royal Exchange Hotel, they had words with a James Moran on the footpath. A fight broke out between Johns' mate and Moran, who was getting the better of the other when Johns joined in the brawl.

Among the crowd who had gathered to watch was William Mortimer. He stepped up and told Johns not to interfere. Johns broke loose, moved to the road, pulled out his revolver, and shot Mortimer dead.

He ran off down Albert Street pursued by two policemen who had just arrived. There they found Johns in a laneway, hiding behind a large wooden case. They overpowered the man, and dragged him out. His gun was found on the ground where he had hidden it.

Found guilty of murder, Sidney Johns was sentenced to death by Justice Real on 12 August, later commuted to life in prison.

1915

Ambrose Butwell
Crime: Murder
Location: Graceville
Penalty: Death
commuted to 15 years hard labour

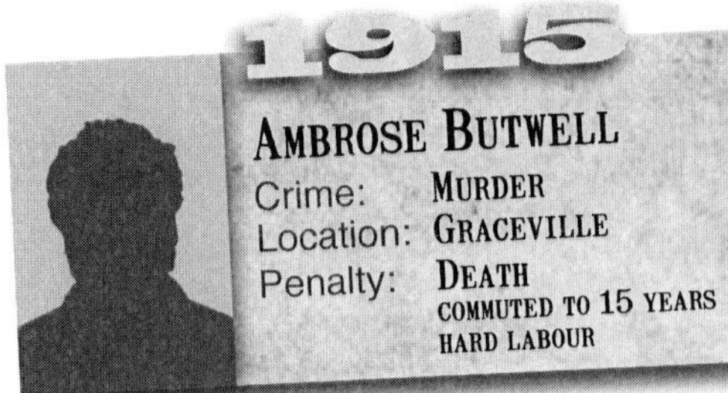

The Oxley Creek infant murder

Around 5.00 p.m. on Sunday 28 November 1915, a motor cycle pulled up outside the Corinda Police Station in Brisbane. A young man told police that something puzzling had happened at nearby Graceville a few hours earlier.

A constable went to Graceville where he spoke with several concerned farmers in the area. He pieced together the following information:

> At around 1.30 that afternoon, a young man and woman were seen walking through farmlands from Graceville Railway Station, in the direction of the isolated junction of Oxley Creek and the Brisbane River. The woman was carrying a child; the man a parcel. On their way back to the station some thirty minutes later, they no longer had the baby. One of the residents, Fred King, said the pair had called in to his farm around 3.30 for a cup of water, on their way back to the train. He offered them tea and sandwiches and in conversation was told that the young woman was living in a boarding house in Wharf Street in the city.

A telephone call to city police resulted in a visit by Detective James Farrell to a city boarding house that night. There he interviewed a 17-year-old Florence Stephens…

"Did any person stay with you last night?"

"Yes, a friend of mine, Ambrose Butwell. He's 19 years old."

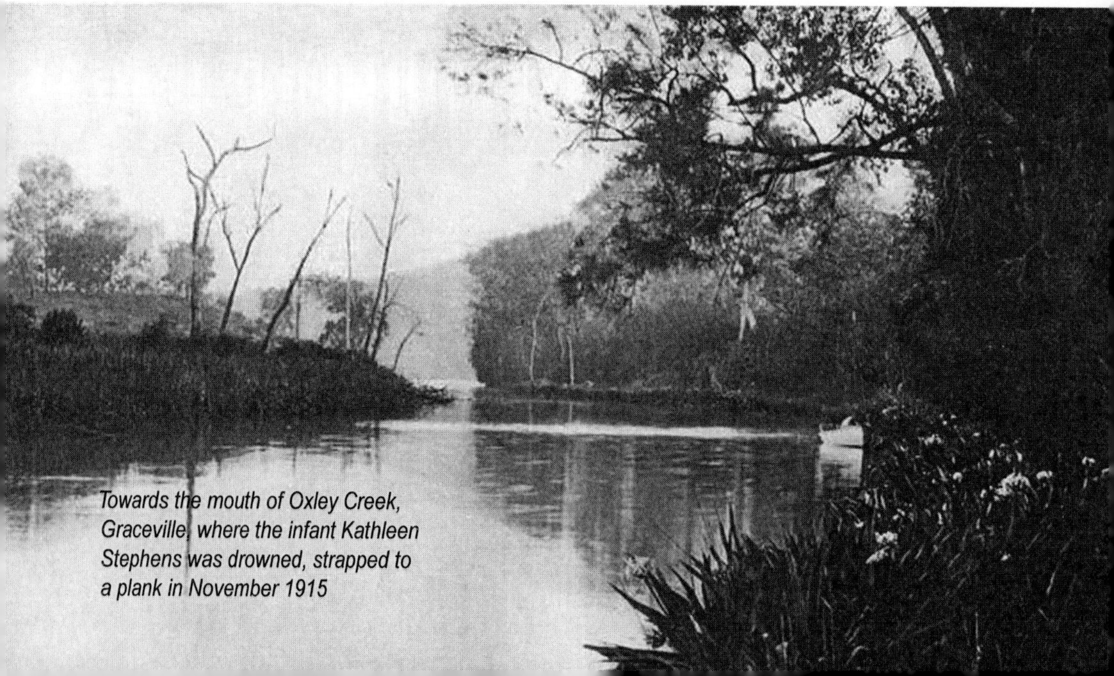

Towards the mouth of Oxley Creek, Graceville, where the infant Kathleen Stephens was drowned, strapped to a plank in November 1915

"Did you have a child with you"

"Yes"

"Is Butwell the father of your child?"

"Yes."

"Where does Butwell live?"

"At Paddington with his sister."

Sgt Farrell outlined the Graceville incident to her.

"Were you and Butwell the two people involved?"

"Yes."

"What did you do with the child?"

"Ambrose got a board and we tied the baby to it and he threw it in the creek."

"Was the child alive when Butwell threw it in the creek?"

"Yes."

"Did you not protest against him doing that to your child?"

"I did not want it."

"Who suggested throwing it into the creek?"

"Ambrose mentioned it to me the night he brought me from the Lady Bowen Hospital a fortnight ago, and we had spoken about it since..."

Returning to the scene

FARRELL took Florence to the city C.I.Branch, and by 3.00 a.m. detectives had also picked up Ambrose Butwell at Paddington. He denied all involvement: "We were at the city gardens at the lower end of Edward Street from 2.00 to 7.30 ."

At daylight, three detectives took Butwell and Stephens by car to the Oxley Creek junction. Water Police were already on the scene searching for the child.

Again Florence Stephens was taken over, and confirmed, the events of the previous afternoon. Butwell continued to deny everything.

Later that morning, the detectives asked several local farmer-witnesses to identity the pair. Yes, these were yesterday's visitors - and the young man was even wearing the same coat, with its distinctive row of buttons on the front.

The evidence mounts

THE child's decomposed body would be found a quarter of a mile down river two days later. A post-mortem confirmed she had died of asphyxia from drowning. The body was tied to a 6-foot plank with a strap, on which was clearly inscribed 'Miss A. Stephens, Roadvale Station, Fassifern Line". An identical strap, similarly marked, was found in Florence's bedroom.

The staff at Lady Bowen Hospital confirmed that Florence entered the hospital on 12 November and the female child was born five minutes later. She remained at the hospital for 14 days, was visited at least twice by a young man resembling Butwell - the same person who accompanied her in a cab when she was discharged on 25 November.

Boarding house keeper Louisa Gromodecki recalled helping Florence dress the baby on the fateful Sunday morning - in the same garments that were found on the infant body later recovered by the Water Police. As they were leaving, Florence said she was catching the train to visit relatives in Ipswich. The Ipswich line passed through Graceville.

The police had sufficient evidence. Ambrose Butwell and Florence Stephens were arrested and charged with the wilful murder of two-week old Kathleen Stephens.

The trial

ON 21 February 1916, the trial of Butwell and Stephens was held at the criminal sittings of the Supreme Court

Judge Patrick Real: "This is a very sad case indeed."

in Brisbane, before Justice Patrick Real.

The jury retired at 4.35 p.m. on the second day, and returned late in the night. It found Butwell guilty of murder, 'with a strong recommendation for mercy on account of his youth', and Stephens not guilty 'on the ground of her having taken no part in the act'.

When asked if he had anything to say before sentence, Butwell replied, "I am very sorry, your Honour."

In passing sentence, Judge Real said that Butwell seemed to lack any sense of responsibility and he appeared to hardly realise the gravity of the offence and its terrible consequences. Although the judge acknowledged that it would have been exceedingly painful for the jury to find the accused guilty, he was compelled to pass the sentence of the law – and that was the sentence of death.

One month later, a special meeting of Executive Council was held to consider Ambrose Butwell's death sentence. The Council was advised that, if the accused had been found guilty of manslaughter, Justice Real would have sentenced him to 15 years imprisonment. And thus it was that, after reading the judge's notes and considering the evidence of the case, Executive Council commuted Butwell's death sentence to one of 15 years imprisonment with hard labour. ■

Fragments from the FILES of FELONS

1915. A year of robberies, among them:

ON 1 April a horse and cart stopped outside the drapery shop of Heaslop & Sons, Stanley Street, South Brisbane at 1.30 p.m. Two men snatched a roll of flannelette from an outside display and drove off. Police were advised. At 5.00, the pair returned and began loading several more rolls. Staff ran outside, grappled with the thieves, but both managed to run off. A large crowd witnessed the ruckus and 'there was considerable excitement'. By evening both men had been apprehended.

ON Friday 9 July, at 4.45 p.m. a youth named Lehane was carrying in a purse £72 in wages for the employees of Taylor & College, wholesale chemists. As he passed down the lane from George Street to William Street in Brisbane, between the Government Printer and the Executive Building, a man approached, threw cayenne pepper in Lehane's eyes, snatched the purse and ran off, never to be caught.

LATE at night on Tuesday 9 November, a tramway conductor and his motorman were sitting in their tram at the Paddington terminus, talking, and waiting for their re-starting time. They took little notice of the footsteps behind them on the tram – an entering passenger, no doubt.

"Hand over your money while I count to ten!" They found themselves looking down the barrel of a six-chamber revolver in the hands of a masked man.

The man was soon running off into the night clutching the conductor's bag with less than £5 in small change. Later the empty bag was found by the road. The man was never found.

Acid attack on the Victoria Bridge

Robert Smith was walking across the Victoria Bridge in the company of his brother Bert and a soldier mate, George Bamford. It was late afternoon on 10 June 1916.

An hour earlier, at a pub in Stanley Street, South Brisbane, Smith had run into Denis Buckmaster, with whom he had had trouble some time earlier.

"I'm going to give you a hiding," said Smith, "because it was you who burned my tent!"

Buckmaster ran off.

THE three were halfway across the bridge when…

"Hey!"

Robert Smith turned round.

"Take that, you bastard!"

It was Buckmaster. He had come up behind the three and had thrown the contents of a small bottle into the face of Robert Smith.

It was sulphuric acid.

Smith fell to the footpath and yelled for water, which took some minutes to bring. In the meantime, Buckmaster walked off.

Smith was taken to the C.I.Branch where the incident was reported.

There it was found that the acid had destroyed the upper parts of his coat, and eaten through the fibre of his hat. An attending doctor recorded that Smith was also 'suffering from burns from a corrosive fluid on the left side of his face and head. The substance could cause permanent injury to his eyes. The skin would heal, but I

According to the trial judge, the acid attack on railway worker Robert Hall, while he was crossing the Victoria Bridge in Brisbane, in June 1916, was 'a most detestable crime'.

cannot express an opinion as to his left eye'.

Robert Smith, a railway worker, was laid up for three weeks.

THE trial of Denis Buckmaster was held in August at the Supreme Court in Brisbane, with the Chief Justice, Sir Pope A. Cooper presiding.

Buckmaster was charged with 'having thrown a corrosive fluid upon Robert Smith, with intent to maim, disfigure, or disable him, or to do him some grievous bodily harm'.

The jury retired at 2.15 p.m. on 14 August 1916. They returned within forty minutes with a guilty verdict.

"This was a most detestable crime you committed, and one that made you a noxious animal in the sight of other men... I sentence you to hard labour for 15 years."

– Chief Justice Sir Pope Cooper

NOT that the victim Robert Smith was without past blemishes. During the trial, Buckmaster's defence counsel had police admitting that they knew Smith well: "He has been convicted over 30 times for various offences - including garotting." ■

Fragments from the FILES of FELONS

1916. THE judge was 'very sorry indeed for her' as Elsie Shaw was led from the court, crying. He commented on the 'sordid nature of her miserable life and expressed astonishment that her brothers and sisters had not taken an interest in her'.

Elsie Shaw had just been convicted of manslaughter and sentenced to five years imprisonment.

The judge had heard that from an early age she had led 'an immoral life with Chinamen and other aliens, and was at one time removed from a certain house in Fortitude Valley occupied by a negro'.

In 1916, Elsie, aged 26, had been living for several weeks with a separated man, William Nielson, in the house of his brother's family at Spring Hill in Brisbane.

As dinner was being prepared, around 5 p.m. on 1 March, the family heard an argument in the upstairs bedroom – then a frantic call: "Duck for the Ambulance, Toby. I have killed Bill. Forgive me, forgive me, I did not mean to do it."

On the bed lay the body of William Nielson, in military uniform, with a single stab wound to the chest. A bloodied knife, used for repairing shoes, was found in the bath.

The judge counselled Elsie:

"On your release after two years, you will lead a far happier life if you live away from your bad associates'.

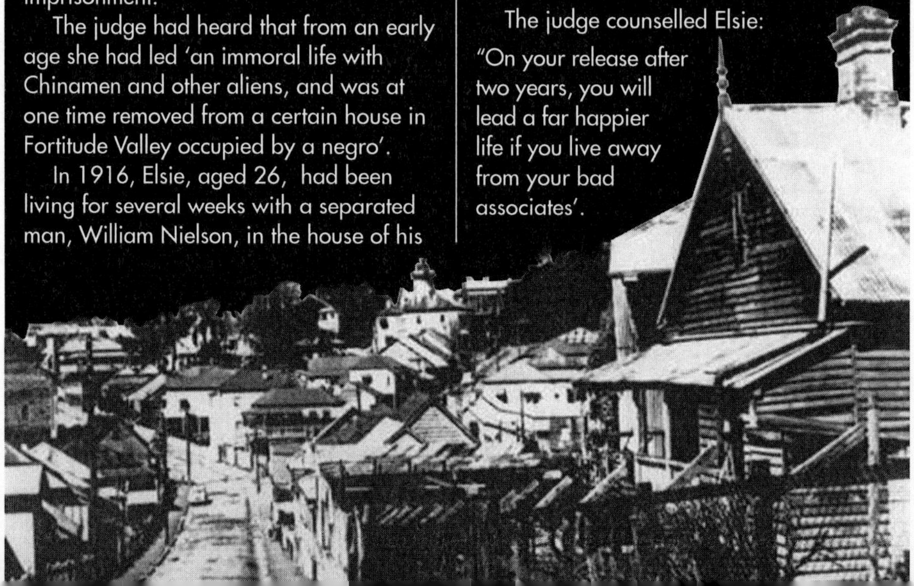

The missionary murderer

In the early 1900s, the Presbyterian Church was granted permission to establish a mission station on Mornington Island in the Gulf of Carpentaria.

The Rev. Robert Hall, accompanied by his wife and two assistant missionaries, Mr and Mrs Owen, proceeded to the lonely island full of enthusiasm.

Right from the start, the missionaries had great success with the natives. Given the Aborigines' earlier reputation, it was thought that they would have proved hostile. Instead, they appeared willing and friendly. Indeed, after the missionaries had erected their headquarters—a large building of corrugated galvanised iron with a veranda all round—they even managed to get some of the natives working at building fences and cottages for themselves and their families, and planting vegetables.

IN 1917, the Burketown district, on the mainland, had been greatly troubled by an unruly and very large Aborigine who had been given the name of 'Burketown Peter'. Semi-civilised and ostracised by his own tribe, this native was considered a very unsavoury character. He had been employed on a cattle station, but had been dismissed for stealing tobacco, for which he had acquired a passionate fondness.

After his dismissal, Burketown Peter embarked on a career of crime, raiding station homesteads and other dwellings, from which he stole all manner of articles - but chiefly tobacco. Tobacco was the one thing above all else that he cherished, and he would do anything to get 'baccy', as he called it.

He always managed to evade arrest, but ultimately he became such a pest that the police set out after him. He managed to evade his pursuers, but then, to the great relief of all, left the district.

No one knew where he had gone—and, needless to say, no one cared; but his destination was revealed only a few weeks later, when his name was blazoned forth as the perpetrator of a shocking crime on lonely Mornington Island.

What prompted the native to go to Mornington Island was never found out, and his method of getting there was likewise a mystery.

His arrival at Mornington marked the beginning of serious trouble for the missionaries. Burketown Peter was a born leader, and on the island he soon gathered about him a band of savage bush warriors, who readily obeyed his orders.

A week or so passed, and then, craving tobacco, Burketown Peter, believing the missionaries would have ample supplies, decided to take his warriors with him and visit the mission headquarters. There they were met by the Rev. Hall, who told Burketown Peter that all the missionaries were non-smokers, and that there was not an ounce of tobacco at the mission.

The Aborigine did not believe this and, scowling savagely and muttering ominous threats, he left with his cronies and disappeared into the bush.

The missionaries did not worry about the incident, and early next morning the Rev. Hall embarked on a trip into the interior of the island, where he hoped to win the friendship of some of the bush dwellers.

He expected to be absent for some days, and took with him a sleeping-bag and a shotgun for shooting game.

All that day he walked through dense bush, now and then halting for a chat at the isolated camps of friendly natives – and the whole time, although he did not know it, he was being closely followed by Burketown Peter and his band of warriors.

On the first night the missionary camped alone in the heart of the bush and, as soon as he had fallen asleep, Burketown Peter and his men crept up and decapitated the missionary with a tomahawk. After Burketown Peter had searched the dead man's clothes for tobacco without finding any, he seized the shotgun and, ordering his warriors to follow him, he headed for the mission headquarters, intending to kill the other missionaries and ransack the place.

That night, however, Owen, the assistant missionary, was sleeping alone on the front veranda of the house. Burketown Peter fired at the sleeping man, tearing away part of Owen's left shoulder.

In an instant Owen was out of bed, dashed inside and slammed the door just as Burketown Peter fired again.

Hastily bandaging his wounded arm Owen, with the assistance of his wife and Mrs Hall, then barricaded every door and window in the building, keeping the hostile natives at bay.

Burketown Peter and his men made several attempts to break in that night, but they promptly withdrew when met by a fusillade of shots through loopholes, which the missionaries had hurriedly cut in the galvanised iron walls.

Then began a siege which lasted for several days. Day and night the natives watched the mission house, with their spears in readiness to attack any person who ventured outside. Every night they renewed their attempts to break into the building, which they bombarded with stones of all sizes, but they were always driven back by rifle and revolver fire from the loopholes.

Burketown Peter had driven all the friendly natives away from the precincts of the mission, and seemed determined to kill the missionaries or starve them to death.

As the days passed, the missionary trio suffered greatly. Owen's injured arm throbbed painfully, and all grew weaker and weaker from lack of sleep. Fortunately they had plenty of food in the house, but water was becoming scarce and, when the supplies were all but depleted at dawn on the tenth day, the three were prepared for the inevitable.

But at sunrise, when Owen went to one of the loopholes to take over the monotonous and terrible task of watching out for the natives, his gaze wandered out to sea where he saw a motor launch travelling at full speed towards the island.

He readily recognised the vessel as being one from Burketown; and so did Burketown Peter who, accompanied by his cronies, dashed away into the bush.

Aboard the launch were police from Burketown. Unbeknown to the besieged missionaries, one of the friendly natives had heroically paddled his way to the mainland in a tiny bark canoe to report the siege.

The wounded missionary and the two women were immediately taken to Burketown, while the police stayed on the island to arrest Burketown Peter, who, with his offsiders, was captured after a short chase.

Peter was sentenced to death, along with his prime accomplice, Dick, a penalty later commuted to imprisonment for life at the penal settlement on St Helena Island, in Moreton Bay. ■

On St Helena Island

ON St Helena Burketown Peter's love of tobacco persisted. The son of a warder who resided on the island remembered the prisoner:

"The prisoners used to tend the fields of corn and lucerne, or work in the vegetable garden opposite our house. There were a lot of Aborigines there then, including a couple of bad ones. Burketown Peter was one. On one occasion he came into our house and tried to force my mother to give him some tobacco. Fortunately there was a gang working in the field on the other side of the road and the warder in charge came in and grabbed this bloke and hoyed him out."[1]

And like many of the Aborigines confined on the island, Burketown Peter yearned for freedom. After nearly three frustrating years in prison, he made a desperate bid for liberty in 1921 by setting out to sea on an old target frame that the warders used for rifle practice. It would be his target frame to eternity.

Rather than be recaptured, the escapee, according to one cryptic recollection, 'chose to jump into the water to be drowned... though I think that he may have been despatched by other means.'[1]

ESCAPEE'S TRAGIC DEATH.

DROWNED IN MORETON BAY.

Burketown Peter, the aboriginal convict who escaped from St. Helena on Sunday, was drowned in Moreton Bay yesterday afternoon under somewhat tragic circumstances. The Comptroller-General of Prisons (Captain Peirson) received advice during the day that at 1.30 p.m. the captain of the dredge tender Pumba, when about a quarter of a mile west of the old Pile Light, which is approximately three miles from St. Helena, saw the aboriginal floating on a target frame. The Pumba was steered alongside the frame, and the captain said, "Come along, Peter; I take you on my ship." The aboriginal replied, "No; you no want take me on your ship." The captain then endeavoured to pull the target frame alongside the ship by means of a boat hook, but Burketown Peter jumped into the water. A boat was immediately lowered and an endeavour made to save the escapee, who was obviously in difficulties. Just as the boat reached him, however, he sank, evidently completely exhausted. One of the crew endeavoured to obtain a hold of the aboriginal's hair, but was unsuccessful, as it was too short. The Pumba remained in the vicinity for some time, but the aboriginal was not seen again, and the conclusion was arrived at that he had been drowned.

Murder on the breakwater

At a little before 8.00 p.m. on 21 January 1918, ferryman James Jenkins carried a man and woman across Ross Creek from South Townsville to the Harbours and Rivers Wharf. He remembered the couple clearly: the man had spent the trip trying to fix the young woman's gold-rimmed spectacles – and he ended up doing so with his teeth.

At the landing, the pair walked towards the recently reclaimed land, passing the cottage of the Harbour caretaker John Fines, who was sitting on the verandah, and disappeared into the post-dusk darkness. The man was carrying an umbrella.

About fifteen minutes later, Fines jumped to his feet. Two shots came from the direction of the reclamation, followed by a woman's screams. Through the darkness he made out the young woman; she was running towards a car that had just parked some 50 yards from his cottage.

"Let me in! Let me in!" she yelled to the driver. "He's coming!"

More shots.

Commercial traveller Robert Garraway jumped from his car and took hold of the woman as she ran towards him. She was bleeding from the head and neck.

"Tommy. Thomas. Tomorrow Charters Towers," she shouted several times.

Another shot.

"Oh, he's coming. He's coming. He will shoot us!"

Garraway pushed her into the car and drove the short distance to caretaker Fines' cottage.

By now the girl had become delirious and slipped into unconsciousness as she was quickly driven off to hospital.

A walk to the watch-house

A FEW minutes later a man entered Fines' cottage: "For God's sake take me to the lock-up. I done it. I shot her."

The caretaker set off with the man walking to the watch-house, but, approaching the Criterion Hotel, the man gave Fines half-a-crown, and asked to share with him the best brandy he could buy. "This will be my last drink for a few years," he added.

In discussion with Fines, the man disclosed that he had thrown his gun into the creek and that he had left his umbrella at the scene of the shooting.

As they walked past the Tattersall's Hotel, the man had second thoughts: "Look here, mate. I have had a change of mind. I'll go up to my room and stop there till they arrest me."

They parted and, as Fines would later admit, "I was in truth very thankful to get away from him."

Arrest and trial

GERTRUDE Dillon was dead on arrival at Townsville Hospital.

At 11.00 that night John La Hay turned up at her ward, announcing to the nurse: "I'm the bloke that shot the girl."

Police in attendance took him to the police station where he made a statement, saying that her mother had driven him to it. He had in his possession the girl's gold-rimmed spectacles.

La Hay was arrested for the murder of Gertrude Dillon. His trial took place in Townsville before Justice Real in March. He pleaded not guilty.

Gertrude's mother revealed that in November she had told La Hay, who had been 'keeping company' with her daughter, that 'his disposition would not suit Gertrude' and that he should break off the relationship.

La Hay did not take it well. He told Gertrude: 'If I catch you walking or keeping company with anyone else I'll break your head off your shoulders... If I don't get you by fair means, I'll have you by foul means."

Mrs Dillon claimed that, on the family's return from Charters Towers after a Christmas visit, her daughter showed constant fear, and always locked her windows at night.

Other witnesses testified to La Hay's obsession with Gertrude. A salesman John Rogers spoke of La Hay's threats against the girl 'if she went to the altar with any other man'. John Shepherd had driven La Hay to the hospital on 21 January, when La Hay said: "I am the one that shot the girl. She has tormented me long enough."

And ironmongers George Manton and James Ferguson testified that La Hay had purchased from them a revolver and cartridges on the afternoon of the shooting.

On 10 March 1918, after a short retirement, the jury found John La Hay guilty of murder. Justice Read sentenced him to death. ■

La Hay appeals

IN April 1918, Chief Justice Pope Cooper and Justices Shand and Lukin heard an appeal by John La Hay against his conviction. The grounds for the appeal included: that the words of the dying girl ("Tommy Thomas has shot me") were ignored; that on the night of the murder, a man named Thomas left Townsville by boat for Brisbane; that Gertrude's mother had threatening letters from Thomas, that would prove La Hay's innocence; that police did not take seriously a second statement by La Hay that he had struggled with a second man (Thomas?) at the murder scene.

The Criminal Court of Appeal found there was 'abundant evidence' to justify the finding of the original jury. The death sentence would stand. It was later commuted to life in prison.

The Red Flag riot

"I had been playing out in Merivale Street, South Brisbane, with a group of other children that evening in 1919 when our game was brought to an abrupt halt by a terrifying, unearthly sound. We stood transfixed. We had never heard anything like it before. It was the roar of a rampant mob of around 7-8000 adults, principally men, rushing across Victoria Bridge and down Melbourne, Grey and Russell Streets en route to attack the Russian community headquarters. Their wild cries were underscored by the thunder of thousands of marching and running feet; and as this cacophony approached a crescendo, we could see the front ranks of the crowd pouring into Merivale Street as well as lines of foot- and mounted-police rapidly taking up their positions to defend the Russian Hall. We ran away in terror…"[1]

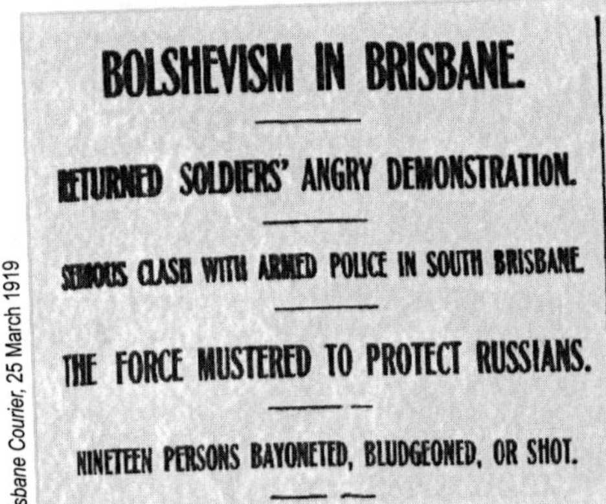

BOLSHEVISM IN BRISBANE.

RETURNED SOLDIERS' ANGRY DEMONSTRATION.

SERIOUS CLASH WITH ARMED POLICE IN SOUTH BRISBANE.

THE FORCE MUSTERED TO PROTECT RUSSIANS.

NINETEEN PERSONS BAYONETED, BLUDGEONED, OR SHOT.

Brisbane Courier, 25 March 1919

During World War 1, Merivale Street in South Brisbane was 'a restless centre of urban, proletarian life, filled with tenements, boarding houses, workers' cottages and corner stores', and included a small Russian ghetto, stretching across several blocks, and surrounding the Russian Hall. This building would be the focus of a major riot on 24 March 1919.

The gathering storm

AT the height of World War 1 came the extraordinary news of the 1917 Tsar-deposing Russian Revolution.

When Leon Trotsky signed a truce with Germany, Brisbane Russians were branded enemy aliens. Many returned to the country of their birth, while all further immigration into Australia from Russia was stopped.

The working people of Brisbane became divided over the use of red flags, which had now become a dangerous symbol of rebellion. While some union organisations proudly flew the flag, and opened and closed their meetings with the red-flag anthem, others bitterly opposed what the flag represented. At one meeting in the Brisbane Domain in 1918 there was a rowdy clash between loyalist returned soldiers chanting 'Rule Britannia' and radicals singing 'The Red Flag'. Reports of riots between red-flag sympathisers and returned soldiers in Hughenden, Toowoomba and elsewhere began to filter in. Red leftist posters were being slapped over War Loan advertisements as fast as they could be removed. Boarding houses in Russian areas of South Brisbane were raided, and red propaganda and printing blocks were seized.

In protest, a large, peaceful march wound its way through Brisbane's streets, led by members of the Russian community. After the march, lists of 'dangerous Russians' who had taken part were compiled. The local conservative press fed the rising frenzy, depicting revolutionary Russians as 'Bolshevik swine', guilty of 'repulsive bestiality, lawlessness and lust'; as well the leaders of the Catholic and Protestant churches preached against the alarming spread of ungodly, atheistic communism.

In one raid the Russian Club on Stanley Street was wrecked and protest banners and other revolutionary material were seized. New headquarters were established by the Russians in Merivale Street.

By the end of 1918, a new law made it illegal to march under a red flag.

The day before

AT 2.30 p.m. on Sunday, 23 March 1919, a subdued assembly of 400, including sympathetic Queensland workers, met outside Brisbane Trades Hall. Police looked on. Surveillance agents mingled with the crowd. Suddenly Alexander Zuzenko and his followers emerged and unwrapped three large red banners, hoisting them high. A cheer went up as a hundred small red pennants were also distributed.

The march began. It grew and gathered momentum as the marchers approached the Domain. There, speaker after speaker took the podium. Police on horses and on foot attempted to intervene, but they were hopelessly outnumbered. For

The Red Monday riot of 1919 with police confronting anti-communist factions in Merivale Street, Brisbane

the moment the radicals had won.

That night, several thousand returned soldiers violently attacked a union meeting at North Quay. Russians and radicals were 'seized, mauled and stabbed'. Then two thousand men crossed Victoria Bridge to attack the 'Bolshevik headquarters'. Police stood by and watched. It took warning shots from inside the building, and a heavy downpour, to disperse the mob.

The Merivale Street riot

ON the next night, 24 March, fuelled by alcohol, exaggerated anti-Russian editorials, and an inflammatory meeting at North Quay, seven thousand loyalists and returned soldiers again marched on the Russian Club chanting 'Burn their meeting place down!' and 'Hang them!'

In Merivale Street, finding their way blocked by a force of between 40–60 police mounted on horseback and armed with rifles and bayonets, a violent clash broke out. Palings, bricks, home-made bombs and bottles rained down. Sporadic gunfire broke out. The fighting lasted for two hours – over 100 men received bayonet wounds, nearly 20 police officers were injured, including Police Commissioner Frederick Urquhart, and three police horses were shot, one of which later died, while 19 ex-servicemen needed to be evacuated by ambulance. Incredibly, no one had been killed. The Russian hall was virtually demolished.

After the *Brisbane Courier* defended the actions of the loyalist mob, violent disturbances and demonstrations continued for three days, much to the dismay of a repressed and terrified Russian community. On the fifth night a mighty storm put a stop to further large scale violence.

The riots were followed by months of intimidation and individual assaults upon people who spoke or even looked Russian.

The trial

IN April-May, sixteen men accused of displaying the Red Flag were brought to trial, painfully presided over by Police Magistrate Archdall, who had been bayonetted in the groin during the battle of Merivale Street. Only one of these, a Labor MLA, Edgar Free, escaped with a fine. The rest were sentenced to various periods of imprisonment – three for seven months, ten for six months, one for two months, and one for one month.

Aware that the verdict was virtually a foregone conclusion, most of the defendants struggled to turn what was basically a political trial into a political forum to air their radical beliefs. Five of the accused were Russians and typical of their defence were the words of Herman Bykov, as he stated in halting English, amidst peals of derisive laughter from the body of the court:

> "As a Russian Maximalist... I consider I am not a criminal, but merely a political prisoner of Australian capitalists. I was stabbed and beaten with sticks by some ignorant and probably drunken soldiers who do not realise what Bolshevism really is... I spent seven years in the Tsar's dungeons and in exile in Siberia... I am glad to come in prison again for the victory of the Red Flag... " ■

Sidelight

During these turbulent two months a new conservative organisation had formed – the Returned Sailors and Soldiers Imperial League of Australia (RSSILA); it continued to gain popularity, later becoming the RSL.

The empty chamber

In 1920, the small township of Emu Vale was the social hub of its surrounding wheat-growing district in the southern Darling Downs.

The Commercial Hotel in town had only recently been taken over by a new proprietor, a married 38-year-old James Comerford, who had already 'built the reputation of conducting the establishment in a thoroughly respectable manner'.

In December 1920, the hotel had been broken into on two occasions by local lads John Long and Michael Kennedy, but Comerford warned both, rather than opting to 'make trouble' so early into his ownership.

Both Long and Kennedy were part of a team of men who worked with a local grain-threshing outfit.

Trouble in the bar

ON 30 December, the 18-year-old Long, in the company of a few of his workmates, having already 'indulged too freely in liquor', turned up at the hotel and began making trouble. It was not for the first time.

On this occasion, the proprietor Comerford asked Long to leave, but he refused. The youth was forcefully ejected through the front door and on to the road, where he had an altercation with another patron.

Early the next day, New Year's Eve, Comerford rang the police at Tannymorel, six miles away, informing them of the issue and seeking their involvement. We'll talk it over with you in the new year, he was told.

The threshing team finished work at 6.00 p.m. on New Year's Eve and set about consuming five gallons of beer, which they had previously purchased.

By 9.30 p.m. Long and several of his rowdy drinking mates had walked the mile to the hotel.

On arrival, a drunken Long declared to bar patrons: "I've come to

Shooting victim John Long was one of several workers of a grain threshing machine operating in the Emu Vale district in 1920.

The Commercial Hotel in Emu Vale, where publican James Comerford shot dead the rowdy 18-year-old James Long on New Year's Eve 1920

fight Jim Comerford. I'm going to bring him out in the yard and it will be all in… I'll fight him dirtier than I fought that chap on Boxing Day. I'll put him in the dirt…"

Comerford said to Long: "You get out of my bar. I do not want you here. You are under 21, and undesirable."

"I'll not leave. You come and put me out, you rotten bastard!"

"If you do not go outside, I will not use my fists," said Comerford, reaching under the bar.

"I'm not frightened by your bloody piece of wood. I've got my push with me tonight, and we'll take the damn pub apart!"

"We're with you," shouted one of his mates.

Comerford gave them three minutes to leave the hotel.

He then went upstairs, took a revolver out of his dresser and put five bullets into it – leaving one chamber empty. His intention was to pull the trigger over the empty chamber, in the hope that, if he were forced to fire, the 'click' would be enough the frighten off the troublemakers.

He returned to the bar.

There Long and his men still refused to leave, and began swearing at and threatening Comerford's wife.

There were more heated words and threats of violence.

A fearful Comerford decided it was time to call the troublemakers' bluff. He raised his revolver, took steady aim at Long, fired – and, instead of a 'click', there was a loud retort. Long fell dead, with a bullet to the heart!

"My God, I've shot him… The cylinder must have turned!" and, stunned, Comerford slumped into a chair. A bar assistant took the gun from the shocked proprietor. Shortly afterwards, Comerford himself rang the police, who arrived after midnight and arrested him.

UNLIKE his fellow publican, Robert Denner of nearby Boonah, who was sentenced to five years penal servitude for shooting a drunken patron in 1904 [see page 156], a jury before Justice Lukin found Comerford not guilty of John Long's murder. He was discharged a free man on 15 February 1921. ■

> Nothing is easier than to denounce the evil doer; Nothing more difficult than understanding him.
>
> – **Fyodor Dostoevsky in *Crime and Punishment***

Commit the Crime, Do the Time...

QUEENSLAND'S MAJOR PRISONS: The colonial years and beyond

The six decades covered by this book

1850 1860 1870 1880 1890 1900 1910 1920 1930 1940 1950

The Colonial Years (1859-1900)... ...and beyond

Brisbane Gaol, Petrie Terrace 1860-1883

St Helena Island Penal Establishment 1867-1933

Brisbane Gaol, Boggo Road 1882-2000

At the time of Separation in 1859 there was in the new colony only one prison, located in a former convict building on the present site of the GPO in Queen Street, Brisbane. In the following years, the major purpose-built prisons at Petrie Terrace, St Helena Island and Boggo Road were supplemented by smaller gaols and lock-ups – the prison hulk *Proserpine* at Lytton (1863), Fortitude Valley (1863), Rockhampton (1864), Toowoomba (1864), Roma (1872), Townsville (1878), Mackay (1888)... and elsewhere.

Brisbane Gaol, Petrie Terrace

QUEENSLAND was declared a separate colony in 1859 and its first purpose-built building – a gaol – was opened a year later, just outside town on a ridge at Green Hills (Petrie Terrace).

The suitability of the structure as a prison was immediately criticised, the massive stone walls doing little to alleviate the sweltering heat of Brisbane's sub-tropical climate. With an initial capacity of 108 male and 36 female prisoners, the new gaol was at once subjected to a barrage of complaints due to the excessive heat and the desperate overcrowding, especially when the prison admissions exceeded 500 annually – some prisoners were even being accommodated in the gaol's office! As early as 1863 warders began petitioning the government to improve their 'harrowing spectacle'. To ease the situation, smaller gaols were opened at such places as Rockhampton and Toowoomba – and on St Helena Island.

The gaol closed in 1883, by which time some 31 hangings had taken place within its walls.

St Helena Island Penal Establishment

LYING several kilometres from the mouth of the Brisbane River, for more than 60 years from 1867, St Helena Island became colonial Queensland's foremost prison for men. The island prison gained a largely unwarranted reputation as 'the hell-hole of the Pacific' and 'Queensland's own Devil's Island'. On the other hand, it was held in high regard by visiting penologists, churchmen and journalists, for it was a 'self-supporting' prison where men could also be rehabilitated through learning such trades as tailoring, bootmaking, saddlery and farming pursuits. Primarily a prison for men serving long sentences – murderers, rapists, bushrangers, rebels, and thieves, at its peak the gaol could accommodate over 350 prisoners.

The prison closed in 1933. No hangings ever took place on the island.

Brisbane Gaol, Boggo Road

THE first cell block at Boggo Road in Annerley opened in1883 using materials from the demolished Petrie Terrace gaol, and over the years many other buildings were added to the site. The gaol was originally designed to cater for 64 male prisoners, awaiting transfer to the colony's main prison on St Helena Island. The Boggo Road gaol would grow to become Queensland's largest and, from 1883 to 1913, was the scene of 42 hangings.

In 1903 an 80-cell facility was built on the site to hold female offenders. In 1921, women inmates were moved to other buildings on the reserve, their former prison used for the detention of long-term male prisoners from St Helena when, during the 1920s, the St Helena inmates and workshops were transferred to Boggo Road.

In the 1990s, the prison closed, with most of the facilities then being demolished, to make way for the creation of an urban village. Part of the old gaol remains as a heritage-listed site.

These three major prisons and a smaller gaol network were supported by lesser, police-managed facilities, larger than the usual lockups attached to police stations throughout Queensland, and holding short-term prisoners serving two weeks or less. Police gaols could be upgraded to official prisons (or such prisons downgraded to police gaols) according to local requirements and population fluctuations, resulting, for example, from the growth or decline of such colonial industries as sugar growing and gold mining.

From prison records. . .

QUEENSLAND. 779/07

No. 105.07 Name August Millewski

Native place Germany | Education R & W.
Year of birth 1855. | Height 5' 7½
Arrived in Colony { Ship Unknown | Weight 9st 10lbs
{ Year 1887 | Colour of eyes Blue
From where Germany | Colour of hair Drk Bro.
Trade or calling Farmer | Complexion Fresh
Religion Lutheran. | Build Prop.

Date when Portrait was taken. Oct 22.07.

Offence Wilful Murder.

When and where tried 15 Oct. 07 SC Maryborough.

Sentence Death

Executed. Dec 16.07

No. of previous Portrait ( )

Marks and special features Large mole & small birthmark rt side stomach, Small blue spot between shoulders, Small mole under rt armpit, Large Scar inside 2nd + 3rd lt finger; Varicose veins both legs.

PAST CRIMINAL HISTORY.

Where Convicted	When.	Offence.	Sentence.

No. 109 Name Polly Logomea S.I.

Date when Portrait was taken, 5. 10

Native place Solomon
Year of birth 1857
Arrived in Colony. { Ship Helena { Year 1885
Trade or occupation previous to conviction } Laborer
Religion
Education, degree of
Height 5 feet 7½ inches
Weight in lbs. { On committal 9 3 { On discharge
Colour of hair Blk
Colour of eyes Bro
Marks or special features 2 crosses left arm " " " "

Where and when tried Bunda...
Offence Mur...
Sentence Death
Remarks

(No. of previous Portrait)

PREVIOUS CONVICTIONS:—

Commuted to 5 Yrs P.S.

No. Name Ellen Thompson

Date when Portrait was taken, 17 May 1887

Native place Ireland
Year of Birth 1846
Arrived in Colony } Ship Joshua } Year 1857
Trade or occupation previous to conviction } Wife of Murdered man
Religion Roman Catholic
Education, degree of Nil
Height 4 feet 9 inches
Weight in lbs. } On committal 106 } On discharge
Colour of hair Gray
Colour of eyes Gray
Marks or special features

Where and when tried } Townsville 27 April 1887
Offence Murder
Sentence Death
Remarks Strenuously denied her guilt upon the gallows and insisted that her innocence would be established. She was a very talkative woman, of a cheerful temperament. Had led a rough hard life in the northern part of Queensland and had probably learned to attach little value to life. Not a bad dispositioned woman, very temperate in her habits. Capable and industrious. Died instantaneously.

(No. of previous Portrait

No. 93 Name Gibson Stewart

Date when Portrait was taken, 3 July

Native place Queensland
Year of birth 1864
Arrived in Colony. } Ship — } Year —
Trade or occupation previous to conviction } Carpenter
Religion C. of E.
Education, degree of Raw
Height 6 feet 0½ inches
Weight in lbs. } On committal } On discharge 159
Colour of hair Bro
Colour of eyes Grey
Marks or special features Scar small toe r foot

Where and when tried } Rockhampton 16 ...
Offence Bigamy
Sentence 2 yrs H...
Remarks

(No. of previous Portrait)

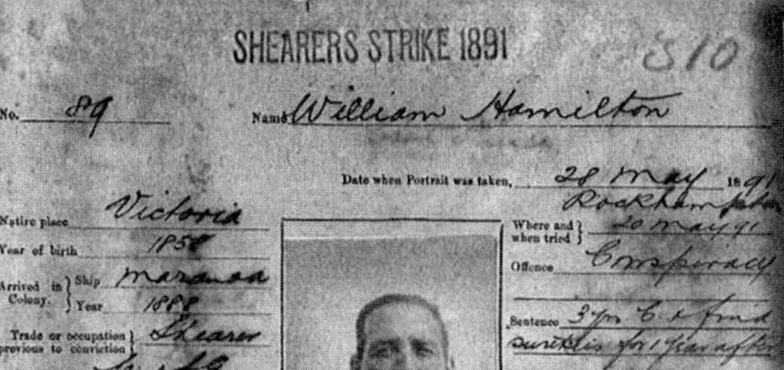

SHEARERS STRIKE 1891 810

No. 89 Name William Hamilton

Date when Portrait was taken, 28 May 1891

Native place Victoria
Year of birth 1858
Arrived in Colony. } Ship Maranoa } Year 1888
Trade or occupation previous to conviction } Shearer
Religion C. of E.
Education, degree of R & W.
Height 5 feet 11½ inches
Weight in lbs. } On committal } On discharge
Colour of hair Bro.
Colour of eyes Bro.
Marks or special features Wart on right cheek.

Where and when tried } Rockhampton 20 May 91
Offence Conspiracy
Sentence 3 yrs C. & find sureties for 1 year after
Remarks Convicted of Conspiracy in connection with SHEARERS STRIKE 1891 in Queensland was prominent in interfering with the free labourers

(No. of previous Portrait)

No. 200 Name Arthur Hollingswor...

Date when Portrait was taken, 5. 12.

Native place Queensland
Year of birth 1867
Arrived in Colony. } Ship } Year
Trade or occupation previous to conviction } Clerk
Religion C of E.
Education, degree of R & W
Height 5 feet 7 inches
Weight in lbs. } On committal 10.8 } On discharge
Colour of hair Bro
Colour of eyes Grey
Marks or special features

Where and when tried } Stanthorpe
Offence Larceny
Sentence 18 Mos.
Remarks

(No. of previous Portrait)

QUEENSLAND.

Name Donald (an aboriginal)

Date when Portrait was taken, 6th April 18

Native place Queensland
Year of birth About 1863
Arrived in Colony: Ship / Year
Trade or occupation previous to conviction Stockman
Religion Church of England
Education, degree of None
Height 5 feet 7¾ inches
Weight: On committal 10.9 / On discharge
Colour of hair Black
Colour of eyes Brown
Marks or special features

Where and when tried Roma, 13th March 18
Offence Rape
Sentence Death
Remarks Executed 25 April

(No. of previous Portrait)

PREVIOUS CONVICTIONS.—

18th July 1881. Toowoomba. Bestiality. Ten years. C.

QUEENSLAND.
Z.
"THE CRIMINAL CODE."

85

Name BONNY. (Aboriginal.)
No. 25-199 District ROCKHAMPTON.
Place and date of arrest Cleve Station, Marlborough. 14/12/1920.
Offence Grievous bodily harm.
Where, by what Court, and when tried Rockhampton. Supreme Court. 2nd March 1920.
Name of Judge or Magistrate by whom sentenced Judge Lukin.
Sentence 2 years hard labour
Date released under "The Criminal Code" 2/3/1920.
By whose authority released Judge Lukin.
Where and to whom ordered to report Rockhampton. O. C. Police.
How often ordered to report Once every three months.
For how long a period ordered to report Two years.
Date when first report made after release 2/3/1920.
Amount of Recognizance Nil.

Date when Portrait was taken: 2nd March 1920.
Name and Address of Photographer: The Irving Studios. East Street. Rockhampton.

Arresting Constable Const P A Salagari.
Married, single, or widower Widower.
Age 63 years.
Height 5 feet 9 inches.
Build Slight.
Colour of Hair Black turning grey.
Eyes Brown, white pupil in the left eye.
Beard, etc. Black moustache turning grey.
Complexion Black.
Native Place Croydon Station. St Lawrence. Queensland.
Trade or Calling Stockman, labourer, & scalper.
Religion Nil.
Marks, Scars, or Special Features Mole under right nostril & right cheek bone. Warts back left thumb, back left hand & left wrist. Six raised aboriginal scoring across chest down to abdomen also on both arms near the shoulders.

Offender's Signature

236

No. 186 Name Francis J. Gallagher

Date when Portrait was taken, 24 Dec 1890

Native place Ireland
Year of birth 1861
Arrived in Colony: Ship South Esk / Year 1888
Trade or occupation previous to conviction Laborer
Religion R.C.
Education, degree of R & W
Height 5 feet 9 inches
Weight: On committal 11/9 / On discharge
Colour of hair Black
Colour of eyes Brown
Marks or special features

Where and when tried Croydon 17 Nov 90
Offence Horsestealing
Sentence 3 yrs 10 mos. P. S.
Remarks

(No. of previous Portrait)

170

No. 156 Name Fredk. Andrews

Date when Portrait was taken, 23 Oct 1900

Native place Queensland
Year of birth 1865
Arrived in Colony: Ship / Year
Trade or occupation previous to conviction Assistant
Religion C. of E.
Education, degree of R & W
Height 5 feet 5 inches
Weight in lbs.: On committal 9/5 / On discharge
Colour of hair Red
Colour of eyes Grey
Marks or special features Minus big toe r foot

Where and when tried 21 Oct 00 Brisbane
Offence Forgery Uttering
Sentence 12 mo. H.L.
Remarks

Name James Gardner alias James McMahon

Date when Portrait was taken, 24th Septr 1883.

Native place Scotland
Year of birth 1864
Arrived in Colony: Ship unknown / Year unknown
Trade or occupation previous to conviction Cab Driver
Religion Roman Catholic
Education, degree of Read & Write
Height 5 feet 6½ inches
Weight: On committal 9 lbs 4 oz / On discharge
Colour of hair Brown
Colour of eyes Grey
Marks or special features: ... joints lower limbs ... in speech

Where and when tried Rockhampton 19th September 1883
Offence Murder
Sentence Death
Remarks:—

(No. of previous Portrait)

QUEENSLAND.

836

Name Irene McFarlane
No. 25-29
Native Place New South Wales
Year of Birth 1897
Arrival in State (Ship and Year)
From Where New South Wales
Trade or Calling Housewife
Religion R C
Education R & W
Height 5' 4"
Weight
Hair Fair
Eyes Blue
Complexion Fair
Build Stout
Finger Print Classification 28 / 16 (10 / M1)
Date Portrait Taken 29/9/19
Previous and Subsequent Portraits
Reference to Police Gaz. Phot. / Disch. Prisoners Supplement
Marks and Special Features scar rt cheek, scar centre f'head, long scar palm lft hand, birth mark ins rt f'arm

CRIMINAL HISTORY.

WHERE CONVICTED.	WHEN.	OFFENCE.	SENTENCE.
D.C. Brisbane	29-9-19	Bigamy	12 months h.l. sentence sub-

REFERENCES

ix Introduction
1. Irving, H.B., *A Book of Remarkable Criminals*, Cassell, London, 1918, p.1.
2. Bloch, H.A. & Geis, G., *Man, Crime and Society*, Random House, NY, 1962, p.3.
3. McCartney, C., Lincoln, R., & Wilson, P., *Justice in the Deep North*, Bond University Press, Gold Coast, 2003, p. ix.
4. Irving, H.B., p.2.
5 McCartney, C. et.al, p.43.
6. Irving, H.B., p.2.

2 **1859 *The slaughter of three St Helena fishermen***
Moreton Bay Courier, 29 January, 2, 12 February, 5, 12 March, 9 April, 29 June 1859; Petrie, C., *Tom Petrie's Early Reminiscences of Early Queensland,* Angus and Robertson, 1904, p.8.

5 **1860 *They didn't need the hangman***
Sydney Morning Herald, 22 December 1860, 4 March 1870; *Moretion Bay Courier*, 23 February, 2 March 1861, 17 December 1910; *The Argus*, 7 February, 12 March 1861; www.cqhistory.com/people/powell_2

8 **1860 *The ex-convict killer***
Moreton Bay Courier, 14 April, 19 April, 17 November, 8, 15 December 1860.

10 **1861 *That tell-tale bump***
The Courier, 19, 22, 23, 24, 26 October, 19, 22 November 1861.

12 **1862 *Three for the gallows***
The Courier, 6 February, 6, 18 March, 2,3,4, 21, 26 April, 3 May 1862.
Illustration: S.Woodcock, 1988.

15 **1863 *Death on a sheep station***
The Courier, 11 March, 8 April, 17 July, 3, 18 August 1863.

18 **1864 *Murder most cowardly on the Darling Downs***
Uebergang, G., 'The History of Owen's Scrub Road', *Australian Heritage*, Vol. 1 No. 3, 1983, pp. 84-98; *Toowoomba Chronicle*, 14 July 1864; Queensland State Archives CCT4/N11, Trial of Alexander Ritchie.

21 **1864 *When Fagan's gang ran wild***
Rockhampton Bulletin, 15, 18 October 1864; *Brisbane Courier,* 22 October 1864; Grabs, C., *Queensland Desperados: Wild tales of bushranging days*, Angus & Robertson, Sydney, 1983, pp. 67-91.

24 **1865 *The Wild Scotchman***
QSA, Col Sec A140 1094/70; *Brisbane Courier*, 7, 18 April 1866, 12 April 1870; McCarthy, P.H., *The Wild Scotsman*, Hawthorn Press, Melbourne, 1975.

27 **1866 *Man overboard!***
Brisbane Courier, 30, 31 August, 19, 26 November 1866.

29 **1866 *The Frenchman, bushranger***
Brisbane Courier, 2 October 1866.

31 **1866 *Assault on the high seas***
Brisbane Courier, 4 July, 23 August 1866.

33 **1866 *The Crocodile Creek Chinese riots***
The Queenslander, 6 April 1867.

35 **1867 *The Ipswich mail hold-up***
Ipswich Punch, Vol. 2 No. 2, 15 December 1866; *Brisbane Courier*, 7 January 1867, 17 August 1868, 4 July 1918; *Sunday Mail,* 4 June 1939; http://www.ipswich.qld.gov.au/documents/heritage/education_kit_transport.pdf

38 **1867 *The Clermont gold escort killings***
Hill, W.R.O., *Forty-five Years' Experience in North Queensland,* Pole & Co, Brisbane,1907, p. 131; MacMaster, H., 'The Gold Escort Murders', *Mostly Murder*, North Rockhampton, 1999, pp. 35-55;
http://www.cqhistory.com/wiki/pmwiki.php/Events/MurderOfTheClermontEscort

41 **1868 *The Imbil incident***
Brisbane Courier, 10, 25 April, 5 May, 9 July, 8 August, 1 September, 3 October 1868; *The Queenslander,* 11 April, 21 November 1868.

44 **1868 *The avenging public servant***
Brisbane Courier, 25 November, 4, 23, 29 December 1868, 2, 3 March 1869, 10 December 1894.

47 **1869 *The lure of Halligan's gold***
Brisbane Courier, 30 October 1869; *Rockhampton Bulletin*, 25 November 1869; Hill, W.R.O., *Forty-five Years' Experience in North Queensland*, Pole & Co, Brisbane,1907, pp. 132-135; Fitzgerald J.D., *Studies in Australian Crime:* 'The Morinish Murder', see http://gaslight.mtroyal.ca/gaslight/austrX03.htm
1. Bird T.S., *The Early History of Rockhampton*, The Rockhampton Bulletin, 1904.

50 **1870 *The hunt for Herrlich, the Hun***
Brisbane Courier, 16, 21 February 1870; *Toowoomba Chronicle*, 26 February, 13, 20, 30 April 1870.

53 **1871 *The murder of Simon Zieman***
Brisbane Courier, 30 November, 1, 11 December 1871; 11, 14, 17, 30 May, 11 June 1872; *The Queenslander*, 23, 30 December 1871, 3 February, 4, 18 May 1872.

56 **1872 *The pure white bull***
Sydney Morning Herald, 1 March 1873; *The Queenslander*, 22 February 1873; *Brisbane Courier*, 13 January 1872, 7 March 1873; *The Argus*, 5 March 1873; Holthouse, H., *Up Rode the Squatter*, Rigby, 1970.

59 **1873 *The downfall of a young nipper***
The Queenslander, 5 April 1873; *Brisbane Courier*, 1 January, 13, 29 March 1873.

61 **1874 *The Ipswich riot***
Brisbane Courier, 9, 10, 21 November 1874; *The Queenslander*, 12, 19 December, 1874, 20 February 1875.

63 **1875 *The stranger who never was***
The Queenslander, 15, 22 May, 6 November 1875; *Brisbane Courier*, 1 November 1875; *Gympie Times*, 30 October 1875.

66 **1876 *The brute from the Belyando***
The Queenslander, 29 April, 20 May, 9 October 1876; *Australian Historical Studies*, no. 123, April 2004, pp. 84-105; 'You'll get nothing out of it'? *The inquest, police and Aboriginal deaths in colonial Queensland*, Finnane M. and Richards J., Griffith University, Brisbane, Australia; Copland M., *Calculating lives: The numbers and narratives of forced removals in Queensland 1859-1972*, A thesis submitted to Griffith University, School of Arts, Media and Culture for the degree of Doctor of Philosophy, February 2005.

69 **1877 *The missing bank notes***
Brisbane Courier, 7, 10, 15 May 1878; *The Queenslander* 11, 18 May 1878.

71 **1878 *Gory goings-on at Gilbert River***
Brisbane Courier, 15 June, 2 October 1878.
1. *The Queenslander*, 8 June 1878.
2. *The Queenslander*, 15 June 1878.

74 **1879 *Caught... down a mineshaft***
Hill, W.R.O., *Forty-five Years' Experience in North Queensland*, Pole & Co, Brisbane,1907, pp. 82-85.

76 **1880 *The tree-climbing bank robber***
Brisbane Courier, 24 January, 20 February 1880.

79 **1881 *The tell-tale letter***
Brisbane Courier, 11-13, 19, 22-26 October, 23-26 November, 2-3 December 1881, 25 February, 1-4 March, 6-8 March 1882.

82 **1882 *Murder in the fowl house***
Brisbane Courier, 13, 28, 29 June, 15, 21, 22 July 1882; *The Queenslander*, 17 June, 22, 29 July, 5 August 1882.

84 **1883 *The Mackay Racecourse riot***
Moore C.R., 'The Mackay Racecourse Riot of 1883', http://espace.library.uq.edu.au/eserv/UQ:207961/DU270_J33_1978_pp181_196.pdf.
1. Cutting from *Mackay Standard* contained in P.M. Captain W.R. Goodall to Col. Sec, 8 January 1884, Queensland State Archives Col/A378, 495/1884.

86 **1884 *The South Sea slavers***
Brisbane Courier, 17, 18, 20 October, 25, 27, 28 November, 2, 4, 5, 12 December 1884, 20 February 1890; Holthouse H., *Cannibal Cargoes*, Rigby, Adelaide, 1969; Docker E.D., *The Blackbirders*, Angus & Robertson, Sydney, 1970.

89 **1885 *The Muttaburra murder***
Brisbane Courier, 20 May, 4 November 1885.

91 **1886 *A brotherly bullet?***
Queensland State Archives, Wong Tong's prison record sheet; *Brisbane Courier*, 7, 13 May, 22 June 1886.

92 **1886 *A woman on the gallows***
Stevenson, B., 'Ellen Thompson: The only woman hanged in Queensland', *Sunday Mail*, 9 February 1986, pp. 8-9; Matthews, T., 'Blood Lovers', *The Picture*, n.d, pp. 62-63.

95 **1887 *The American killer***
The Queenslander, 4 June 1887.
1. Harvey, J.R., *Hangman's Clients*, Invincible Press, Sydney, 1948, pp. 57-63. *passim.*

98 **1888 *A right royal ruckus over stolen boots***
Brisbane Courier, 10 September 1888; *Sunday Mail Magazine*, 28 January 1940.

101 **1888 *Murder – and the Normanton riot***
1. Donegan, J. and Evans, R., 'Running amok:

the Normanton race riots of 1888 and the genesis of white Australia', *Journal of Australian Studies*, Vol. 25 No. 71, 2001, pp. 83-98.

104 **1889 *The strychnine scones***
Brisbane Courier, 26 September 1889, 22, 28 February, 20 March 1890; *The Argus,* 22 March 1890.

107 **1890 *It's only a pumpkin I found***
Brisbane Courier, 11 September 1890.

108 **1890 *The law would show no mercy***
Rockhampton Morning Bulletin, 28 February, 25 April, 3 June 1890; *Brisbane Courier,* 27 February, 15 May, 2 June 1890.

109 **1891 *The Union conspirators***
The Argus, 26 March, 17 April, 11 May, 16 June 1891; *Brisbane Courier,* 9, 15, 29 November, 6, 21 December 1933.
1. Queensland State Archives, Col. Sec 2926/92.
2. From *Lunchroom to Boardroom*, Women in the Labor movement, 1930-1970. Interview: 'Ida Welsh, Townsville. Daughter of William Hamilton, striking shearer 1891', Fryer Library, University of Queensland.
3. Bernays, C.A., *Queensland: Our Seventh Political Decade 1920-1930,* Angus & Robertson, Sydney, 1931, p. 300.

112 **1892 *Bones in his bed***
Harvey, R.H., *Hangman's Clients*, Invincible Press, Sydney, 1948, pp. 73-78; MacMaster, H., *Mostly Murder*, North Rockhampton,1999, p. 156.

114 ***1892 Death among the pearl divers***
Harvey, R.H., *Hangman's Clients*, Invincible Press, Sydney, 1948, pp. 73-78.

116 **1893 *The burning body***
Brisbane Courier, 19 May, 24 October 1893; MacMaster, H., *Mostly Murder*, North Rockhampton,1999, pp.81-83.

119 **1894 *Death of a swagman***
Bundaberg Mail, 14 January 1895; *Brisbane Courier,* 15, 23 April, 21 May 1895.

121 **1895 *The hallucinating husband***
Brisbane Courier, 19, 23, 26 July, 23 August 1895.

123 **1896 *The Snob***
Finger, J., *The St Helena Story*, Fernfawn/ Boolarong, Brisbane, 2010, p.120.
1. MacMaster, H., *Mostly Murder,* North Rockhampton, 1999. p.32.

126 ***1896 Marie, the mission matron***
Brisbane Courier, 26, 29, 30 September, 18 November 1896; Gouglas, S. & Weaver, J.C., 'A Postcolonial Understanding of Law and Society: Exploring Criminal Trials in Colonial Queensland', *Australian Journal of Legal History,* Vol. 7 No. 4, 2003; Walker, F., 'Useful and Profitable: History and Race Relations at the Myora Aboriginal Mission, Stradbroke Island, Australia, 1892-1940', *Memoirs of the Queensland Museum,* Cultural Heritage Series, Vol. 1 No. 1, pp. 137-175, 1998.

127 **1897 *Double death at the asylum***
The Queenslander, 30 January 1897; *Brisbane Courier,* 5 February, 23 March 1897; *Sydney Morning Herald,* 8 April 1897.
1. Goodall J. B., *Whom nobody owns: The Dunwich Benevolent Asylum, an institutional biography 1866 - 1946,* PhD Thesis, University of Queensland, 1992.

128 **1898 *The murder of Warder Dodd***
Queensland State Archives, Col Sec 3696/98; *Brisbane Courier,* 19, 21 February, 1, 2, 10 March 1898; Finger, J., *The St Helena Story*, Fernfawn/ Boolarong, Brisbane, 2010, pp. 179-180.
1. *Courier Mail,* 18 May 2007, p.22.

131 **1898 *The Gatton mystery***
The Queenslander, 30 December 1898; 7, 24 January, 10, 25 March 1899.
1. *The Gatton Mystery* by James and Desmond Gibney; *The Gatton Murders: A true story of lust, vengeance and vile retribution* by Stephanie Bennett; *Gatton Man* by Merv Lilley; *Captivity Captive* (novel) by Rodney Hall (Victorian Premier's Literary Award, The Vance Palmer Prize for Fiction 1989).

134 **1899 *The Woolloongabba murder***
Brisbane Courier, 9, 10, 12, 14, 15, 16, 17, 21, 22, 24, 29 June, 1 July 1899.

138 **1900 *The fake suicide***
Brisbane Courier, 21 February, 20 May 1901; *The Queenslander,* 19, 26 January, 2, 16 February 1901; *Townsville Bulletin,* 6 March 1901; *Sydney Morning Herald,* 14 May 1901; MacMaster, H., *Mostly Murder,* North Rockhampton, 1999, p. 158.

140 **1900 *The jockey who sought revenge***
The Queenslander, 11 August 1900; *Brisbane Courier,* 5 September 1900, 5 February 1902; MacMaster, H., *Mostly Murder,* North Rockhampton,1999, p.97.

142 **1901 *Bullets in the boardroom***
Brisbane Courier, 11, 20 July, 3, 10 December 1901; *Truth,* 15 December 1901.

145 **1902 *The railway rascals***
Brisbane Courier, 5 November 1902; *Telegraph,*

3-5 November 1902; Blakie, G., *Great Australian Scandals*, Rigby, Adelaide, 1979, p. 43.

146 **1902 *"The very man I wanted to meet"***
Queensland State Archives PRI A143; *Brisbane Courier*, 15 February 1900, 1 March 1919; *Bundaberg Star*, 17 October 1901; *The Patriot*, 19 February 1919.

148 **1902 *The last of the bushrangers***
Brisbane Courier, 13 January 1903.
1. Fitzgerald, J.D., 'The Kenniffs', *Studies in Australian Crime*, Cornstalk, Sydney, Vol. 2, 1924 pp. 292-293.
2. Heap, E.G., 'The Ranges were the Best: The Kenniff Story', *Queensland Heritage*, Vol 2 No. 1, November 1969, pp. 3-23.

151 **1903 *One killing was not enough***
Brisbane Courier, 23 June 1903; *Truth*, 28 June 1903.

154 **1903 *The Longreach Cinderella***
Brisbane Courier, 1, 4 March, 6, 7 May 1904; *The Queenslander*, 5 March 1904; *Toowoomba Chronicle*, 3, 5 March 1904.

156 **1904 *The Boonah publican***
Truth, 8 May, 14 August 1904.

158 **1905 *One crime too many***
Brisbane Courier, 25, 27, March, 8, 12 April, 25 May, 17 July 1905; Irving, H.B., 'The Bloodthirsty Butler', in *A Book of Remarkable Criminals*, Cassell, London, 1918.

161 **1905 *Death of a Policeman***
Brisbane Courier, 15 May 1906; *Truth*, 7 January, 8 April, 15, 20 May 1906.

164 **1906 *Dobbed in by his wife and son***
Brisbane Courier, 17 December 1907; *Truth*, 18 August, 22 September, 22 December 1907.

167 **1906 *The threepenny murder***
Truth, 30 December 1906, 6 January 1907; *Brisbane Courier*, 2 January 1907.

168 **1906 *A killing in the kitchen***
Brisbane Courier, 15 May 1906; *Truth*, 20 May 1906.

169 **1907 *The Townsville railway station robbery***
Brisbane Courier, 27 December 1906, 12, 19 February, 13, 16, 19, 21 March, 6 June 1907.

171 **1908 *The bungling bank robber***
Brisbane Courier, 7 June 1909, 8 June 1909; *Truth*, 2 May 1909, 13 June 1909, 22, 29 November 1909; *Sunday Mail*, 22 September 1991.

174 **1909 *The Carron River killings***
Truth, 17 April 1910; *Brisbane Courier*, 14 June 1910.
1. MacMaster, H., *Mostly Murder*, North Rockhampton, 1999, p. 164.

177 **1909 *Bismark, the murdering blacktracker***
Brisbane Courier, 20 April 1909; *Truth*, 25 April 1909.

179 **1910 *Tragedy in a tent***
Brisbane Courier, 29 March, 21 April 1911.

181 **1911 *Butchery on a Sarina cane farm***
Brisbane Courier, 11 June 1912; *Truth*, 16 June 1912.

184 **1912 *The Turkey Station mystery***
Brisbane Courier, 13, 26 February, 9 March, 2, 27 August, 4 September, 29 November 1912; Gibney, D., *The Turkey Station Tragedy*, Alderley, Qld, 1995.

185 **1913 *The last man to hang***
Brisbane Courier, 23 September 1913; *Truth*, 15, 22, 29 June, 6 July, 31 August 1913.

188 **1914 *The Mayne timber yard tragedy***
Brisbane Courier, 19, 20, 28 January, 19 February 1914.

190 **1915 *The Oxley Creek infant murder***
Brisbane Courier, 14, 23 December 1915, 22, 23 February, 27 March 1916.

193 **1916 *Acid attack on the Victoria Bridge***
Brisbane Courier, 15 June, 15, 22 August 1916.

195 **1917 *The missionary murderer***
Brisbane Courier, 21 November 1917, 8 March, 10 May 1918, 18, 19, 20 January 1921; *Sydney Morning Herald*, 7 November 1917; *The Queenslander*, 16 February 1938.
1. Murrie F., in *Moreton Bay People: The Complete Collection*, Peter Ludlow, Brisbane, 2000, p. 96.

198 **1918 *Murder on the breakwater***
Townsville Bulletin, 30, 31 January, 9 March 1918; *Brisbane Courier*, 29 January, 11 March, 12 April 1918.

200 **1919 *The Red Flag riot***
Brisbane Courier, 25, 27 March, 4 April 1919; *The Queenslander*, 29 March 1919; R.L. Evans, *The Red Flag Riots: A study of intolerance*, University of Queensland Press, St Lucia, 1988.
1. Evans, R. & Ferrier, C., *Radical Brisbane*, Vulgar Press, Carlton North, 2004. Ch. 26. *passim*.

203 **1920 *The empty chamber***
Brisbane Courier, 3, 4, 11, 12, 16, 17 January 1921.

INDEX

A

Abduction, 184
Abolutionist Movement, 173
Ackroyd, John, 124
Alligator Creek, 181
Anderson, Alfred, 138
Anderson, Edie, 184
Anderson, John, 34
Andrews, Fred, 209
Ango, Tommy, 127
Antonio, Guido, 78
Apis Creek, 23
Arabury Station, 137
Archdall, PM Hewan, 202
Archer, Alexander, 69
Archer, William, 128
Arson, 85, 157
Assault, 31, 45, 84
Attempted murder, 121, 140
Austin, Ernest, 185
Australian Labor Party, 111, 187
Australian Republican, 115
Avondale, 119

B

Baker, Thomas, 67
Ballow, 2
Banana, 25
Banchory Station, 67
Banks
    Australian Bank of Commerce, 142
    Bank of New South Wales, 69, 123
    Commercial Bank, Gayndah, 171
    Queensland National Bank, 76
    Union Bank of Australia, 123
Barcaldine, 109
Barnett, Joseph, 116
Barney, 155
Barry, Michael, 108
Battery, The, 70
Beckett, William, 53
Beckman, Charles, 138
Behan, Michael, 23
Belmont, 125
Belyando Station, 67
Bennett, William, 110
Benson, Dr John, 63
Berry, Joseph, 76
Bigamy, 146
Bigge, F.E., 13
Billy, 168
Billy, Kipper, 12
Billy Dingy, 3
Birksgate, 103
Bismark, 177
Blackall, 57, 85
Blackbirding, 86
Blacktrackers, 39, 51, 132, 133 137, 149, 177.
Blackwell, Hugh, 110
Blake, Arthur, 179
Blake, Joseph, 41
Blantern, George, 116
Bob, 112
Boggo, 59
Boggo Road Gaol, *see* Prisons
Boldrewood, Rolf, 56
Bond, William, 78
Boney, 209
Bonnor, William, 135
Boonah, 104, 156, 204
Botanical Gardens, 46, 70, 78
Boulton, Robert, 90
Bowen, 138
Bowerman, Frank, 44
Bowlea, 139
Bowton, Fred, 184
Boyler George, 148
Bradshaw, Arthur, 174
Brandy, 10
Breaking and entering, 90, 118
Bribie Island, 3
Briggs, Fanny, 5
Broom, Billy, 137
Brown, Arthur, 68
Brown, David, 142
Buckmaster, Denis, 193
Bundaberg, 91, 100, 119, 146
Bunning, Walter, 89
Bunya Mountains, 3, 17
Burgess, Richard, 132
Burke, Michael, 36
Burketown, 26, 195
Burketown Peter, 195
Burns, Garrick, 9
Burns, James and Leslie, 175
Bushranging, 23, 24, 29, 30, 35, 41, 78, 148
Butterworth, Robert, 157
Butwell, Ambrose, 190
Bykov, Herman, 202

C

Cahill, Patrick, 38
Callaghan, Dr William, 40
Campbell, Archibald, 8
Campbell, John, 145
Candiottis, Dr Spiridion, 40
Canning Downs Station, 17
Canoona, 38
Carnarvon Range, 148
Carnarvon Station, 150
Carnill, James, 11
Carron River, 174,
Cassey, 126
Cattle duffing, 56
Cavanagh, Michael, 116
Chandler, William, 32
Charleville, 137
Charlie Gos Ano, 159
Charters Towers, 115, 142
Charters Towers Pyrites Company, 143
Childers, 137
Chinese, 33, 38, 83, 91, 92, 101, 151, 155, 162, 167,184, 194
Ching, Charles, 181
Christensen, Marie, 126
Clermont, 22, 38, 67, 109
Clifton Station, 9
Clint, Arthur, 90
Cobb & Co, 35, 78
Cock Tow, 91
Cockerill, John, 60
Coffey, Nellie, 157
Cogzell, Arthur, 184
Collins, Patrick, 53
Collins, Robert, 2
Comerford, James, 203
Condamine, 30
Conley, William, 169

Connolly, James, 15
Connors, Thomas, 17
Conroy, William, 120
Conspiracy, 110
Cooktown, 68, 113
Coonambula Station, 8
Corbett, John, 23
Corrie, Robert, 34
Counterfeiting, 78
Crocodile Creek, 33
Crothers, Jack, 41
Croydon, 174,
Cutsy, Abraham, 85

D

Dahlke, Albert, 148
Dalby, 17, 100
Dale, Elizabeth, 130
Daniels, George, 184
Darr River Station, 89
Davey, 166
Davidson, Gordon, 15
Davis, J.P., 102
Dawes, Archdeacon Nathaniel, 96
Day, Thomas, 132
Day Dawn mine, 115
Dee River, 6
Denner, Robert, 156, 204
Denton, William, 179
Dillon, Gertrude, 199
Dispersal raids, 73
Dodd, Henry, 129
Domane, William, 27
Donald, 209
Downie, William, 129
Downing, Henry, 104
Drayton, 20
Dugandan, 104
Dululu, 6
Dumbleton, 180
Duncombe, William, 29
Dunwich, 126, 153
Dunwich Benevolent Asylum, 125, 127

E

Eaves, William, 28
Elliott, Sub-Inspector, 40
Emmerson, Martin, 95
Emu Vale, 203
Erin Go Bragh, 16
Eventide, Sandgate, 127
Evitts, Janet, 177
Execution, *see* Hangings

F

Fagan, Peter, 21
False pretences, 146
Farrell, Detective James, 190
Farrington, John, 180
Fassifern, 66
Ferguson, James, 199
Fernvale, 12, 168
Fines, John, 198
First Offenders' Act, 98
Fisher, Andrew, 111
Fitzgerald, Edward, 34
Fitzgerald, John, 102
Flying Cloud, 20
Fogg, James, 186
Foran, Sub-Inspector, 21
Forgery, 123
Forrester, A., 110
Fothergill, William, 110
Fraud, 145
Fred, 166
Freeman, Thomas, 86
'Frenchman, The', 29

G

Gabriel, Frederick, 118
Gallagher, Francis, 209
Galvin, Daniel, 33
Gaols, *see* Prisons
Gardener, James, 209
Gardiner, Frank, 21
Garraway, Robert, 198
Gatton, 131
Gatton Cemetery, 133
Gayndah, 8, 25
Gayundah, 70
Georgetown, 73, 155
Georgie, 10
Gerlee, John, 59
Gibson, Helen, 121
Gilbert, John, 24
Gilbert River, 71, 155
Gill, Tom and Jim, 41
Gin Gin, 25
Gipsy's Creek, 138
Gladstone, 2, 66, 184
Gleeson, George, 114
Gogango, 38
Gordon, Walter, 89
Goyner, George, 84
Graceville, 190
Gray, Edward, 180
Great Shearers' Strike, 109, 115
Green, James, 34
Greyrock, 124
Grievous bodily harm, 193
Griffin, Paddy, 110
Griffin, Thomas, 38
Griffith, Albert 169
Griffiths, Israel, 63
Griffiths, William, 31
Gromodecki, Louisa, 191
Gulliver, 5
Gunde Gunda Creek, 53
Gunning, Alice, 151
Gympie, 41, 48, 63, 78, 147

H

Habana, 151
Hall, Ben, 25
Hall, Benson, 69,
Hall, Rev. Robert, 195
Halligan, Patrick, 47
Hallingworth, Arthur, 208
Hamilton, William, 109, 208
Hammond, Dr Samuel, 158
Han, Eliza, 34
Hangings, 9, 14, 16, 20, 49, 51, 55, 75, 78, 90, 91, 92, 96, 103, 108, 113, 115, 118, 120, 137, 139, 141, 144, 150, 153, 159, 163, 166, 167, 168, 173, 176, 178, 183, 187, 206-7
Hansen, Christian, 186
Hardgraves, Thomas, 17
Harding, John, 159
Hardwick, Fanny, 141
Harris, Sub-Inspector, 52
Harrison, John, 92
Harry Redford Cattle Drive, 57
Hartigan, Edward, 123
Hasted, Henry, 137
Hawk, 2
Haygarth, Graham, 142
Henderson, James, 145
Henderson, John, 141
Hennessy, Police Constable, 158
Herbert River, 86
Herrlich, James, 50
Hessell, Dr, 31
Highlands, 51
Hill, Alfred, 130, 135
Hill, W.R.O., 74
Hobbs, Dr William, 20
Holberg, John, 94
Hooper, Harry, 37
Hopeful, 86
Hopgood, Henry, 188
Horrocks, Frank, 113
Horton, Billy, 12
Hotels
  British Empire Hotel, Brisbane, 189
  Clarence Hotel, Brisbane, 94
  Commercial Hotel, Emu Vale, 203
  Criterion Hotel, Townsville, 199
  Dunmore Arms, Brisbane, 27

Exchange Hotel, Brisbane, 180
Maryvale Hotel, 85
Royal Exchange Hotel, Boonah, 156
Royal Exchange Hotel, Brisbane, 189
Royal Mail Hotel, Tingalpa, 79
Samford Hotel, 185
Tattersall's Hotel, Townsville, 199
Treasury Hotel, Brisbane, 27
Victoria Hotel, Mackay, 162
Waterloo Hotel, Brisbane, 90
Howson, Thomas, 21
Hughenden, 100, 109
Hunter, Bob, 2
Hunter, Henry, 29
Hurley, Tom, 63
Hyde, Albert, 104
Hyde, Elizabeth, 104

I

Ikin, Edward, 178
Illicit still, 85
Ingham, 100
Iogomea, Polly, 208
Ipswich, 35, 61, 105
Irvine, Charles, 115
Irvinebank, 66
Irwin, Michael, 82
Irwin, Thomas, 90

J

James, Reg, 168
Jandowae, 23
Jemmy, 67
Jenkins, James, 198
Jenkins, William, 35
Jensen, Christopher, 78
Joe, 155
Johannes, 161
Johnny Reid, 5
Johns, Sidney, 189
Johnson, Caroline, 17
Johnson, David, 152
Johnson, Sam, 149
Jondaryan, 179
Jones's Camp, 179
Judges/Justices
Blakeney, Charles W., 58
Chubb, Charles, 170, 189
Cockle, James, 17, 23, 25, 43, 55
Cooper, Pope A., 93, 96, 103, 166, 172, 187, 194, 199
Griffith, Samuel, 86, 88, 99, 122, 137, 150
Harding, George, 81, 91, 110, 118,
Lilley, Charles, 62
Lukin, Lionel, 182, 199, 204
Lutwyche, Alfred, 20, 28
Macnaughton, Allan, 175, 180,
Mein, Charles, 106, 108,
Miller, Granville, 168
Noel, Arthur, 98, 115, 136
Power, Virgil, 141, 178
Real, Patrick, 126, 150, 189, 192, 199
Shand, William, 199
Sheppard, Edmund, 75
Julian, James, 39

K

Kanakas, 84, 86, 119, 139, 151, 159, 161, 168, 184
Kangaroo Point, 121
Kelly, George, 179
Kelly, Ned, 30
Kennedy, Michael, 203
Kenniff, James, 148
Kenniff, Patrick, 148
Kidnapping, 86
Kimberley, 66
Kimboo, 9
King, Fred, 190
Kitt, Benjamin, 98
Klein, Michael, 50

L

La Hay, John, 198
Lang, George, 12
Larceny/Theft, 17, 59, 69, 94, 98, 109, 153, 155
LeBlowitz, Mary, 137
Lee Chay Yuen, 167
Lefu, Budlo, 126
Lenham, Fritz, 16
Lethbridge's Pocket, 148,
Lever, George, 69
Leyburn, 18, 44
Lilley, William, 132
Linke, Amelia, 168
Little Ipswich, 10
Livingstone, Alexander, 31
Lonergan, Maurice, 107
Long, John, 203
Longland, Jonathan, 125
Longreach, 154
Longreach Cemetery, 154
Look Tow, 167
Luggage Point, 2
Lunn, Walter, 116
Luther, Martin, 61

M

Macdonald, Angus, 154
Macdonald, Florence, 154
Macdonald, Grace, 154
Mackay, 32, 84, 151, 161, 180
Macpherson, James Alpin, 24
Madden, William, 30
Mahoney, Michael, 29
Manning, Arthur W., 44
Manslaughter, 17, 23, 27, 50, 63, 68, 79, 137, 141, 156, 194
Manton, George, 199
Marks, Dr A.H., 189
Marlborough, 23
Marlborough Station, 116
Martin, John, 152
Maryborough, 12, 25, 31, 91, 166, 157, 173
Matchett, Jimmy, 143
Matthews, Percy, 107
Mayne, 188
McCormick, John, 17
McDonald, Flora, 116
McDonald, John, 45
McFarlane, Irene, 209
McGovern, John, 54
McGuinness, Matthew, 16
McIlwraith, Sir Thomas, 99
McKenzie, John, 57
McKiernan, Paddy, 114
McNeil, Neil, 86
McNeil, William, 131, 132
Medetoo, 85
Meriga, Christian, 102
Merivale Street, Brisbane, 200
Meston, Archibald, 126
Mi Orie, 119
Millewski, August, 164, 208
Minnie, 141
Minnis, Michael ,79
Missionaries, 195
Mitchell, Ivy, 185
Mitchell, James, 185
Mitchell Downs, 15
Moncardo, Leonardo, 112
Morell, Gabriel, 8
Morinish, 47
Morningside, 125
Mornington Island, 195
Mortimer, William, 189
Mossman River, 92
Mount Morgan, 7, 118
Murray, John, 28
Muir, Edmund, 171
Munday, William, 158
Munro, Bill, 168
Murder, 2, 5, 8, 9, 12, 14, 18, 38, 47, 51, 53, 66, 71, 74, 82, 86,

89, 91, 92, 95, 101, 104, 112, 113, 114, 116, 119, 120, 124, 125, 127, 128, 130, 131, 134, 137, 141, 142, 148, 151, 154, 155, 158, 159, 161, 164, 166, 167, 168, 171, 174, 177, 179, 181, 184, 185, 188, 189, 190, 195, 203
Murphy, Daniel, 110
Murphy, Ellen, 131
Murphy, G, 110
Murphy, Michael, 131
Murphy, Norah, 131
Murphy, William, 76
Murrarie, 113
Murray, James, 90
Musgrave, Governor Sir Anthony, 99
Muttaburra, 89
Mutter, Joseph, 74
Myora Mission, 126

N

Nabby, Wallum, 164
Nanango, 44, 164
Narasemai, 119
Neagh, 139
Neddy, 137
Nielson, William, 194
Normanton, 100, 101

O

Ohley, William, 159
Old Man, 155
Otter, 153
Owen, Charles, 18
Oxley, 130, 136
Oxley Creek, 35, 190
O'Callaghan, Bridget, 188
O'Sullivan, John, 33
O'Sullivan, Michael, 175

P

Pacific Island labourers, *see* Kanakas
Palmer, Sir Arthur, 115
Palmer, George, 47
Paluma, 70
Parker, Henry, 28
Parsons, John, 159
Patton, Henry, 22
Pender, William, 51
Perry House, Brisbane, 189
Perseverance Station, 50
Peter, Burketown, 195
Petrie, Andrew, 3
Petrie, John, 3, 13, 24
Petrie, Tom, 3
Petrie Terrace, 28
Pickford, Christopher, 95
Pierce, John, 18
Pillinger, William, 79
Pinnock, PM Philip, 107
Porteus, Rev. D, 61
Pottinger, Sir Frederick, 25
Potts, William, 94
Poulton, James, 134
Power, John, 38
Preston, James, 86
Price, Albert, 161
Price, Mary, 161ff
Princhester, 22, 23
Prior, James, 121
Prisons
  Boggo Road, 75, 78, 90, 92, 96, 103, 113, 115, 118, 120, 130, 139, 141, 144, 146, 152, 153, 155, 159, 166, 167, 168, 173, 182, 187, 206-7
  Fortitude Valley, 206
  Mackay, 151, 206
  Petrie Terrace, 9, 12, 37, 206
  Proserpine, 25, 31, 32, 60, 206
  Rockhampton, 21, 108, 206
  Roma, 206
  St Helena Island, 1, 3, 23, 25, 26, 30, 45, 52, 54, 94, 98, 111, 120, 123, 125, 128, 137, 148, 153, 155, 175, 197, 206-7
  Toowoomba, 206
  Townsville, 206
Pritchard, Charles, 63
Proserpine, see Prisons
Pumba, 197

Q

Queensland Criminal Code 1899, The, 137
Queensland Native Police, 5, 66, 71, 82,
Queensland Railways, 145
Quinn, Bishop Dr James, 62

R

Rape, 10, 12
RSL, 202
Rae, Edward, 13
Rae, Jane, 12
Rapido, 103
Ravenswood, 74
Ravenswood Junction, 95
Red Flag Riot, The, 200
Redcap, 141,
Redford, Harry, 56
Redman, Edward, 41
Renshaw, Edwin, 126
Reubens, John, 141
Richards, Edwin, 158
Riotous assembly, 28, 33, 62, 84, 115, 200
Ritchie, Alexander, 18
Robbery Under Arms, 56
Robbery, 11, 32, 76, 168, 169, 192
Robbery under arms, *see* Bushranging
Robber's Tree, The, 78
Roberts, Eliza, 174
Robinson, Arthur, 59
Rockhampton, 5, 21, 33, 34, 47, 67, 100, 108, 111, 117, 123, 140, 172, 178
Rocky Waterholes, 59
Rogers, Edward, 86
Rogers, John, 199
Roma, 25, 57, 100, 137
Roma Street Markets, 107
Rooney, Alexander, 27
Ross, Andrew, 32
Ross, Arthur, 171
Ross, Billy, 11
Ross, William, 140
Royal Commission 1885, 87
Royal Commission 1899, 132, 135, 136
Ruddy, John, 59
Russian Club, 201
Ryan, Bridget, 10
Ryan, T.J., 111

S

Salvation Army, 174, 176, 183
Samuels, John, 125
Sandiford, George, 20
Sarina, 181
Scanlan, Jeremiah, 11
Schofield, Harry, 86
Scholes, Jacob, 78
Scrubby Creek, 6
Scuthorpe, Elizabeth, 57
Seaview Plantation, 91
Sedin, 101
See Ong, 127
Settler, 20, 27
Sewell, William, 27
Seymour, Alfred, 178
Shaw, Elsie, 194
Shaw, Lewis, 86
Shepherd, John, 199
Silva, George, 181
Simpson, Job, 78
Sketty Belle, 112

Smith, Jack, 140
Smith, Robert, 193
Smith-Barry, H.C., 110
'Snob, The', 123
Soloman, Abraham, 33
Sow Too Low, 151
Spillane, Margaret, 82
Spring Hill, 194
St George, 53
St Helena Island, *see* Prisons
Stable, J.W., 48
Stack, Walter, 15
Stanford, Sam, 134
Starkey, Arthur, 178
Starlight, Captain, 56
Stephens, Florence, 191
Stewart, Gibson, 208
Stone, John, 33
Strauss, Frederick, 11
Stuart, Julian, 110
Suicide, 46, 68, 159, 178
Sutherland, Alice, 175
Sutherland, George, 175

T

Tak Lung, 33
Tannymorel, 203
Tartulla Station, 53
Taylor, George, 110
Thackeray, Rev. William, 19
Thompson, Andrew, 127
Thompson, Billy, 92
Thompson, Ellen, 92, 208
Thornhill, William, 85
Thursday Island, 114, 120
Tierney, Thomas, 153
Tingalpa, 79
Tinyana, Frank, 120
Toby, 5
Tommy, 12
Tommy, 141
Tommy Chin Mow, 155
Toowong, 158
Toowong Cemetery, 129, 130, 159
Toowoomba, 16, 17, 51, 100, 145
Toroom, 25
Town and Country Timber Yard, 188
Townley, PM Captain William, 62
Townsend, John, 120
Townsend, Victor, 69
Townsville, 75, 100, 139, 159, 167, 198
Townsville Railway Station, 169
Troden, William, 41
Turkey Station, 182
Turley, Michael, 15
Twadiga, 168
Twine, Captain, 2
Tynan, Peter, 180
Tynan, William, 180

U

'Unfortunate Nine, The', 36
Urandangi, 141
Urquhart, Frederick, 202

V

Vickers, Henry, 78
Victoria Bridge, Brisbane, 193
Vosper, Frederick, 115

W

Wallerderine Station, 56
Walloon, 22
Wanti, 139
Ward, Tom, 71
Warry, T.S., 14
Warwick, 17
Warwick, 100
Wassell, Inspector James W., 60
Watchorn, Henry, 85
Weaber, Sarah, 134
Webster, Daniel, 21
Webster, William, 186
Weissmuller, Rudolf, 113
Wells, Joseph, 76
Westwood, 21
Wharton, James, 158
Wheeler, Lt Frederick, 66
Whelan, Michael, 63
White Australia Policy, 168
Whitehouse, Edgar, 146
'Wild Scotchman, The', 24
Williams, Bernard, 86
Williams, John, 47
Wilson, Edward, 130
Winton, 100
Wong Tong, 91
Woods, Thomas, 8
Woolloongabba, 135, 136
Wounding with intent, 34
Wright, John, 21

Y

Yaamba, 23
Yandilla Station, 18
Yous, Manuel, 71

Z

Zieman, Simon, 53
Zuzenko, Alexander, 201

About the author

Jarvis Finger is a prolific and award-winning author of a range of management books, magazines and online resources including *Management in a Minute, Just about Everything a Manager Needs to Know, The Management Bible, Managing Your School, The Classroom Teacher's Book of Management Essentials,* www.justasktom.com, www.thesthelenastory.com.au, *The Australian Educational Leader,* and several entertaining paperbacks on matters educational.

His interest in Queensland's crimes and criminals was aroused in the late 1970s when he was asked by the then Queensland Department of Education to investigate the feasibility of re-establishing a school on St Helena Island, at the mouth of the Brisbane River. St Helena was the location of colonial Queensland's major prison for men from 1867 to 1933. The intention was for groups of school children to visit the island to learn a little of the island's penal history and environment. At the time he found that published material relating to the island's absorbing past was non-existent – the outcome being his publication in the 1980s of a series of small books for schools and tourists, including *True Tales of Old St Helena, More True Tales of Old St Helena, The Wild Men of St Helena,* and *The Escapes from St Helena.* The award-winning *The St Helena Story: An Illustrated History of Colonial Queensland's Island Prison,* published in 2010, was a further step in bringing to fruition his desire to reawaken public awareness of the fascinating role this small island played in Queensland's history.

In researching material for *The St Helena Story,* he became intrigued by the files and episodes relating to the men serving their terms of punishment in that colonial prison.

A Cavalcade of Queensland's Crimes and Criminals: The Colonial Years and Beyond is the product of that interest.

Boolarong Press
Brisbane, Queensland
2012

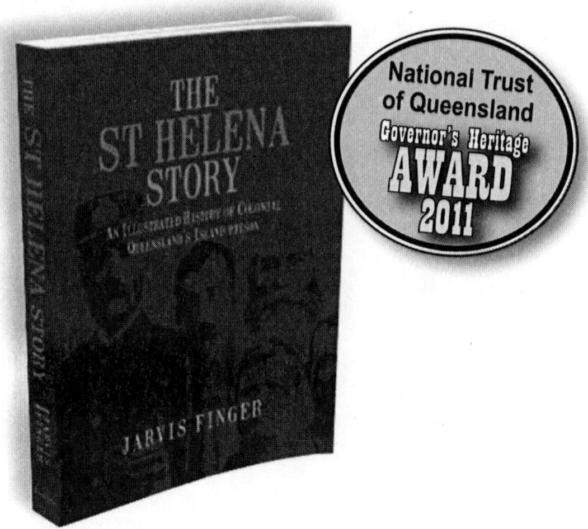

The St Helena Story

An Illustrated History of Colonial Queensland's Island Prison

Jarvis Finger

This well-presented 300-page full-colour history of colonial Queensland's island prison is rich in eyewitness accounts, anecdotes, historic photographs and documents, illustrations and absorbing tales of prison life, mayhem and escape. The material is presented in 18 illustrated chapters – an historical treasurehouse for student, general reader and historian.

The St Helena Story:
An Illustrated History of Colonial
Queensland's Island Prison
by Jarvis Finger

300 pages; References and Index; Full-colour throughout;
Hundreds of photographs and illustrations; Gatefold cover;
250mm x 200mm; ISBN: 9781921555442
$39.95 plus postage

Available through your local bookstore
or online from:
www.boolarongpress.com.au